P9-DGX-832
3 6021 00085 4699

The Invisible Drug

William Everett Bailey M.S.

Mosaic Publications, Inc.
Houston

The Invisible Drug

by William Everett Bailey M.S.

printed in the United States of America

Publisher's Cataloging in Publication
(Prepared by Quality Books Inc.)

Bailey, Everett William
The invisible drug / William Everett Bailey.
p. cm.
Includes bibliographical references and index.
Preassigned LCCN: 96-77886
ISBN 0-9653793-3-7

1. Tobacco--Health aspects. 2. Smoking-- Health aspects. 3. Tobacco habit-- United States--Prevention 4. Tobacco Industry--United States. I. Title

RA1242.T6B35 1996 362.29'6

QBI96-40466

Table of Contents

Acknowledgment

I wish to thank each person listed below for their generous contributions to, and encouragement in the preparation of this manuscript: Dr. Herbert L. DuPont M.D., Peggy DuPont, Sharna C. Kruse, Anthony J. Paviglianiti, Jeffery Roy, Anne Sheldon, Dr. James H. Steele D.V.M., M.P.H, and Les Wolf. I am especially grateful to my loving wife for her undying patience and encouragement.

W.E.B.

Preface

Following the death of the first of four family members who died of smoking related illnesses, I became interested in the tobacco issue. The first died of lung cancer in 1982, which made me keenly aware of the health hazards of smoking. When the second one died of esophageal cancer, I wanted to know why they started smoking and why they continued to smoke when they knew it was bad for them. Both of these men were upper middle class, educated, and sensible adults. With the exception of smoking, they did not abuse drugs or alcohol, and their health otherwise would have allowed them another ten to 20 years of life. They could have quit, after all wasn't nicotine about the same as caffeine, and smoking just a bad habit that anyone could break?

Then near the time of the third death, a sudden heart attack of a 48 year old male, I heard disturbing news reports about the tobacco industry. These were major tobacco and food conglomerates such as Philip Morris and R.J. Reynolds Nabisco. Their names were associated with wholesome food brands like Post, Nabisco, and Kraft. These where legitimate businesses, I thought would not sell a product that killed people. The reports said that they have been targeting children with advertising. That couldn't be, not in America where drug pushers caught selling drugs to children were locked in jail and the key thrown away.

The average American, including myself at that time, did not know enough about the tobacco issue. Even the above average, well educated American is deficient. I was ill-informed despite having studied pharmacology and toxicology in graduate school. What the average American knows can be summed up as: smoking is bad for you, some smokers find it hard to quit, and the tobacco industries trustworthiness was under suspicion. I had many questions, so I went to the library and began my research for *The Invisible Drug*. To my surprise, there were over 50,000 books and articles written on tobacco. I was beginning to believe that I would have to read them all to get the whole story. I could not find one good book that would answer all my questions. Instead, I had to read hundreds of publications: clinical articles that doctors wrote for other doctors published in medical journals, newspaper articles, many that were very good, but were limited in depth and breadth, books stressing some aspect of the issue, either political, or about the tobacco industry, but little on the health issues.

I wanted to know why smoking was apparently so lethal. How many people die from smoking compared to those who are murdered, or die from AIDS, or from heroin? I thought smoking must be less of a risk than being killed in an auto accident. Could it be that other factors were killing smokers? I knew smoking caused lung cancer, but I only knew a few that actually got lung cancer.

What was in cigarettes that made them killers? Tobacco is a legally grown and sold, government subsidized plant. Could it be as toxic as it seemed and if so why would the government allow it to be sold? Furthermore, being familiar with the pharmaceutical industry, and knowing how drugs are strictly regulated, tobacco must surely have passed safety tests. It just did not make sense to me that smoking could be that bad. It's use was so widespread, and was a normal part of life.

About the time the fourth family member died, the second one from lung cancer, my research had formed an unpleasant picture in my mind. The tobacco issue is an ugly story of the worst public health disaster in American history. The public's health has been seriously and negligently jeopardized. American smokers are dying at an unbelievable rate, 0.2% of the U.S. population every year. The daily body count is enough to fill three jumbo jets. A new view of the issue is necessary to fully realize the magnitude of this tragedy, because most do not have it in proper perspective.

Why is it that a defective product, a dangerous poison, continues to be promoted and sold? The tobacco industry has invaded the government and manipulates it to protect their business at the expense of the citizens whom the government is dutifully bound to protect. There is no democracy where tobacco is concerned. Today nonsmokers outnumber smokers three to one. Yet, since the Surgeon General's Report in 1964, when smoking was announced to be the cause of cancer, heart attacks and premature death, Congress has voted down almost every major tobacco control legislation. Small steps have been taken, but little has been done to stop the unnecessary deaths and human suffering which continues unimpeded at the rate of one every 72 seconds.

Taking poisons and dying a slow painful death is not normal. Why then is smoking so socially acceptable? The tobacco industry, like the government, has a tight grip on the minds of most Americans. They spend $24 for every man, woman and child in the United States annually to "brain-wash" us into believing smoking is a normal part of life. They bombard us with a plethora of very effective advertising associating smoking with good health, fun, popularity, independent life styles, and individual's rights. Billboards, magazine advertising, movies, and ads at sporting events constantly besiege the subconscious telling us that smoking is a normal part of life. The industry calls it "friendly familiarity," and that has been one goal of tobacco advertising that has been very successful. So we shrug it off and say let the smoker smoke, they know its bad for them. We also say that secondhand smoke doesn't bother us.

Tobacco advertising has been successful in another arena. The tobacco messages start getting through to children before they learn to read. After years of constant repetition, and at the vulnerable age of ten to 12, 25% start smoking. For the most part, tobacco advertising only works on children, therefore it must be designed to attract the one audience it is most effective in reaching. Yet this systematic culling of the America kid, killing one of every three that starts smoking, goes unnoticed by most people. The tobacco companies fight hard to continue advertising that is directly responsible for smoking initiation. Worst of all, it's illegal to sell tobacco to minors, however, despite the law it continues unimpeded.

There was no single book that gave me a concise summary of all of these issues: the health hazards of tobacco use and secondhand smoke, nicotine addiction, tobacco industry corruption, tobacco advertising and promotion, and the political-social dilemma we are in because of it. Nothing I read put the magnitude of the human suffering and loss of life attributed to tobacco use into a proper perspective. I wrote *The Invisible Drug* to answer the questions that no book could answer until now. I wanted to bring a new perspective to the tobacco tragedy, and de-normalize tobacco use.

The Invisible Drug is written primarily for readers with no science or medical background. However, it was necessary to include some science and medicine in the text. The impact of the deadliness of tobacco use, and the tenacious grip of nicotine addiction can't be fully realized without some explanation of the scientific basis for it. In some cases I had to use ridiculously long chemical names, using abbreviations whenever possible. For readers without a science background, reading through the medical information, even if not fully understood, will greatly increase your awareness of the essential dangers of tobacco use. For those readers with a science or medical education, many questions will be answered. Furthermore, for your reading convenience, I omitted the footnote biographical references, and instead combined them in the bibliography section.

Why would a nonsmoker be interested in the tobacco issue?

The reason is because it affects your life dramatically. Although you have chosen a healthy life style and don't smoke, tobacco affects your health and can kill you. You pay more taxes. You have lost your representation in Congress, because the representatives you elected to serve you, serve the tobacco industry instead.

Secondhand smoke may kill you.

Secondhand smoke kills one person every 6 ½ minutes, and many are infants. It effects 87% of the population, yet most are unaware they have been poisoned. Some say secondhand smoke doesn't bother them, and the tobacco industry says it is about as harmful as eating Oreos and milk. The truth is secondhand smoke is more dangerous that asbestos. More nonsmokers die from passive smoking that those killed in car wrecks and by gun shots combined. Passive smoking is the fifth leading cause of preventable deaths in America.

Your children are being stalked.

Tobacco advertising is responsible for 3,000 children and teens starting to smoke every day. One of every three will die from smoking related disease.

Smoking kills your loved ones, families members and friends.

Since 1964, ten million people have died from tobacco related illness. Every year 430,000 spouses, children, mothers, fathers, uncles, aunts, cousins, and friends die prematurely. Tobacco smoke aborts 140,000 fetuses in the womb every year. The cause of these needless deaths go unnoticed publicly, yet the 35,000 that are shot to death each year make the front page.

You pay more taxes.

Other people's nicotine addiction costs you money. Every time a pack of cigarettes is smoked, it cost American taxpayers $2.59 for health care for the smoker. Furthermore, taxpayers pay over $15 million a year to help tobacco farmers support the price of tobacco.

Your rights and freedom are being denied.

Smoking policies today, except for a few isolated cities, deny nonsmokers their rights and freedom. You are being denied the freedom to enter any public building in the United States and be accommodated with a safe, tobacco smoke free environment. You have the right to demand safe indoor air free of poisons. It is your right to be accommodated with a smoke free indoor environment in all public buildings.

You have lost your fair representation in Congress as the majority.

The majority of Americans are nonsmokers, yet your fair representation in Congress is being denied. Instead, Congress unfairly sides with the tobacco industry. Tobacco lobbying has hampered every tobacco control bill and every government agency that has tried to curtail tobacco advertising and promotion, or smoking in public. Tobacco has killed our democratic process.

Your health is being compromised by a lack of government protection.

One of the fundamental duties of government is to protect the public's health, safety, and well being. Tobacco is legal, but it is also lethal and an addictive drug. Tobacco companies manipulate the government to protect its $45 billion annual tobacco business, at the expense of the public's health. They make campaign contributions to members of Congress, then they stymie the governments efforts to protect the public from tobacco promotion and secondhand smoke.

Why would a smoker be interested in the tobacco issue?

Smokers are victims of the largest and most lethal hoax perpetrated on the public in the history of the United States— that smoking is OK. Advertising is largely responsible for the lack of concern and the positive image of smoking. Advertising gets you started and nicotine hooks you.

You need to accept the truth.

You need to believe the truth you have never fully been told about the health hazards of tobacco use. Knowing will not make quitting easy, but it may help. Seek the help of a smoking cessation counselor and the support of a group of others that want to others that want to quit. Discuss what you read in this book with the group. Then, after you quit smoking, read chapter 17 again and take some action to help stop this madness, so future generations will not be duped and hooked on *The Invisible Drug*.

Introduction

This book is about an invisible drug—the world's most dangerous, most widely used substance of abuse. Forty-six million Americans are addicted to the invisible drug. It is as addictive as cocaine, it's sellers liken it to a "snack." The invisible drug makers put a candy label on the package, but when peeled away we find a skull & crossbones underneath.

More people have been killed by the invisible drug than from crack, heroin, World Wars I & II, and Vietnam combined. Since 1964, the invisible drug has killed ten million Americans. Every year the same number of people that live in the city of Albuquerque, New Mexico perish by the invisible sword—their deaths are invisible too. Some drop dead suddenly – others die painfully slow, miserable deaths. Their deaths go unnoticed because they don't die at the same moment, and they are not buried in a mass grave. Ten million premature, preventable deaths, all caused by the same poison.

Millions still live on with a lower quality of life— a silently growing tumor—an impending cardiac arrest. Their disease is invisible—like observers of a hydrogen bomb explosion—far enough away not to be blown apart, but close enough to die slowly from it in time.

The invisible drug hides diabolically within the leaf of a plant. When smoked, it releases two thousand chemical poisons, and a drug that is highly addictive. The killer is tobacco—the invisible drug is nicotine.

While the public has been asleep, money has exchanged hands—Congressional representatives have taken millions from the invisible drug cartel. Deals have been cut, votes have been traded, and the poison billows freely. The invisible drug cartel operates legally in America. Congress and the best lawyers money can buy have protected them for over 30 years. The Federal government has failed to protect the public from the hazards of the invisible drug.

Three thousand children a day, enough to repopulate Dallas every year, are seduced into addiction by advertising with an invisible purpose. To these children, the hazards are invisible. A deadly addiction will write "the cause of death is cancer" on the death certificates of many of the children that try it more than five times. We turn our heads as children become addicts, doomed at the age of 12 to a short life ended in misery by cancer, or suddenly from a heart attack. America, when are you going to stop this crime in progress!

The poisons, the ineffective warnings, the magnitude of the deaths, the tremendous suffering from cancer and heart disease, and the tenacious grip of addiction—the horror—all denied by the invisible drug cartel and rationalized by the average American. This book, like a microscope that reveals deadly bacteria, will help you see the invisible drug. You, too, will then ask,

Why are there not angry mobs in the streets?

Invisible drug users and non-users alike will be disgusted and angry when they discover how they've been deceived and manipulated into complacency. Advertising keeps us all believing the invisible drug is a normal part of life. The cartel has made a syringe look like candy—keeping us friendly and void of concerns.

Smokers, prepare for a shock that may motivate you to save your life. Nonsmokers, beware of the "White Serpent"—the chemical warfare cloud of the invisible drug that kills one American every 6 ½ minutes, some of them infants. Everyone knows that smoking is bad for you. This is a major understatement. To those that think they know why, or those that don't know, this is the untold story.

Chapter One

Origin of the United States Epidemic

American Indians were the first people known to cultivate and use tobacco. It was inhaled, smoked and used as snuff as early as 100 CE. But it has only been since the 1500's that the use of tobacco started to become more widespread. Over the next 200 years, Spanish and Portuguese sailors distributed the tobacco plant around the world.

Precious Stink

Although they were ignorant about the health effects of tobacco, it had many foes from the beginning. King James in 1604 referred to tobacco as the "precious stink." Many countries and religious groups forbid the use of the foul bane.

The modern tobacco plant had its beginnings in America in 1609, when the Englishman John Rolfe arrived in Jamestown. Dissatisfied with the native tobacco found there, *Nicotiana rustica*, he first cultivated *Nicotiana tabacum,* the tobacco species grown today. Compulsive tobacco users in

Virginia, preoccupied with its cultivation, produced 20,000 pounds by 1618. Tobacco was bartered for the passage of mail-order brides. Tobacco farming continued to grow and the plantation owners became wealthy. Tobacco plantations had huge labor requirements, so slaves were purchased to do the farming. It was the sweat and blood of Africans that built the economic foundations of early America. African slaves did the work, but the credit was given to "tobacco."

In the early 1900's, cigarette smoking gained tremendous popularity. The annual per capita cigarette consumption increased to 54 per person in 1900. The invention of high speed cigarette making machines made smoking cigarettes cheaper, easier and more readily available. In 1913 the first modern cigarette was introduced: Camels.

Tobacco Farming in America

Today, there are about 160,000 tobacco farms. The leading tobacco growing states are North Carolina, and Kentucky, followed by South Carolina, Tennessee, Virginia, and Georgia. Two-thirds of flue-cured tobacco is grown in North Carolina, and two-thirds of burley tobacco is grown in Kentucky. About one half of the U.S. tobacco crop is exported to other countries.

Flue-cured Tobacco - *Class one, bright tobacco. It is cured for 3 days in airtight barns, which are heated from exterior fires.*

Burley Tobacco - *Class three, light tobacco. It is air cured naturally, by hanging in the sun or in ventilated barns.*

The Tobacco Support Program

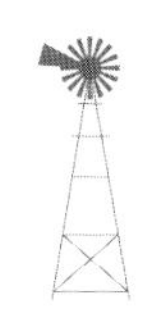

Beginning in 1938, the Federal Government guaranteed the tobacco farmer a minimum price for his crop—the birth of the Tobacco Support Program. The U.S. Department of Agriculture (USDA) sets a maximum quota for all tobacco that can be grown. Tobacco is sold by bid. If the bid is less than the minimum price, the crop is taken by one of the farmers' cooperatives and the farmer is given a "loan" for the minimum price of the tobacco. The co-op sells it, then uses the money to lend. Farmers borrow from the Commodity Credit Corp., which is part of the USDA.

The tobacco subsidy allows farmers to make more money from tobacco than food crops. Based on 1979 prices, the profit per acre is $1,198 for tobacco; $233 for peanuts, and $72 for soy beans or corn. Today, a tobacco farmer can make up to $4, 000 per acre for flue-cured or burley tobacco. The Federal Government encourages production of tobacco for the benefit of the tobacco industry by keeping their raw materials (tobacco) in good supply.

From 1930 to 1985, the U.S. government lost $3.5 billion in principal and interest charges from the program. During about the same time taxpayer's paid $200 million for the tobacco support program, compared to only $12 million for dairy support.

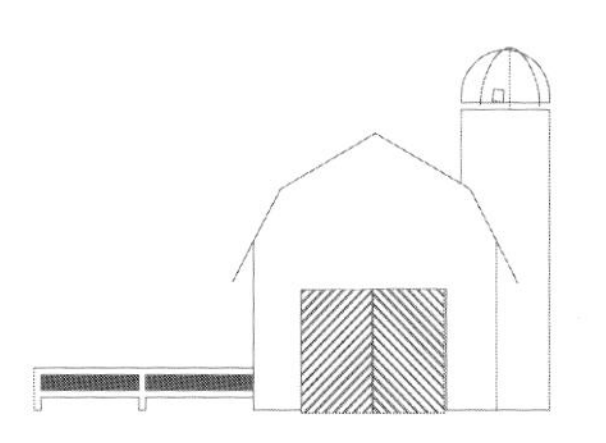

"Our Fighting Men Rate The Best"

During W.W. I, smoking was associated with war, fighting, and freedom. Cigarettes were given to almost all of our soldiers. Camels, Lucky Strikes, and Chesterfields were the most popular brands in 1917.

One Chesterfield advertisement stated:

"Our fighting men rate the best...see that they get plenty of milder cooler-smoking Chesterfields. Everybody who smokes 'em likes 'em."

This began a smoking trend in the military. By 1987, 47% of military personnel were still smoking.

The Romancing of Tobacco

After W.W.1, men started smoking by the millions. Advertising in national magazines made smoking attractive. Camel advertisements associated smoking with sexual appeal, sophistication, pleasure, and the good life. Until the 1920's, tobacco advertising mainly targeted men.

On the other hand, the industry was missing a huge segment of the population the women. American Tobacco Company's Lucky Strike campaign of 1927 finally broke the social barrier that looked down on women smoking and Lucky Strikes became the best seller. By the 1950's, advertising had promoted smoking to a new level, it became as "American as apple pie." Smoking was normalized.

The AGE of *IGNORANCE*

In the age of ignorance, tobacco was smoked with no concern about health or death. Smoking, as the cause of lung cancer, heart disease, and nicotine addiction, was unknown. Intelligent decisions cold not be made about the risk of smoking. Americans did not have available the 50,000 articles and scientific papers written on smoking and health that we have today.

The First Health Concerns

In 1950, one of the first scientific papers was published on the connection of smoking and lung cancer. In 1952 *Readers Digest* ran an article that spread the cancer scare. Later in 1953, Dr. Ernest Wynder, a scientist at Sloan-Kettering, applied tar to the skin of mice. The mice developed cancer. To that news, the public reacted with fear. Cigarettes were nicknamed Cancer Sticks. Sales of cigarettes declined over six percent. Philip Morris responded to the health scare by honing their aggressive style, and coined this slogan:

"Philip Morris -the cigarette that takes the

FEAR out of smoking"

Introduction of the Filtered Cigarette

"There is no such thing as a safe cigarette."

-Dr. Julius B. Richmond, former U.S. Surgeon General

In 1952, tobacco companies developed and marketed the first filtered cigarettes in an effort to counter health concerns. One and one half million people who quit during the health scare of the 50's, started smoking again, but this time filtered cigarettes. One filter cigarette was promoted as:

"Just what the doctor ordered."

Filters do not make smoking safer. Instead, it was later proven that filters may also be a health hazard, compounding the risks of smoking.

Early Worries

One of the first public announcements from the government about the safety of smoking was in 1957:

> "...The weight of the evidence is increasingly pointing in one direction: that excessive smoking is one of the causative factors in lung cancer."
>
> -Dr. Leroy Burney, former U.S. Surgeon General

In response to the Surgeon General's statement, television advertising for cigarettes jumped from $40 million in 1957 to $115 million in 1961. Young, healthy people in television commercials were running the fifty yard dash and jumping through hoops to get a cigarette. With the increase in tobacco advertising came a corresponding increase in the annual per capita cigarette consumption. It increased dramatically to 4,345 per person by 1963.

Consumers Union warned their readers in 1963 about the hazards of smoking in *Report on Smoking and the Public Interest.* Few other reports on the hazards of smoking were available to the public. Then in 1964 came the report some call the bombshell.

The 1964 Report of the Surgeon General

By 1964, 42% of all adults smoked. Cigarettes became the most successfully marketed product in American history. Everyone was puffing, until the report that shocked the world.

On January 11, 1964, the U.S. Surgeon General, Luther Terry, gave the first report on Smoking Hazards. The report linked smoking with an increase in lung and other cancers, emphysema, bronchitis, heart attacks and premature deaths.

Immediately following the bombshell, smokers quit by the thousands. National sales of cigarettes dropped 20%-25% overnight. Much of that drop was thought to be due to smokers cutting back, rather that quitting. What then followed was a terrifying aftershock.

The Great Relapse of 1964

Then came the first warning of the tremendous addictive power of nicotine: "The Great Relapse of 1964." Within two months, sales returned to normal. People discovered they could not quit smoking easily. This great nicotine addiction experiment in 1964 proved on a grand scale that nicotine is addictive, by demonstrating three hallmarks of drug addiction:

1. **Continuation despite knowledge of the harmful health effects.**
2. **Relapse after withdrawal.**
3. **A low quit rate.**

■■■■■■■■■■■■■■

The year 1964 is a turning point in history — the year the tobacco zealots were born.

"A custom loathsome to the eye, hateful to the nose, harmful to the brain, dangerous to the lungs, and in the black, stinking fume thereof nearest resembling the horrible Stygian smoke of the pit that is bottomless."

King James I

Chapter Two

The Tobacco Zealots

First Awareness

When did the tobacco industry first become aware that smoking caused cancer and heart attacks? Was it at the time of the first Surgeon General's report in 1964? No, tobacco companies knew about the dangers of smoking before the Surgeon General's report. As early as 1957, tobacco industry researchers discussed data on the link of smoking to cancer.

Internal Brown & Williamson Tobacco Co. (B.A.T.) documents written in the 1960's, refer to nicotine as an addictive drug. "Smoking is a habit of addiction that is pleasurable," explained Sir Charles Ellis, Research and Development for B.A.T., in 1962, "Nicotine is a very fine drug..." Smoking was also discussed as the probable cause of heart disease, emphysema, and cancer.

"The probabilities are that some combination of constituents of smoke will be found conducive to the onset of cancer."

—Addison Yeaman, General Council, B & W, 1963.

Choices

The tobacco industry was faced with a dilemma. They had two choices. One, they could work with doctors and public health officials to initiate a national cessation program, and gradually withdraw tobacco products from the market. Second, they could defend tobacco and continue selling a dangerous product.

Rumor has it that some tobacco executives suggested closing down the business if it was confirmed that smoking caused cancer or health problems. They could have halted all advertising and promotion. They could have discouraged smoking; provided cessation programs for smokers. They could have established a product liability fund to care for the ill, dying, and their surviving families. Their companies could have survived if they diversified into other kinds of business. This choice would have been a decent, moral, responsible thing to do in the interest of public health. That was not the path they took.

The Decision

"Nicotine is addictive. We are, then, in the business

of selling nicotine, an addictive drug."

—Addison Yeaman, general council, B.A.T., 1963.

The decision they made, as you know, was to continue business as usual. Despite the tobacco industry keeping the health hazards of smoking a secret for seven years, the age of innocence was over in 1964. Thereafter, someone must be held accountable for the deaths. The government can be excused for deaths before 1964 because they did not know about the dangers of tobacco. The tobacco industry and the government must bear the guilt for the death toll that starts in 1964.

Year One, 1964: Death toll: Zero.

Denial

The tobacco industry began challenging the 1964 Surgeon General's report. They disputed the health risks and addiction claims, even though they knew them to be true. The Council for Tobacco Research was established to dispute the truth.

"We have to stand firm on the health issue."

-Joseph Cullman III, Philip Morris

The Putrefaction of a Legitimate Business

Their decision changed the tobacco industry forever. They were never to be a legitimate business again. There were 75 million loyal addicted smokers serving the empire that they had created. They advertised more, and gave away more free samples. Consequently, with nicotine as their hook, cigarettes became the most successful product in American history.

Smoking caused cancer and heart disease, but it would not show up overnight. It took years, and that made it hard to prove and easy to defend in court. No one could sue them for liability and win. They had enjoyed a status with little or no government regulations, and they fought to keep that status. It would take the Congress to change it. The tobacco industry had the money and the people to began a multimillion dollar lobbying effort. The industry was confident they could continue to operate as they always had.

Tobacco industry people had to come face to face with the reality of who and what they had become. They were "born again," proud sellers of the perfect drug, the invisible drug— nicotine. Selling tobacco made huge profits, and it was legal.

Today, the men who run the largest tobacco companies of this $45 billion industry are some of he highest paid executives in America. The total compensation of the top three in 1995:

Philip Morris	**Geoffrey C. Bible**	**$2,475,000**
RJR Nabisco	**Stephen F. Goldstone**	**$841,600**
Loews	**Laurence A. Tisch**	**$861,800**

The Future of the Tobacco Industry?

The State of Mississippi was the first state to file suit against the tobacco industry to recover Medicaid health care costs to treat diseases caused by smoking. Following Mississippi's lead, eight other states have filed suit which could pose a greater liability for the tobacco firms. Warren Buffett, an investor who once praised the tobacco industry as a profitable business, now says that the economy of the business may be fine, "But that does not mean it has a bright future." If you own shares in mutual funds, see Appendix G to find out which funds have a large number of shares of tobacco company stocks, and those that don't.

The Tobacco Industries Future is Brighter in Foreign Countries

The future of the tobacco industry in the rest of the world is bright. Consider that there are 1.1 billion smokers worldwide. The World Bank reported in 1996, that there are three million deaths a year caused by tobacco use worldwide. By 2025, if current smoking trends continue in developed nations, there will be ten million deaths a year from tobacco, making it the number one cause of preventable deaths in the world.

Tobacco companies will continue to export cigarettes to developing nations. In 1992, 10.2 billion packs of cigarettes, valued at $4.2 billion, were exported from the U.S. The top five countries buying American cigarettes are: Japan, Belgium, Hong Kong, Russia and Saudi Arabia. They are busy now, building and operating cigarette factories in South America, China, and Eastern Europe. This will enable tobacco companies to gain back lost sales from an impending decline in their domestic cigarette business.

■ ■ ■ ■ ■ ■ ■ ■ ■ ■ ■ ■ ■ ■

Bottom line, if the tobacco cartel truly cared about the public's health, in 1957 when they first learned of the health hazards of smoking, they would have worked with doctors and public health officials on a national cessation program, and gotten out of the tobacco business. The tobacco cartel fought back, and they showed us they will do anything to continue distributing their lethal biological weapon, even if it tears at the fabric of the constitution of the United States. Today the drug war continues, and the American public is losing.

The acid test of how much power the cartel has in Congress is whether an investigation into their activities appears fair to the American people. Are there representatives in Congress that are acting as agents of the tobacco industry?

"Nicotine is addictive.

We are, then, in the business of selling

nicotine, an addictive drug."

Addison Yeaman, B.A.T.

Chapter Three

The Deceit

When the gavel slammed on the first Congressional hearing to investigate the tobacco industry on April 14, 1994, some believed the government was finally going to expose the truth about the tobacco cartel. The cartel laughingly called it a witch hunt. It is important to know what was behind the headlines. The six tobacco industry representatives standing before Congress:

William I. Campbell	CEO, Philip Morris Co.
James W. Johnston	CEO, R. J. Reynolds
Edward Horrigan	CEO, Liggett Group Inc.
Andrew Tisch	CEO, Lorillard Tobacco Co.
Joseph Taddeo	CEO, U.S. Tobacco Co.
Donald S. Johnston	CEO, American Tobacco Co.
Thomas Sandefur Jr.	CEO, Brown & Williamson Tobacco Corp., (B.A.T. Industries)

The cartel stood before God, Congress, and the American public and denied nicotine is addictive, denied nicotine is a drug, denied smoking causes death and disease, denied they spike cigarettes with nicotine, and denied they promote tobacco to children. This was another battle of the invisible drug war.

Three of the biggest tobacco allies on the Congressional subcommittee, were recruited among others, to aid their cause:

Thomas J. Bliley Jr., R-VA
Alex McMillan, R-N.C.
Dennis Hastert, R-Ill.

Rep. Bliley, an undertaker from Virginia, is one of the tobacco cartel's biggest assets. They wanted to deliver propaganda, and Bliley was their messenger.

He read questions designed to put them in a positive light. Most of his questions were leading "yes" questions, beginning with "Isn't it true that...." For the most part, he appeared to be reading the questions for the first time, and was not involved in writing them. He did not appear to understand the answers given if they went beyond "yes."

One question he asked about nicotine concentrations was obviously planted by R.J. Reynolds (RJR), because James W. Johnston was ready with an answer. He answered it with a lengthy, well-prepared response using visual aides.

Bliley battered Dr. Victor DeNoble, a former Philip Morris drug scientist, about his research. Bliley, a politician-undertaker, was trying to communicate about nicotine addiction on the same level as DeNoble, a scientist. He read question after question, stumbling on words like denicotized and acetaldehyde, "let me try this one, acet-al-d-hyde."

Many of his questions were about what DeNoble told his supervisor while he was employed at Philip Morris. How could he ask about something DeNoble allegedly told his supervisor 15 years ago unless he was primed by someone at Philip Morris? He also asked about specific internal research done at Philip Morris. How could Bliley have known about this confidential, internal company business if Philip Morris had not helped construct the questions?

In another bit of foolery, Bliley asked DeNoble about a potentially damaging paper Philip Morris blocked from being published in the *Journal of Psycho-Pharmacology.* This is not a journal undertakers would typically read. Furthermore this scientific paper was written 15 years ago but was never published! Nonetheless, Bliley said "The title of your paper, as I recall, was *Nicotine as a positive reinforcer in rats, the effects of infusion dose and fixed ratio size.*" Under these circumstances, Bliley was speaking for Philip Morris, not personally, not as an undertaker, and not as a House Representative.

Spies were investigating the enemy. The Health and the Environment subcommittee hearings were rigged.

During the First Six Hours of the Congressional Hearings — 745 Teens Started Smoking, and 296 Americans Died from Smoking Related Diseases

Congress has protected the cartels drug production, distribution, sale, and promotion in this manner for over 30 years. The booty from the sale of their dangerous addictive drug enables the cartel to buy politicians, and maintain extravagant life styles. Immoral politicians take sides with the tobacco cartel. They turn their backs on the health and well-being of the American people, in exchange for campaign money, vacations, golf trips, and power.

Over the years, the cartel has weakened government regulatory agencies for their own gain. The Federal Trade Commission (FTC) was crippled by Congress when they tried to stop the tobacco companies from deceptive advertising. The Department of Health Education and Welfare's budget to investigate children smoking was stripped. And finally just today as the Food and Drug Administration (FDA) is going to regulate tobacco, Congressional representatives are talking about dismantling the agency. Is this merely a coincidence?

The cartel also uses our justice system for their own benefit. B.A.T. legal strategy has been to avoid liability for smoking related diseases and deaths. While lawsuits are being prepared against them for product liability, Congress began debating legislation to limit damages from product liability.

The cartel blatantly used television and the press to make a mockery of Congress's efforts to protect the health of the public by regulating tobacco. At the heart of the deceit, is the cartel's accusation that the government is trying to ban tobacco. One Philip Morris internal memo explains their concerns about the catastrophe that would result if they had to stop selling nicotine, "The cigarette market would collapse, Philip Morris would collapse and we'd all lose our jobs and our consulting fees." James W. Johnston, RJR, suggested,

"If tobacco is too dangerous to be sold,

and is addictive, then ban it."

He quoted inflated numbers on potential job losses, and claimed it would lead to a black market. He appealed—painting an emotional picture, "where cigarettes are sold out of the trunk of cars to children. Criminals don't care who they sell to." Johnston called the Congressional inquiry on nicotine "An attempt at tobacco prohibition." This grandstanding, scare tactic attempted to rally the industry and their 46 million nicotine addicted smokers, to fight a phantom—the prohibition of tobacco.

When asked "Do you believe nicotine is addictive?" the cartel bosses unanimously answered "No." Contrary to their answer, Philip Morris and B.A.T.s executives had evidence in the 1960's that nicotine was addictive. An internal B.A.T. report in 1963 stated "Nicotine appears to be intimately connected with the phenomena of tobacco habituation (tolerance) and/or addiction." B.A.T. withheld the proof they had on nicotine addiction from the scientific community, and keep it secret from the world. Furthermore, they never labeled their cigarettes with a warning on addiction.

The CEO's had several unconventional reasons why they thought nicotine was not addictive. "Saying nicotine is addictive is a disturbing allegation," explained James W. Johnston, "rather it is an enjoyable activity like watching TV, or drinking coffee." Mr. Johnston claimed that nicotine is not addictive, based on the argument that some people are able to quit smoking. Apply that logic to heroin and cocaine, and they too, would not be considered addictive. On the contrary, research over the last decade shows that the quit rate for tobacco is only 2.5% per year, much lower than the 30% for cocaine and heroin.

"Smokers are not addicted," explained Edward Horrigan, CEO of Liggett Group, Inc., "because they do not have to go to the Betty Ford Clinic to quit." Some were more blunt with their dissatisfaction with the whole ordeal. The late Thomas Sandefur Jr., B.A.T., said "Dr. Kessler's FDA investigation into nicotine addiction was foolish."

All of the tobacco executives objected to calling nicotine a drug. "Chewing tobacco," said Joseph Taddeo, U.S. Tobacco Co. (UST), "is not a drug, it is a tradition." In Peru, chewing coca leaves is a tradition. According to Taddeo's logic, cocaine is not a drug.

Tobacco companies don't like being called a drug company even though they sell a drug, do drug research, maintain drug laboratories, employ drug scientists, and study the drug effects of nicotine. A scientist at B.A.T., wrote about nicotine in drug terms, in a report to company officials in 1969, "Nicotine has well documented pharmacological action."

"Nicotine is not a drug," explained Campbell, of Philip Morris, because it does not "make you drunk." Fortunately, nicotine does not cause intoxication, but it is addictive. Despite his testimony, a Philip Morris memo from 1992, refers to nicotine as a pharmacologically active organic chemical similar to the drugs "cocaine, morphine, atropine, and quinine."

"Nicotine is not a drug," says Edward Horrigan, Liggett Group Inc., reasoning that "it is a natural occurring product." If naturally occurring products are not drugs, then antibiotics, coca, opium, marijuana, and most of the pharmaceuticals on drug store shelves are not drugs.

William I. Campbell, of Philip Morris, said nicotine is a taste component of tobacco. "Smokers are satisfied by its taste," said Campbell, "Philip Morris must strive to meet consumer demands or we will fail in the market place." Campbell did not mention the Philip Morris memo that states the primary reason people smoke is, "to deliver nicotine into their bodies."

RJR's CEO joined in with Campbell. "Our products maintain taste customers expect," explained James Johnston, "R.J. Reynolds manufactures cigarettes with consistent concentrations of nicotine." These comments suggest if taste is satisfied, the tobacco companies will continue to sell cigarettes.

Contrary to the tobacco executives testimony, nicotine does not satisfy taste. It satisfies a drug craving in the brain. Research has shown that when nicotine receptors are blocked in the brain, smokers can't taste cigarettes. Furthermore, smokers reject cigarettes that contain no nicotine, because their drug cravings are not satisfied.

When Congress asked the CEOs about cancer and heart disease, none would say that smoking is linked to health problems.

"I am not convinced that smoking causes deaths."

-Andrew Tisch, Lorillard Tobacco Co.

"Oral tobacco has not been established as

a cause of mouth cancer."

-Joseph Taddeo, U.S. Tobacco Co.

"The Surgeon General's numbers on

tobacco deaths

are computer generated."

-James W. Johnston, RJR

Despite their pleas of ignorance to the truth, recently discovered internal tobacco documents reveal the cartel bosses and their predecessors have known for decades that smoking causes lung cancer and heart disease. More interestingly, they were aware of these hazards long before you, your parents, any U.S. Surgeon General, or your family doctor were.

These documents prove B.A.T. was aware of the health hazards in the early 1960's. These documents are in the archives at the University of California, San Francisco

(UCSF) library, under the supervision of Dr. Stanton Glantz. (The B.A.T. documents can be viewed at this Internet address: http://www.library.UCSF.edu/tobacco/bw.html).

When the documents were first opened to public scrutiny, B.A.T. planted private detectives at the UCSF library. They harassed and intimidated anyone trying to study the documents. When the detectives were removed, they filed a law suit to have the documents removed from the library. Nothing they could do could stop the flow of documents into the hands of the hungry public. B.A.T. then turned to their allies in Congress. Congress obliged B.A.T. by removing Dr. Glantz's federal funding to study the documents.

This "book burning" mentality is flagrant terrorism, orchestrated by B.A.T. and members of the U.S. Congress. The tobacco cartel does not want you to know the truth about the health hazards of tobacco, or the power of nicotine addiction. They do not want you to read this book. This is what a drug war looks like.

Is the tobacco cartel concerned about the public's or smokers' health? Consider the 1995 Philip Morris recall of pesticide contaminated cigarettes. The recall was about money and market share. The real agenda was to prevent a big drop in market share because the pesticide made people cough and dizzy. People will not smoke cigarettes that make them cough and dizzy. Movement of product is paramount—not the health of the user.

When the cartel bosses were asked, "Do you spike your cigarettes with nicotine?" they all answered "No." Andrew Tisch, Lorillard Tobacco Co., said "Nicotine is extracted from tobacco, then it's put back in. This is not spiking."

William I. Campbell, Philip Morris, explained that denatured alcohol and tobacco extracts contain nicotine, and both are used in the processing of tobacco. However, he says it adds "too little to be called spiking."

None of the manufactures admitted spiking cigarettes with nicotine. However, all CEOs agreed they manipulate nicotine concentrations by blending tobaccos, and they do this consistently. Thomas Sandefur Jr., of B.A.T. said "B.A.T. manipulates nicotine in cigarettes, but only for taste."

The FDA concluded that nicotine concentrations in cigarettes are manipulated. James Johnston of RJR disagreed, saying "The FDA calculations are incorrect." He explained that "We manipulate tar levels, not nicotine levels. Tar is a health risk factor."

RJR was questioned about promoting cigarettes to children. In defense of their Joe Camel cartoons, Mr. Johnston said that cartoons don't sell to children. As an example he cited MetLife's use of Snoopy cartoon character. In contrast to Joe Camel, MetLife's Snoopy advertising does not prey on the psychological vulnerabilities of children, selling sex appeal, popularity, and adult activities. MetLife's cartoons target adults. In any case, they do not have 3,000 twelve year olds calling every day to buy life insurance.

RJR Nabisco and Philip Morris are experts at marketing. They also have had extensive experience in selling breakfast cereal and cookies to children. Mr. Johnston was asked about an American Medical Association (AMA) study that shows Camel ads increased market share of those under 18 years old by 32%. Johnston said, "The AMA numbers are false. If there was proof that Joe Camel tempted children to smoke, I would pull the ad in a heart beat." There is proof, and there is common sense, which both support pulling the ads.

When asked about UST's marketing practices that target children, Taddeo said

"Our ads are not intended to attract children.

We advertise it is an adult custom for adults only."

For adults only—this is precisely the point. It's what kids want. They want to do adult things. UST's smokeless tobacco is used by children, which belies their alleged advertising intentions. "We want to start a fad," said L.F. Bantle, at a 1968 UST meeting. "We must sell the use of tobacco in the mouth and appeal to young people."

Despite the White Knight effort by a few Members of Congress, Henry Waxman (D-CA), Ron Wyden (D-OR), and the late Mike Synar (D-OK), the Congressional hearings of 1994 eventually came to an abrupt halt. Deals were made—money exchanged hands behind closed doors. Tobacco industry contributions helped elect new republican representatives that would follow Representative Newt Gingrich's plan. Powerful Congressional representatives were quickly and quietly shuffled. Speaker of the house Newt Gingrich appointed Thomas Bliley as the new chairman of the Energy and Commerce Committee investigating the tobacco cartel. This sealed the Republican's web that protects the tobacco industry.

"I see no reason to continue

the tobacco hearings."

-Rep. Thomas Bliley (R-VA).

Will the Congressional Hearings on Tobacco be Reopened?

The American Cancer Society's President, Dr. LaMar McGinnis, asked Congress to reopen the hearings in June 1995. However, with the replacement of Henry Waxman (D-CA) as the chairman of the Energy and Commerce Committee with Thomas Bliley, (R-VA), it is doubtful this will ever occur. Bliley has stated publicly that he does not see any reason to continue the tobacco hearings. He has taken a total of $126,976 from the tobacco industry as of December 1995, more than any other member of Congress. It is important to note that Bliley's appointment was an instrumental part of Newt Gingrich's plans to control the government. Meanwhile, tobacco related deaths continue at the rate of one every 73 seconds.

Criminal Charges Pending

On May 27, 1994, Rep. Martin Meehan (D-MA), and six members of Congress sent a written request to the U.S. Attorney General, Janet Reno, to begin a criminal investigation against tobacco companies. Evidence was collected for the "prosecution memo" by the House Subcommittee on Health and the Environment. It was not until July 1995, after secret Philip Morris documents appeared, that the Justice Department began a full blown investigation. Their New York office convened a grand jury, and Philip Morris was subpoenaed on July 25, 1995.

Some of the allegations cited in the 111 page document:

"Tobacco companies—through their executives, their lawyers, their advertising agencies, their lobbyist, their public relations agents, their scientists and their trade associations officials—have committed a series of serious crimes over a period of several decades."

Some of the possible offenses the tobacco companies will be charged with:

- **PERJURY**
- **CONSPIRACY TO OBSTRUCT CONGRESS**
- **CONSPIRACIES IN RESTRAINT OF TRADE**
- **CONSPIRACY TO DEFRAUD THE PUBLIC**
- **MAIL FRAUD**
- **WIRE FRAUD**
- **RACKETEERING**
- **FALSE ADVERTISING**

Signed:

Martin T. Meehan, D-MA
Henry Waxman, D-CA
Mike Synar, D-OK
Pete Stark, D-CA
James V. Hansen, R-UT
Peter J. Visclosky, D-IN
Thomas M. Foglietta, D-Pa.
Richard J. Durbin, D-IL

Richard Daynard, law professor at Northeastern University, and member of the Tobacco Products Liability Project, said "I don't see the stopping point between here and bankruptcy for the tobacco companies." Daynard also had these comments regarding the criminal charges:

Contempt of Congress —"Contempt of Congress is based on false statements, (made by the CEO's)."

Antitrust violations —"They got together and decided not to come out with safe products and not to tell the truth about the dangers."

Reckless endangerment —"They made deliberate decisions that they knew to a certainty would cause millions of Americans to become addicted and hundreds of thousands to die."

The tobacco companies are not going to roll over and plead guilty. They have the best lawyers money can buy, including a former federal judge.

■ ■ ■ ■ ■ ■ ■ ■ ■ ■ ■ ■ ■

How has the tobacco industry made such a harmful product one of the most successfully marketed products in America? Nicotine keeps them smoking, but advertising gets them started. Advertising directly induced millions of women to start smoking Lucky Strikes. Today's cigarette advertising strategies deserve a careful look—how they lure and target children, minorities and women.

Doctor,
be your own
judge...
try this
simple test

With so many claims made in cigarette advertising, you, Doctor, no doubt prefer to judge for yourself. So won't you make this simple test?

Take a PHILIP MORRIS and any other cigarette

1. Light up either one first. Take a puff—get a good mouthful of smoke — and s-l-o-w-l-y let the smoke come *directly* through your nose.
2. Now, do exactly the same thing with the other cigarette.

You will notice a distinct difference between PHILIP MORRIS and any other leading brand.

PHILIP MORRIS

Philip Morris & Co. Ltd., Inc,. 100 Park Avenue, New York 17, N.Y.

This advertisement appeared in a medical journal in 1950.

Chapter Four

Advertising Normalizes an Addiction

"Advertising affects everyone.

We just do not like to admit it."

- Professor Edward Popper, North Eastern University

What made cigarettes the most successful product in American history? Advertising. No one likes to admit that advertising has an affect on them. Most people will agree that they do not like to be "sold." Despite this, advertising works. It makes people buy brand name products, and products on sale.

Cigarette advertising reached an unprecedented high of $3.27 billion in 1988. Since then, the budget steadily increased, and by 1993 was $6.2 billion. That is $24 spent for every person in the U.S., or about $135 per smoker. This is the largest ad campaign in the history of any product.

Tobacco Companies Spend $ 24.00 on Advertising for Every Man, Woman and Child in the U.S.

The tobacco industry must replace the smokers that die or quit. Tobacco companies claim they use tobacco advertising to attract two classes of buyers. Brand competition advertising is designed to switch existing smokers away from another brands. The other class of buyer is the new smoker or starter. The easiest and most vulnerable new smoker is the teenager.

Guy Smith, a Philip Morris public relations executive, explains "Our studies, and anti-smokers research say the top three reasons people start smoking are: 1) Advertising, 2) Friends smoke, and 3) Family members smoke."

Creating a Desire to Smoke

"I never saw an ad that made someone

buy something they did not want."

-John O' Toole, President,
American Association of Advertising Agencies

This is true for selling cigarettes. Salespeople will tell you that you have to desire something before you want to buy it. Desire precedes want. Cigarette ads create a desire. Teens desire popularity, acceptance, something in common with a peer group, and to rebel against adults. Women desire equality to men, a sense of importance, and recognition.

Targeting Women

Until the 1920's, tobacco advertising mainly targeted males. Men were smoking, but the industry was missing the female segment of the market. American Tobacco Company's Lucky Strike campaign in 1927 finally broke the social barrier that frowned on women smoking. This campaign started women smoking by creating desire—the desire for women to be equal to men. Smoking was portrayed as the thing to do to give women the equality they desired. When women desired equality, they wanted to smoke.

Torches of Freedom

The advertising genius, Dr. Edward Bernays, was credited for breaking the barrier. (Later, Bernays worked aggressively for pro-health, tobacco control organizations.) Bernays consulted a psychoanalysis, Dr. A.A. Brill, about the challenge. Dr. Brill explained—

> "Cigarettes, to women, are torches of freedom
>
> that they use to dramatize their objection
>
> of the taboo against smoking by men."

At the next Easter Parade, debutantes were solicited to march and smoke, that is to light "torches of freedom," in protest to man's inhumanity to women. Within six weeks of the promotion, the barrier was broken. Smoking by women became accepted, and Lucky Strikes became the best seller. Slogans such as "Reach for a Lucky instead of a sweet" were used. Famous people, like Lucill Ball, Dean Martin, Bob Hope, Henry Fonda, Arthur Godfrey, and Jerry Lewis appeared in advertisements.

One Lucky Strike ad read:

"An ancient prejudice has been removed. Today, legally, politically and socially, womanhood stands in her true light. American intelligence has cast aside the ancient prejudice that held her to be inferior."

The dramatic rise in women smoking can be attributed to that one Lucky Strike advertising and promotion campaign. Advertising did not cause women to switch from one brand to another. Advertising directly induced women to start smoking, a fact the tobacco industry denies.

Janet Sackman began smoking when she appeared as "Miss Lucky Strike" in advertisements. "They kept providing false reassurances," that she says encouraged her to start smoking, "so I had no idea that smoking was so very dangerous." Some years later Ms. Sackman developed throat cancer, and is a tobacco control advocate today.

Tobacco Advertising in Women's Magazines

In the late 1960's and 1970's, major advertising campaigns were initiated for Virginia Slims, Silva Thins and Eve cigarettes. Advertising that targets women uses themes of liberation and feminism, and images of sophistication and slimness. Virginia Slims was introduced in 1968 using the theme "You've come a long way, baby."

Today, women's magazines that run cigarette advertisements have fewer articles on the health hazards of smoking. Some of the most widely circulated magazines today collect more than 25% of their advertising income from tobacco advertising. The editors will not run articles on the hazards of smoking because they do not want to lose the tobacco company's advertising money.

Doctors Were Used to Promote Cigarette Safety

In the 1950's, doctors were solicited to promote the safety of smoking. These ads reassured the public about the safety of cigarettes:

"More doctors smoke Camels than any other cigarette."

"20,679 physicians preferred to smoke a Lucky Strike

because it's toasted."

Philip Morris advertisements targeted physicians. Real doctors appeared in their cigarette advertisements. They appealed to other doctors to recommend Philip Morris to their patients. One such ad appearing in a medical journal stated:

"With proof so conclusive.....(that Philip Morris are less irritating).... with your own personal experience added to the published studies. Would it not be good practice to suggest Philip Morris to your patients who smoke?"

The Marlboro Man — Legacy or Curse?

Philip Morris began the Marlboro country theme in television advertisements in 1964. The Western theme painted portraits of ruggedness and independence, with cattle, boots, cowboy hats, all sprinkled with testosterone overtones. The center piece of the theme was the famous "Marlboro Man".

R. W. Murry, Philip Morris CEO, stated that the Marlboro Man conveys "elements of adventure, freedom, being in charge of your own destiny." Marlboro give the adolescent a badge to identify them as masculine, in the same way a car, clothes or a cologne do. Some kids see the Marlboro man as an outlaw, and smoking Marlboro gives them a way to be "bad."

The Marlboro cowboy is said to be one of the most successful advertising icons ever. The actor that immortalized the Marlboro Man on TV ads, was David McLean, who died of lung cancer on October 12, 1995, at the age of 73. Following the advertising ban on TV, a new Marlboro Man portrayed the famous cowboy on billboards and printed ads. His name was Wayne McLaren. McLaren died of lung cancer on July 23, 1992, at the age of 51. Some of his last words were: "Take care of the children. Tobacco will kill you, and I am living proof of it."

The Marlboro country advertising campaign has made Marlboro the number one selling cigarette. That campaign is still promoted in the 1990's. Today, one third of the 46 million smokers in America smoke Marlboro. In 1995, the brand was honored by the American Marketing Association by naming Marlboro to their hall of fame.

The Marlboro Man is not the only cigarette model that has fallen victim to lung cancer. Alan Landers was a Winston billboard and magazine model in the 1960's. He has since undergone two operations for lung cancer. Mr. Landers is now a spokesman for a pro-health, tobacco control group, Citizens for A Tobacco-free Society.

Smoking in the Movies

Movies in the 50's romanticized smoking. Some of the early Hollywood image makers were Marlon Brando, Humphrey Bogart, and Betty Davis. Smoking became a positive statement of American culture. Most baby boomers, statistically about half, were raised by parents that smoked.

A study of films, from 1960 to 1990, revealed:

- Smoking in films was three times as prevalent as it was in the general population.
- Smokers were portrayed as successful, attractive, white males.
- Smoking was associated with hostility and stress reduction.
- The incidence of young people smoking in films doubled during that time.

The exaggerated prevalence of smoking in films misleads young people to overestimate the real prevalence of cigarette smoking. "Everybody smokes," is an answer often given by adolescents as a reason for smoking.

The high rate of smoking in films is the result of tobacco companies paying producers to 'place' their brand of cigarettes in movies, a common practice before 1990. Tobacco companies often gave payments of cash, cars, jewelry, and even horses to the cast and crew. In the 1980's, Philip Morris paid $350,000 to have their cigarettes in the James Bond movie, License to Kill. Brown & Williamson Tobacco Corp. (B.A.T.) paid almost $700,000 to producers to have Kool in movies, such as Body Heat.

Sylvester Stallone was allegedly paid $300,000 to show a Kool billboard for a few seconds in First Blood. Stallone recently denied ever receiving any money from B.A.T., and says he does not enter into such agreements today.

No movie was immune to paid cigarette promotions—they also appeared in children's movies. Who Framed Roger Rabbit, and Honey I Shrunk the Kids, both Walt Disney movies, had Camel "ads" in them.

Tobacco companies, in response to public outrage in 1990, agreed to stop the practice of paying to have their brands in movies. However, many producers independently continue to glamorize smoking by having leading stars and role models for America's youth smoke. One recent example is Winona Ryder's part as a nicotine addicted youth in the movie *Reality Bites*. Hollywood idols, such as Johnny Depp and Brad Pitt, have also depicted smoking as the trendy, cool thing to do.

Banned from TV, but Still on TV

Cigarette manufactures spent about $300 million on television advertising in 1967. Before 1967, the American TV watching public was exposed to few pro-health, tobacco control messages. Then in July of 1967, the *Fairness Doctrine* required equal time for anti-smoking messages, largely due to the work of the pro-health tobacco control advocacy organization Action on Smoking and Health (ASH). About $75 million in air time was provided for smoking cessation and prevention messages. For the first time, TV watchers saw both tobacco advertising and antismoking messages. That mix continued until January 1971, when all advertising on TV and radio was banned. This also put an end to the smoking cessation and prevention messages. It is most important to note that during the era when health messages encouraged people to quit smoking, cigarette consumption dropped seven percent. Furthermore, once the pro-health messages were eliminated, cigarette consumption jumped back up. This is a mammoth study that provides evidence that advertising works, and that smoking cessation and prevention messages are effective in countering cigarette advertising.

The year following the advertising ban in 1971, the decision was tested by the U.S. Supreme Court and upheld as constitutional. Despite the ban, cigarette advertisements still can be seen today on most televised sports events.

Tobacco Advertising at Sporting Events

Tobacco company sponsorship of sporting events totaled $84 million in 1988. Cigarette billboard ads are prominently displayed at televised sports events like tennis tournaments, baseball, and auto racing. Hanging from the wall surrounding the action, they often appear on TV. One report claims Philip Morris was guaranteed three minutes of TV exposure of it's cigarette advertisement during a Knicks game at Madison Square Garden.

Baseball

Philip Morris is baseball's third largest sign advertiser. One of the most famous signs is their Marlboro Man ad at New York's Shea Stadium. On May 21, 1995, ASH filed a complaint with the Department of Justice about these signs. The Justice Department charged that Philip Morris placed ads in strategic locations to appear on TV. Philip Morris has used this loophole in the ban on TV cigarette advertising for 24 years. They finally complied with the Justice Department's demand to stop the practice, but only after a six month battle.

The Justice Department's agreement with Philip Morris does not include auto racing. Meanwhile, the cigarette logo race cars continue to jump through the loophole in the ban on TV advertising—a loophole the FDA wants to close.

Tobacco Advertising at Auto Racing Events

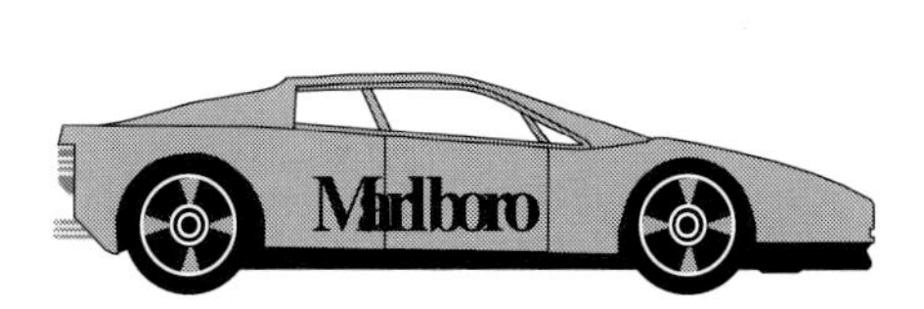

Auto racing is the biggest arena for tobacco advertising. Philip Morris and RJR spend about $30 million a year on auto racing cigarette promotions, filling about 12 hours of air time a week. Sponsorship of the Nascar's Winston Cup gets RJR about 30 hours of TV coverage for Winston. RJR has spent $200 million dollars on Nascar racing since 1971. During a televised Marlboro Grand Prix race tobacco advertising flashed across the screen constantly. Dr. Alan Blum M.D., of Doctors Ought to Care (DOC), had the patience to count the number of times the Marlboro logo appeared—5,933 times.

Free Cigarette Samples

Doling out free drugs is one of the most effective ways to induce drug dependence in a vulnerable person. Free cigarette giveaways at community and sporting events is part of tobacco companies promotional strategy. In 1993, cigarette companies spent $2.6 billion on free samples, coupons and other financial incentives to hook smokers.

At one time, airline food trays were served with a pack containing three cigarettes, even to kids. Today, auto racing is a typical event where cigarettes are given away. Tobacco salesmen have also been known to toss bushel baskets of cigarettes at passersby in the streets of New York City. One witness to this described the cigarette giveaway as causing a near riot.

In 1992, The State of New York passed the *No Tobacco Sampling Law*. Later in 1994, Philip Morris mailed five packages of Marlboro to 44,000 people in New York. If a young person intercepted and smoked all five packs they would have a 94% chance of becoming nicotine dependent, and one of every three would die from tobacco related diseases. Philip Morris paid $250,000 to the state in a settlement, while denying their guilt.

In 1995, Philip Morris announced that it was indefinitely suspending all cigarette sampling. In contrast, RJR spokesperson said we "feel very comfortable" with our current sampling programs, and have "no plans to suspend them."

Funding of Community and Special Events

Event sponsorship increases brand visibility, and associates a particular lifestyle with a brand to create loyalty. In 1994, event sponsorship rose to more than $4 billion.

Concerts are one kind of community activity tobacco companies commonly fund. Youth-oriented concerts are frequently targeted for free cigarette sample giveaways. Tobacco companies also fund minority organizations, such as the United Negro College Fund, which receives $150,000 a year. Some museums also rely on tobacco donations.

The Tobacco Zealots Position in Ads Today

To the tobacco zealots, utopia is selling cigarettes the way they did in the 1950's. At that time, nearly half the country smoked, and the tobacco industry operated with even fewer government regulations. They advertised their tobacco products without restrictions, and denied all the health hazards of smoking.

Past advertising themes were associated with high-style living, healthy activities, economic, social, and professional success. Today, cigarette advertising campaigns are tailored to children, women, blue-collar workers, and minorities. The young and hip are being wooed by RJR and Philip Morris with trendy packaging and artsy imaging, with brands such as Red Kamel, and Moonlight.

Whatever the message, whatever the product, they are all the same old cancer sticks. Ads avoid the health hazards of smoking. They deny the health hazards attributed to ETS and deny that nicotine is addictive. They divert our attention from these issues with institutional advertising that concentrates on rights, freedom, choice and government interference.

The Lowest Form of Free Speech: *Cigarette Advertising*

With help of the American Civil Liberties Union, the tobacco industry has tried to link the ban on advertising with the issue of free speech. They claim First Amendment rights. The ban on TV advertising has been tested, and failed to qualify as a violation of the First Amendment. It is important to note that the Supreme Court ruled that advertising was a "low form of speech," and was not considered at all protected by the First Amendment. Scholars agree that if Congress or the FDA ban all tobacco advertising, the Supreme Court would uphold the ban as constitutional.

Sidestepping the Issue

A study sponsored by the Tobacco Institute in 1978 warned that the most dangerous development to the tobacco business is the public's concern about ETS. The Roper Organization did a public poll on smoking, and made these recommendations:

Summary of The Roper Report to the Tobacco Industry

- The tobacco industry's strategy should be a program of publicity to show ETS is not harmful.
- They should argue that a vote for a new tobacco excise tax is a vote against freedom and rights.
- To take the position that a vote for a Smoke-free Environment Act is a vote for more arrests, and overworked police officers chasing smokers.
- To sidestep the health issue, and draw fire from it by talking about rights, privacy, government intervention, big brother, freedom and civil liberties. (Variation used today: accommodation).

Roper created the "What's Next Defense," a series of sidestepping tactics for the tobacco industry. Their overall strategy attempts to undermine reasonable tobacco control efforts by confusing the issue with exaggerated and sometimes ridiculous claims. The "What's Next Defense" applied to a ban on tobacco advertising would sound like this: "What's next – a ban on coffee advertising?"

The tobacco industry was quick to put Roper's advice into practice to ward off all tobacco control efforts, and is still using it today. Seventeen years after the Roper Report, Guy L. Smith, VP of Philip Morris in 1987, used the "What's Next Defense" when he said:

> ".. If those that oppose tobacco would succeed in dictating which behaviors were acceptable and which were not, ... If they eliminated free choice regarding tobacco, they would affect free choice itself. What would they ban next? Alcohol, red meat, eggs, dairy products?"

Smith's compares taking a poison to eating food. These stale "What's next messages" still appear in editorials, and in tobacco industry propaganda today:

Will alcohol be next?

Will caffeine be next?

Will high fat foods be next?

Ban books, movies, music?

Where will it all end?

A cigarette ban is the beginning of

the end of a free country!

The common thread running through all this sidestepping is to divert the public's attention from the real issues – tobacco use and secondhand smoke kills people!

Nicotine Talk

Beware of the opinions of those tobacco zealots who support smoking in public, deny the health hazards of second hand smoke, or deny that nicotine is addictive. Bob Dole, for example, in July 1996 stated in public that he did not think nicotine was addictive.

Some editorials are written by tobacco industry consultants who are paid to promote their position. Use caution if the source of information quoted is from the Tobacco Institute. If so it is probably biased, misleading, or incorrect. Some of their sidestepping strategy regarding banning smoking in public:

It's an attack on individual rights. An attack on freedom of choice. Not allowing smoking in public is Government intervention, prohibition, discrimination.
(Roper: Sidestep the health issue, by talking about rights, privacy, government intervention, big brother, freedom and civil liberties.)

ETS is not the same as mainstream smoke.
(Roper: The tobacco industry's strategy should be a program of publicity to show ETS is not harmful. Also, this is a half-truth, ETS has more carcinogens that mainstream smoke, and it kills people.)

Smokers will become criminals overnight.
(Roper: Take the position that a vote for banning smoking in public is a vote for more arrests, and overworked police officers chasing smokers. Experience from cities where smoking is banned in public shows that no arrests have been necessary because smokers willingly comply with the ban.)

Not every newspaper reader in every major city is fortunate enough to have newspapers with editorial boards that are pro-health. Consider that many editorial boards are like most folks — they are deficient in their knowledge of the hazards of smoking, secondhand smoke, and nicotine addiction. Furthermore, they have been neutralized by tobacco advertising in two ways. First, tobacco advertising makes them complacent, and they suffer from the "friendly familiarity" syndrome. Second, they have become accustomed to the significant profits made from tobacco advertisements.

On the other hand, some reporters have done a tremendous job in unraveling many of the tobacco companies' deceptions. Alix Freedman, a reporter for the *Wall Street Journal*, won the Pulitzer Prize in 1996 for uncovering deception in the tobacco industry. For that, the tobacco industry has lashed out at reporters:

- Reporters do not trust the tobacco industry, and are one sided on the issue.
- The press is not fair because they allow more space for scientist and doctors to argue the health hazards of ETS than the tobacco industries position.
- They suggest one should trust the tobacco industry, not journalists, for reliable health information on ETS.

Confusing the Issue

The tobacco industry, using expert psychologists as advertising consultants, have found ways to confuse the health issue. One way to confuse the health issue is to call tobacco use a risky activity. They compare smoking to sky diving, eating bacon, having unprotected sex, and drinking beer. Pointing a gun at your head and pulling the trigger can be called a risky activity. Smoking, like Russian Roulette, is also a deadly activity.

Bob Dole, in June 1996, compared the hazards of secondhand smoke to drinking milk. It is no coincidence, that Philip Morris also has an active disinformation program running in Europe, which compares the hazards of secondhand smoke to eating cookies and milk. The message is that secondhand smoke is as harmless to a child as an all-American snack. Recall that in the ranking of preventable deaths, exposure to secondhand smoke was fifth. The truth is that food is essential to life — tobacco ends life.

Whenever a new tobacco excise tax is mentioned, it is called a risky activities tax. Similarly, as the heat is being turned up and several States are preparing to sue the tobacco companies for reimbursement for Medicaid expenses used to treat smokers' diseases, the tobacco companies are doing a double sidestep dance. They try to minimize the death and disease from tobacco use, and their responsibility for it, by saying that States are suing them because tobacco use is a risky activity. The tobacco companies defend smoking as if someone's life was at stake. Smoking is not essential to life – it is a cause of death.

The Legal Product Defense

Whether it is a ban on advertising or smoking in public, the tobacco industry, and all the people that profit from tobacco use often defend their actions by whining "Tobacco is a legal product." Some other legal products are cocaine, morphine, amphetamine, barbiturate, and dynamite. At one time, LSD was a legal product. Most products that are not illegal have some kind of restrictions on their possession or use in the interest of public health and safety. Why should tobacco be any different from other legal products that are restricted to protect the health of the public?

The legal product defense used in this context is saying "you can not restrict the use of a legal product," which is a half-truth. On the other hand, when the legal product defense is used by a tobacco company attorney it may have a different meaning. When asked about the deaths of ten million smokers, they answer with the same legal product defense but with this meaning: "Yes, but tobacco is a legal product and there's nothing you can do about it."

The Smoking is Morally Right Defense

Who knows where the tobacco industry got their moral values. One ad actually touted smoking as morally right. If that is so, then it must follow that it is morally right to poison yourself, abuse addictive drugs, and kill other people by poisoning. Furthermore, what they do must be morally right as well: the manufacture, distribution, promotion and advertising of an addictive drug that has killed ten million people. And selling addictive poisons to children must be morally right. This moral code also implies that if a generous profit is made, it is morally right.

Some people want to stop tobacco advertising because it conflicts with their moral beliefs. One concerned group is The Interfaith Center of Corporate Responsibility, a coalition of Roman Catholic, Protestant, and Jewish institutional investors. Some 275 coalition members advocate corporate responsibility on issues such as tobacco advertising.

Outdoor billboard advertising is one way tobacco advertising reaches children. According to the Outdoor Advertising Association of America (OAAA), the three largest billboard companies are Gannett Outdoor, Eller Media Co., and 3M Media. In May of 1996, the Interfaith Center of Corporate Responsibility led the way to convince 3M that they should stop accepting billboard advertising from tobacco companies.

When Kippy Burns, a spokesperson for OAAA, was asked about 3M's action on tobacco advertising she said that they will continue a "firm and vigilant support of free-speech protections." Once again, the Roper Report strategy was used to avoid the health issue by invoking the first amendment.

Unfortunately, the first and second largest billboard advertisers, Gannett Outdoor and Eller Media Co., are not going to follow 3M's moral decision. Jeffrey Dixon, spokesperson for Eller Media said "As long as tobacco continues to be legal, we will continue to advertise it"— using the legal product defense. Philip Morris' response was a predictable "cigarette ads help adults make choices."

Nonsmokers Lulled by Cigarette Advertising Too

The perception of smoking is conditioned by advertising—by associating smoking with psychological traits. A advertising executive for Philip Morris called this "friendly familiarity." Many nonsmokers also view smoking as socially acceptable. Too many have been lulled into a state of numbness—often sitting in smoking sections with no concern. On the contrary, others are less tolerant in their acceptance of smoking in public. If all 214 million nonsmokers were more aware of the seriousness of the health hazards of secondhand smoke, more would take action to stop smoking in public places; 83,000 lives a year depend on it.

■■■■■■■■■■■■■

Tobacco advertising has one purpose — to get people to smoke. It has been proven to directly induce people to start smoking, as it did women in the 1920's. When cigarette advertising was prohibited from television, the tobacco industry got more creative. But when adults no longer responded to tobacco advertising, they did the unbelievable.

Chapter Five

Seduction of Children into Addiction

The Teen Smoking Crisis

Tobacco advertising has one purpose – to get people to smoke. Advertising was the motivating factor to get masses of women to start smoking in the 1920's. Today, it just so happens that the only group that responds to tobacco ads are children. Advertising is the most potent force in causing children to start smoking. The alarming rise in teen smoking is also attributed to peer pressure, easy access of cigarettes, and the feeling of immortality.

The Alarming Trends in Children Smoking

During a six year cigarette advertising blitz, from 1967 to 1973, there was a tremendous increase in young women starting to smoke. Doctors at the University of California - San Diego, (UCSD) Cancer Center observed this horrifying smoking trend among young girls:

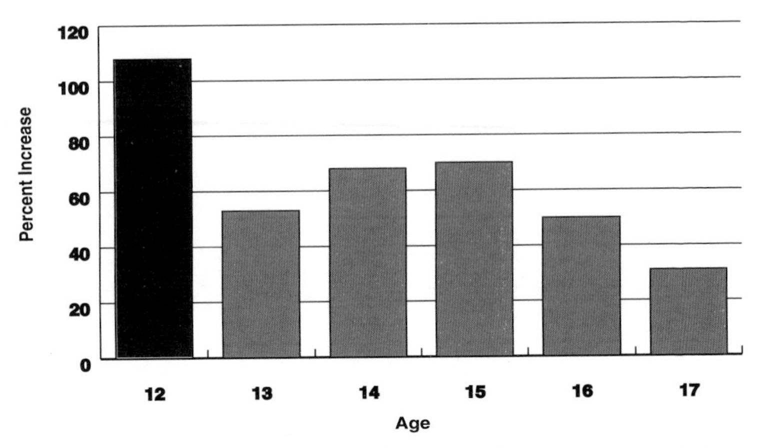

The researchers found twelve year old girls showed the biggest increase in smoking. On the other hand, they found no increase in boys starting to smoke during the same time. They concluded that advertising has an important impact on the uptake of smoking by girls, and does play a role in encouraging long term nicotine addiction. Since that time, girls have started smoking at the same rate, and in some areas higher than boys. The UCSD doctors urged a ban on all advertising and promotion of cigarettes.

Teen smoking dropped from 1976 to 1984, then leveled off. The downhill slide in teen smoking was effectively stopped by a corresponding change in cigarette promotion budgets in 1991 which increased 16%. The following year, teen smoking again started increasing steadily.

In 1996, the Centers for Disease Control (CDC) reported that the percentage of high school teens reporting that they smoked within the last 30 days rose dramatically from 27.5% in 1991 to 34.8% in 1995. By race and sex, the single largest increase in smoking was among black male teens, which increased 14%. Even more alarming, 16% of all teens surveyed reported smoking at least 20 cigarettes per month. One pack a month is enough to induce nicotine cravings, and explains why 20% of high school graduates are addicted to nicotine.

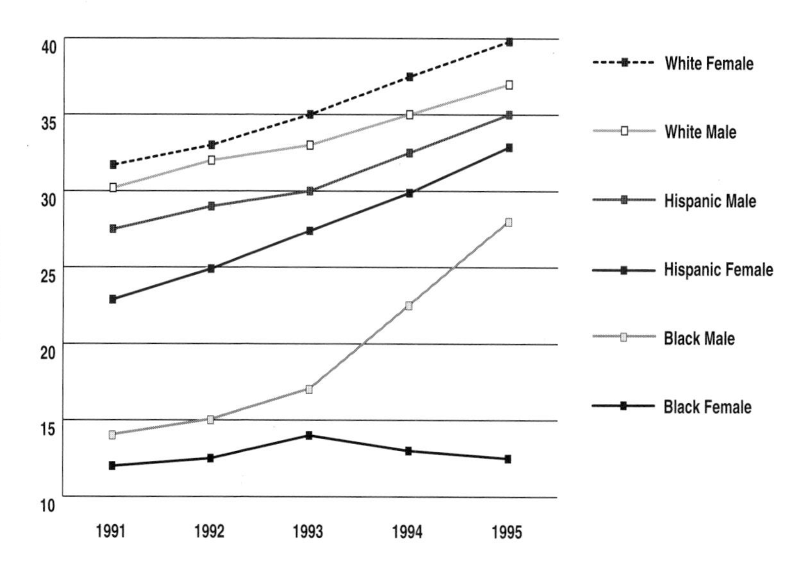

Dr. J. DeFranza, author of a study published in the *Journal of the American Medical Association,* found that adolescents smoke 947 million packs of cigarettes and consume 26 million packages of smokeless tobacco a year. Children eight to 11 years old that smoked daily averaged four per day, and those 12 to 17 years smoked an average 14 a day. It takes millions of children smoking seven to 14 cigarettes a day to spend $1.26 billion on tobacco annually.

Consider these trends:

- Three million kids under 18 smoke.
- 3,000 teens a day, 1.1 million teens a year, start smoking.
- 19.4% of high school seniors smoked daily in 1994, up from 18.5% in 1991.
- Nine percent of eighth graders smoked daily in 1994, up from 7.2% in 1991.
- 75% of adolescent smokers want to quit, but cannot.
- 70% of adolescent smokers say they would not have started smoking if they could choose again.
- 14 1/2 years is the average age when smoking begins.
- 90% of new smokers are under 19 years of age.
- 50% of new teen smokers will smoke at least 16 to 20 years.

Advertising Starts Children Smoking

Decades ago, tobacco advertising attracted new adult smokers. When it no longer attracted new adult smokers, marketing strategies had to change. Tobacco companies had to replace the smokers that quit or died every year with new smokers. Tobacco advertising and promotion took an abrupt turn to address their potential loss of profit. They started targeting kids, and it worked — teens started smoking by the millions. Consider that 90% of smoking initiation starts before age 19. For all practical purposes tobacco advertising only works on teens 19 years old and younger. The National Center for Chronic Disease Prevention says that advertising is to blame for 3,000 teens a day starting to smoke. In contrast, there has been a decrease in the number of children smoking in countries like New Zealand, where tobacco advertising has been banned. In America today, some $1 billion in cigarettes are sold every year to three million teens.

Research shows that advertising does affect the uptake and the continuation of smoking by children. Doctors at the University of California, San Diego, reported in the *Journal of the National Cancer Institute*, that "tobacco marketing may be a stronger current influence in encouraging adolescent to initiate the smoking uptake process than exposure to peer or family smokers." Dr. John P. Pierce, an author of the study, says that "receptivity to tobacco advertising is twice as good an indicator of whether a child will smoke as whether peers or family members are smokers."

If a child is positively influenced by tobacco promotions, they are four times more susceptible to start smoking.

Kids Smoke the Most Heavily Advertised Brands

A report on adolescent smoking by the CDC confirmed they smoke the most heavily advertised brands. Furthermore, adolescents changed brand preferences as brand-specific advertising increased.

A California survey in 1990 found that teens smoke the top two most heavily advertised brands: Marlboro and Camel. The authors concluded that cigarette advertisements do encourage teens to smoke. In the interest of public health, they suggested banning all tobacco advertisements.

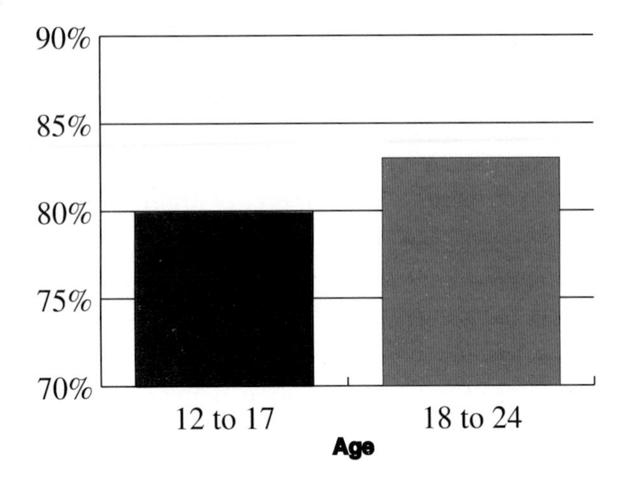

A more recent national survey of teen smokers, age 12 to 18 years, found similar trends in cigarette brand selection. From 1989 to 1993, the most popular brand smoked was Marlboro; Camel was the second, and Newport was third. Most disturbing, 85% of adolescent smokers choose one of these three most heavily advertised brands. And at the heart of the problem, spending on regional cigarette advertising correlates with the brands adolescents smoke in that region. These observations establish a positive link of cigarette advertising to adolescents' brand preference.

One of the most comprehensive studies on cigarette advertising was done by the University of British Columbia. Professor Richard W. Pollay was the lead author of this 20 year study of nine cigarette brands. He found that when the advertising budget for a brand increased ten percent, its market share for adults increased three percent, and nine percent for teens. Below is a summary of some of his findings:

Brand	Advertising Market	Market ShareTeens	Market Share Adults
Marlboro	12.7%	59.5%	21.9%
Camel	4.9%	8.7%	3.7%
Newport	4.7%	11.1%	3.8%

These three brands, Marlboro, Camel, and Newport have a higher teen market share for each advertising dollar spent that other brands. The advertisements for the other brands studied, Kool, Merit, Salem, Virginia Slims, Winston and Benson & Hedges, were less appealing to kids and did not have the same effect on teen market share. Mr. Pollay commented on this data saying it "clearly shows that cigarette advertising for market share is primarily a battle of brands for consumption by the young."

The Culling of the American Teen

Barron's, a prestigious weekly financial publication, first noted on September 3, 1956, that the industry was making a conscious effort to sell to the young. It was known as early as 1956 that teenagers were the easiest and most vulnerable targets for tobacco advertising. Seductive advertising does not strike like a lightning bolt. It is a gradual process that begins when a child is old enough to read.

See spot run. Run spot, run.

See Jane smoke. It's Jane's right.

Smoke Jane smoke.

Absurd? Molding young children's minds is said to be big business today. No one knows that better than K-III Communications Corp., who owns Weekly Reader, a children's newspaper that is distributed primarily in schools. Weekly Reader brings K-III an annual profit of $8 million, which is 44% of their education related business products. It is important to note that K-III was owned by Kohlberg Kravis Roberts & Co. (KKR) from 1989 to 1995. KKR in turn owns R. J. Reynolds Nabisco, the makers of Camel.

Weekly Reader has always had a reputation of being responsibly pro-health. However, in 1989, *Weekly Reader* deviated from their reputation. They suddenly began printing fewer articles on the negative health effects of smoking, and as shocking as it may be, began printing articles that were pro-tobacco.

Investigators at the University of California, San Francisco, analyzed 34 articles on smoking that appeared in Weekly Reader. The principal UCSF researcher, Edith Balback, found 68% of the articles included tobacco industry views. More disturbing, only 38% of the articles contained strong messages against smoking. Furthermore, during that time, Joe Camel appeared in *Weekly Reader* eight times.

Weekly Reader ran a story entitled "Do cigarettes have a future?" in October of 1994. The article included the tobacco industry's position on the tobacco control movement, and how it will cost the country jobs and taxes. It also discussed how the tobacco control movement will effect smokers' rights. The editor of *Weekly Reader,* Sandra Maccarone, said the article gave a "balanced view of the smokers' rights movement." That caused many tobacco control officials to express their disagreement. One was James Bergman, of Stop Teenage Addiction to Tobacco (STAT). Bergman said Weekly Readers' presentation of the arguments of the tobacco industry is "extremely negligent."

Predator Targets Their Prey

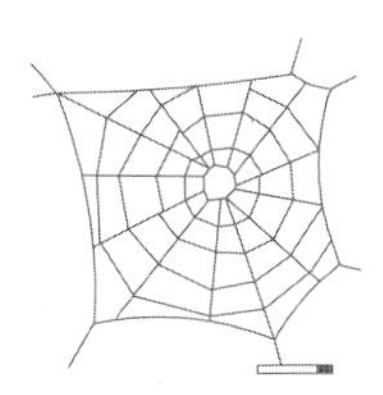

Cigarette advertising strategies today seduce children and teens into smoking by associating it with a protest of authority figures, rebellion, and a symbol of independence. They present tobacco as desirable, socially acceptable, glamorous, something cool, safe and healthy. Smoking is also presented as more prevalent in society than it actually is. The ads are so convincing that smoking will bring happiness, that teenage girls suffering from depression and anxiety will smoke thinking it will relieve their psychiatric symptoms.

Cigarette ads create a desire—a desire to be popular, to be accepted. The ads remind the youngsters of what they lack, and imply that smoking will satisfy that lack. Men and women, real or cartoon characters, are depicted having fun, and doing adult things which teens want to do. Teens project themselves into the picture enjoying those things—taking risks, enjoying adult activities, being comfortable in social situations and smoking.

Selling a Commodity to Starters

The number one rule of selling is: know your customer. That is precisely why the tobacco industry sponsored research to learn how tobacco smoking starts. They identified the major psychological vulnerabilities of children, who they call starters. These psychological vulnerabilities are used to sell perceived social benefits, such as improved self-image and self-confidence, individuality, popularity, and admiration by peers. As one tobacco company memo put it, "At a younger age, taste requirements and satisfaction of a cigarette are thought to play a secondary role to the social requirements."

In 1973, RJR proposed tailoring cigarette marketing to the 21 and under group. "Realistically, if our company is to survive and prosper, over the long term," wrote Claude Teague Jr., RJR assistant director of research and development, "we must get our share of the youth market." "This is clear and convincing evidence", explains Scott Ballin, of the Coalition on Smoking OR Health, "that they are targeting kids." RJR claims they never acted on the memo.

In July 3, 1974, D. W. Tredennick, a RJR marketing research executive, wrote about their advertising and how to attract new smokers: "young smokers wear their cigarette, and it becomes a part of the 'I' they wish to be." He went on to say that young smokers choose a cigarette brand because of "the user image a brand projects and differentiated product characteristics." Even more interesting, Tredennick noted that smoking "generally starts during his teens," and that half became regular smokers by the age of 18. Three years later in 1977, a RJR Marketing Plan positioned Salem to "Emulate personalities and situational elements that are compatible with the aspirations and lifestyles of contemporary young adults."

Tobacco company marketing executives must constantly think of new ways to attract potential candidates for nicotine use. A B.A.T. Viceroy brand market research plan in 1975 revealed a strategy to create a desire to smoke in starters. The Viceroy plan suggested: "For the young, smoking is not a part of day to day life, it is part of an illicit pleasure category." The plan suggested to relate smoking to something "bad," to portray it as part of growing-up.

"Present smoking as an illicit pleasure."

This image was created with ambiguous pictures, to reduce objections and to repress health concerns. Cigarettes were touted to help in tense social situations. B.A.T.'s advertising thrust used to attract starters to Viceroy was:

B.A.T.'s Viceroy Advertising Promotion:

- Present smoking as an initiation into the adult world.
- Present smoking as an illicit pleasure category of product and activities.
- Symbolize growing-up, the maturity process.
- Avoid health concerns!

B.A.T. sued a Chicago CBS anchorman in 1981 for stating that B.A.T.s marketing strategy was to link Viceroy's to illicit pleasures such as marijuana, and to sex.

Peer Pressure Advertising

Peer pressure advertising can apply the same forces that a friend or family member can. Peer pressure advertising must attack at the vulnerable age of 11 to 12 years, when the desire to be part of a peer group is the strongest.

Tempo by RJR, was a peer pressure brand. RJR's marketing strategy was to use positive imagery. An attractive social appearance and peer group acceptance were pitched in the ads—the psychological benefits the insecure child desires. More recently, RJR used Joe Camel peer pressure ads. The ads depict Joe rejecting a cowboy, a Marlboro type man. This switch advertising has a peer pressure twist and says if you smoke Marlboro you are not cool and you are not welcome.

All tobacco advertising targets children, because they are the only group that responds to it predictably.

RJR claims that they never acted on the memos from the 1970's that spoke of targeting teens with cigarette ads. Despite their denial, RJR embarked on a program called (YAS), Young Adult Smokers. YAS consisted of one element to address the fact that a smoker's first cigarette brand is the brand they are most likely to smoke for years. The YAS promotion was intended to target 18 to 24 year olds.

Despite their alleged intentions, in 1990 RJR divisional managers targeted stores frequented by young shoppers for special YAS cigarette logo consumer items. Memos written by two RJR managers, instructed their salespeople to target stores in this manner:

"These stores can be in close proximity to colleges (and) high schools."

"Identify these accounts......in the general vicinity of the high schools."

RJR's YAS program was very effective in capturing the youth market for Camel. Camel became the most popular brand of smokers under 18 years old. Following the first year of the YAS promotion, Camel market share of young smokers rose from three percent to 8.1%. By 1991, it had risen to 13%. Richard J. Durbin, IL-D, Congressional Task Force on Tobacco said "They are going after American kids with a vengeance."

If the industry actually used this sales strategy, more tobacco advertisements would be found in stores near schools. In 1995, the California Department of Health Services studied 5,700 stores in the state. They found an interesting correlation between the number of cigarette promotional items in stores and it's proximity to high schools. Stores within 1,000 feet of a school had an average of 26.5 ads per store, and an average of 5.6 exterior ads. Those over 1, 000 feet, averaged 24.9 ads per store, with only 4.5 ads on the outside. Stores in young neighborhoods, with one third of the population 17 years and younger, had the highest number of ads per store.

Not only were there more ads at the stores closer to schools, and in young neighborhoods, something more shocking was discovered. The tobacco ads were near the candy counters, and placed only three feet above the floor. If these ads were intended for adults to see, they would be at eye level of an adult, but instead are at the eye level of a child. In 1993, tobacco companies spent $1.6 billion on cash slotting fees (a fee paid to the retailer for each carton or package "face" that is visible to the customer), and promotional items, such as caps and T-shirts, to enhance tobacco sales in retail stores.

It should not be difficult for anyone to find a retail store in their neighborhood plastered with tobacco posters and signs that is less than 1,000 feet from an elementary or middle school. These retailers are often targets of local police sting operations, and those caught selling tobacco illegally to children under 18 are fined or jailed.

Joe Camel

RJR'S cartoons are "Very effective in targeting

the most vulnerable, the children."

-Kenneth Warner Ph.D., University of Michigan

The first modern cigarette, Camel, was introduced in 1913. In 1950, advertisements for Camel reported that in a thirty day test by throat specialists, "Not one single case of throat irritation due to smoking Camels!" A testimony from a secretary taking the test said "I found Camels agree with my throat."

Curious! What does a toxic relic like Camel have to do with being cool in the 90's? Music from the 50's, 60's and 70's is history to teens today, but they accept an 80 year old cancer stick. This is an example of the power of advertising. Advertising can transform the ancient into something new and cool.

The government saw the sharpest increase in teen smoking in 1988—the year RJR's Joe Camel ads were first introduced. RJR Joe Camel ads create the desire to smoke using visual pictures. These cartoons cause some teens to perceive smoking as less hazardous, and more socially acceptable. Studies establish that if an ad attracts a teen to be more popular or more attractive, they are 4.7 times more likely to start smoking.

Dr. Joseph R. DiFranza, University of Massachusetts Medical School, conducted a survey in 1991, of school children in five regions of the United States. These 12 to 19 year olds, as well as adults over 21, were asked if they recognized Joe Camel.

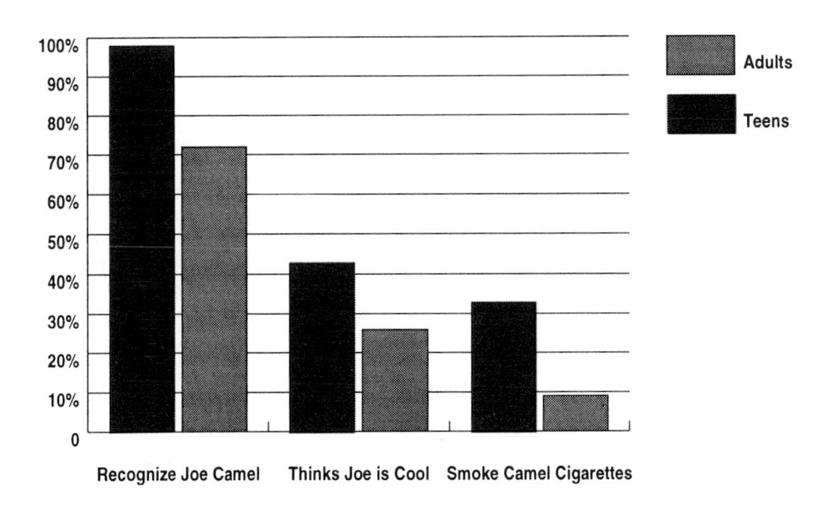

Dr. DiFranza concluded: "Joe Camel cartoon advertisements are far more successful at marketing Camel cigarettes to children than to adults."

Dr. Paul Fisher of the Medical College of Georgia, interviewed 229 children, ages three to six, for brand logo recognition. Among children six years old, Joe Camel was as recognizable as Mickey Mouse.

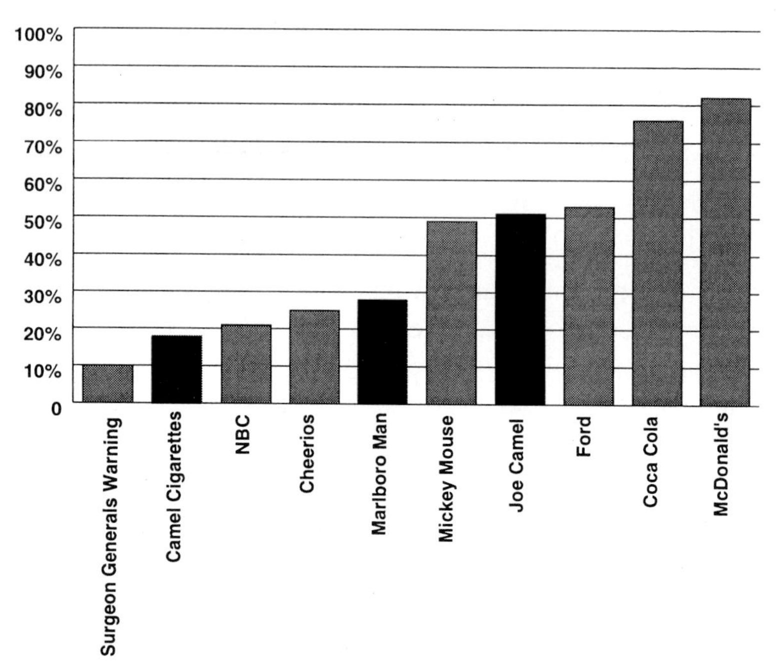

Children Know Adults Take Risks:

"Me Too Daddy!"

Children use tobacco because they believe the benefit outweighs the risks. Teens smoke as a sign of boldness. For some, risk is what they desire. Edward Popper, Professor of North Eastern University, commented on a cigarette advertisement portraying a downhill sky racer. He says the ad says "I want to be like them. They take risks. I will smoke, it's a risk."

One RJR promotion stated: "..young people don't smoke, smoking is an adult custom, it's an adult thing to do." Dr. Popper says that the ad is saying, "If you want to be grown up smoke." Furthermore, the tobacco companies "don't smoke it's the law" campaign says to the child, "if you want to be an outlaw (cowboy), smoke."

Cigarette Ads Tell Children—

If you want to be grown-up —Smoke!

If you want to be an outlaw —Smoke!

If you want to be an adult —Smoke!

The Mode of Seduction is Ever Changing

Teen fads change as fast as their desires. Tobacco advertising must keep up with the teen psyche or they will not sell enough cigarettes. Recent sales figures say they are doing an excellent job of attracting new child smokers at the rate of 3,000 a day. More interesting, until 1993, new white teen smokers out numbered new African-American teen smokers by five fold. It could be as simple as "Smoking is a white thing," or African-Americans could be more adept at spotting a hype that tries to exploit them in some way. Cigarette promotions were clearly not reaching the black teens, that is until 1993. Since 1993, there has been a steep rise in the number of black male teens starting to smoke. The question remains, did advertising and promotion strategies change and become better at targeting black teens, or did black teen psyche change to fit the advertising?

The changing winds and tides of motivational factors that drive teens to drugs and tobacco are not easy for public health professionals to deal with. Especially when trying to develop and stay current with tobacco-health education and tobacco cessation curriculums. Local health departments do not have the same budget as tobacco companies have to survey teens and develop psychological counter measures. The only way this public health menace will stop is when all tobacco advertising is stopped. This measure, considered extreme by the industry, would not be necessary if the tobacco companies were reasonable. However, they are not reasonable, and since

1964 have exceeded all decency. In the meantime, the advertisements continue. And unfortunately, health care professionals are billions of dollars and light years behind tobacco's marketing expertise.

Peer Pressure

Although peer pressure plays a smaller role than advertising, it can be a strong influence after the child's resistance to smoking is broken by advertising. Peer pressure is not usually effective after age 16. Therefore, peer pressure advertising must attack at the vulnerable age of 11 to 12 years, when the desire to be part of a peer group is the strongest.

Smoking may be a way for some kids to enter a desired friendship group. Researchers, studying smoking initiation during adolescence, find the desire for friends is a strong influence to start. Studies at the UCSD, found that adolescents exposed to peer pressure were 90% more likely to start smoking as those who were not. Friends can create peer pressure, and so can family members. Furthermore, if parents want to discourage their children from smoking, they will have a difficult job if they too are smokers.

Teens Confuse Legality with Safety

One teenage smoker said: "They can't be that bad for you, or they wouldn't sell it." Teen myth — if something is legal, it must be safe. Legality is often confused with safety, because it is common knowledge that most products and drugs sold today have passed some safety tests. It makes sense to children that tobacco must be no different, and they think tobacco has passed safety tests as well. As a consequence, many young people are under the false impression that our government is protecting them. This misunderstanding is fueling the teen smoking epidemic, and is a threat to future generations.

Should we expect that a child be responsible for their own actions when it comes to issues like starting to smoke? It is important to note that after a teen starts smoking and becomes addicted, they do not have a second chance to think about starting. Teens do not understand that they can't just change their minds about smoking later. That chance never comes — nicotine makes the decision to start smoking a permanent one.

Educating teens on the health hazards of tobacco and nicotine addiction will prevent some from starting. All teens and most adults are not informed on these issues. Contrary to popular opinion, it is not sufficient to simply say "everyone knows smoking is bad." As the reader should realize, there is much more to it. We can't rely on the tobacco industry to be the only ones to supply health information on tobacco use. We have learned from experience that their "education" is based on half-truths and is a disguise for promotion.

Teens Confuse Accessibility with Safety

"I can buy cigarettes anywhere. They don't care, it's no big deal." Teen myth —if I can buy cigarettes without a hassle, then smoking isn't bad for you. Easy access, either from stores or vending machines, is another reason children start smoking. Despite laws forbidding the sale of tobacco to minors in all 50 states, tobacco is easier than ever for kids to buy. The problem is that the majority of states do not enforce their own laws. In eleven states, the fine for selling tobacco to minors is only $10–$50. This puts the retailer at ease and they don't implement procedures to prevent selling tobacco to children. This fuels the myth that smoking cigarettes must be safe.

According to recent studies by the CDC, in 1995, 62% of minors reported that they could easily buy their own cigarettes, which was up from 58% in 1989. Furthermore, 75% of them were never asked for identification to verify their age. Children as young as 12 said they could buy them from convenience stores, girls reporting more buys than boys. This hard data counters the tobacco industries claims that their "It's the Law" program was stopping kids from buying cigarettes, when in fact access is getting easier.

Self-serve displays of tobacco products also increase access of tobacco products to children. Many times tobacco displays are eye level to a child. To some children, it is easier to steal cigarettes than buy them. In a report by San Diego State University in 1995, 9.3% of minors surveyed said they steal cigarettes from stores as the main way they get cigarettes. Researchers also found that among retailers that have self-serve tobacco displays, 61.4% were more likely to sell tobacco to minors. Compounding the problem, tobacco companies give retailers an extra supply of cigarettes to allow for inventory shortage. Some say this is part of a diabolical plot to encourage children to steal cigarettes, and at the same time compensate the retailer for the loss with free cigarettes.

Vending Machines

Vending machines make cigarettes readily available to children. Although they account for only two percent of the dollar sales of cigarettes, the sheer number of vending machines is staggering. In some areas vending machines are so plentiful, they account for half of the sites where cigarettes can be purchased. This means for every store where cigarettes are bought face to face there is one vending machine that will dispense cigarettes to any child with a fist full of quarters.

Some communities have tried to stem vending machine sales to minors by requiring a lockout device that can be unlocked only by an attendant. One community was partially successful in reducing minor purchases from 91% without locks, to 39% with locks. However, when a vending machine lockout is started, minors just shift their purchases to stores. The investigators concluded that vending machine locks are not a reasonable substitute for law enforcement. Beer is not sold in vending machines, why are cigarettes?

Children Buy Cigarettes Sold on Internet Sites

Children only need a hand full of coins to buy cigarettes from a vending machine. The Internet has made it even easier. Some six percent of all children age two to 18 have easy access to the Internet. They only need daddy's credit card number to buy cigarettes from certain Web sites. A few clicks of a mouse, and with no questions about age asked, the cancer sticks will arrive in the mail. The threat may be small now because these cyber smoke shops don't have a huge volume of sales, but the potential is there for much more in the future. It is most important to note that cigarette advertisements on the Internet are not required to display the U.S. Surgeon Generals Warnings. No warnings, no identification checks, and easy computer shopping all add up to new teen access problems for health authorities.

The Danger of Feeling Immortal

"Minors, children, do not understand the long-term consequences of smoking."

-Dr. J. R. DiFranza, University of Massachusetts Medical School

Why does the military draft young men when they need an army? One reason is that teens believe they will not be killed. Similarly, the threat of having a lung removed or a heart attack sometime later in life is just too remote an idea to shock kids. Research on smoking trends show that boys ten to

14 years old, and girls younger than 21, do not respond to health messages. The health messages that have been effective in stopping adults from smoking have not been effective in stopping teens from smoking. Advertising, psychosocial motives, and peer pressures override health concerns.

Teens Believe They Can Quit Smoking Easily

Kids are not only missing the health warnings, they also have no clue about nicotine addiction. Teen myth – I can quit smoking any time, I am not addicted. Children don't think nicotine is addictive, and even if they did, they think it doesn't apply to them. That leads them to believe they can smoke for a few years and then easily quit. A 16 year old smoker was asked by his Grandmother "Why do you smoke? Don't you know it killed your Grandfather, and your Uncle?" His answer was "Grandmother, I am not going to smoke forever." Research has shown that about half of the teens that start smoking will smoke for at least 16 to 20 years.

Tobacco Companies Defense:

"Ads are not intended to attract kids"

Recently Camel ads introduced Joe's new girlfriend, Josephine. RJR spokeswoman Maura Ellis says that the appearance of Josephine in their advertising is not intended to attract children and young women to start smoking. "Not intended to attract children," this has been the tobacco industries defense for a decade when confronted with the accusations that tobacco advertising is designed to cause kids to start smoking. However, many tobacco company internal documents have surfaced recently, and as you now know, their actions belie their words.

■ ■ ■ ■ ■ ■ ■ ■ ■ ■ ■ ■ ■

Once a person starts smoking, most continue smoking the remainder of their lives. The majority of smokers say they want to quit but can't. Advertising starts people smoking, what makes them keep smoking? The answer is the invisible drug–the addictive hook!

The view from a convenience store across the street from an intermediate school.

Chapter Six

The Addictive Hook

"Cigarettes taste horrible to people who have never smoked and the nicotine kick is not euphoric."

- Larry C. White, author, former smoker.

Nicotiana tabacum, the botanical name for tobacco, is named after Jean Nicot, who promoted its cultivation in the late 1500's. Nicotine, a natural alkaloid drug from the tobacco plant is also named after Nicot.

Cigarette smoke has two basic parts: Nicotine and Poisons. Actually both components are poisons. Cigarette smoke is composed of 2,000 complex poisons and the powerfully addictive drug nicotine.

NICOTINE and 2,000 POISONS

Nicotine: The Poison

Poison: A substance that on inhalation or ingestion, in relatively small amounts, causes structural damage or functional disturbances.

Anyone familiar with botanical insecticides knows that nicotine is a good one. It is sprayed on plants as a freebase concentrate spray. It kills aphids, but it can also kill the person doing the spraying. The lethal dose of nicotine is ten times less that of pyrethrum or rotenone, making it one of the most toxic insecticides.

How much nicotine does it take to kill a human? According to R. H. Dreisbach, author of *Handbook of Poisoning*, one drop of pure nicotine, about 40 mg., placed on the tongue will kill in five minutes. One small drop is the amount of nicotine in about four cigarettes.

A child that eats two cigarettes

will die in less than five minutes.

Nicotine first stimulates, then depresses and paralyzes the cells of the brain, spinal cord, and nervous system. Next, the skeletal muscles and the diaphragm (breathing muscles) are paralyzed. Death results from respiratory failure.

Two men recently found out how dangerous nicotine is during a smoking contest in China. They smoked two or three at a time continuously until one gave up. One smoked 50 cigarettes and lived to tell about it. Unfortunately, the other man smoked 100 and fell dead from nicotine poisoning.

The Power of Nicotine Addiction

Addiction: A behavioral pattern of drug uses, characterized by the overwhelming involvement with the use of a drug (compulsive use), the securing of its supply, and a high tendency to relapse after withdrawal.

Today, there are millions of drug addicts in America. Most are addicted to nicotine, alcohol, cocaine, and opiate drugs, like morphine. Cocaine and morphine have some medicinal uses and they don't cause cancer. Morphine is safe when given in an appropriate dose and by a safe method to a normal, healthy individual. A life of morphine addiction is socially unacceptable. On the other hand, a life of addiction to a socially acceptable poison that causes cancer is a nightmare.

Drug addiction is not only about the stereotypical street junky. "A drug does not have to be intoxicating to be deemed addictive," says Dr. Jack E. Henningfield, Ph.D., Chief of Clinical Pharmacology Research at the National Institute on Drug Abuse.

A drug can be addictive without causing a high

The American Psychiatric Association defines addiction as "a compulsive use of a drug resulting in loss of control over intake." The three hallmarks of nicotine addiction that are present in animal experiments are:

SELF-ADMINISTRATION

TOLERANCE

WITHDRAWAL

The scientific criteria for addiction, met by barbiturates, amphetamines, morphine, heroin, alcohol and cocaine, is also met by nicotine. Nicotine addiction is the reason most people smoke. The characteristics of nicotine addiction, (or dependence), and some common expressions smokers use that demonstrate each, are listed in the table on the opposite page.

Some of these characteristics, such as compulsive use, drug seeking behavior, and physical dependence, can be observed at the entrance of any busy office building. The smokers are huddled outside of their "smoke-free" workplace even in extremely miserable weather, to feed their nicotine addiction.

Most heroin addicts will identify their favorite drug as nicotine. Researchers asked heroin addicts, "What drug do you need the most?," from a list, including heroin, nicotine, marijuana, amphetamine, barbiturates, LSD, and alcohol. They chose nicotine over all other drugs. Heroin addicts say they needed nicotine the most to cope. Despite successful treatment for their dependency of alcohol and/or drugs, most of these patients will not quit smoking, and most will die from tobacco related illnesses. Research done at the Mayo Clinic observed the mortality rate of these patients to be 48.1%, much higher than the expected normal mortality rate of 18.5%. From a clinical point of view, tobacco dependency is the most lethal and the most difficult addiction to control.

Smokers also find it difficult to quit. Seventy percent of people who smoke (some 32,000,000 smokers) want to quit. Even after a heart attack or cancer surgery, most want to quit, but can't. Seventy percent of the smokers who survive a heart attack, start smoking again within one year. Forty percent of the cancer patients who have undergone surgery continue to smoke.

Despite a HEART ATTACK 70% keep smoking.

Despite CANCER SURGERY 40% keep smoking.

Characteristic	Common Expressions of Smokers
Compulsive use.	"I've got to have a cigarette after I eat!"
Drug seeking behavior.	"I've got to run to the store for a pack of cigarettes."
Psychoactive effects.	"It relaxes me."
Drug-reinforced behavior.	"I feel better now that I've had a cigarette."
Use despite harmful effects.	"I know I should quit."
Unsuccessful attempts to quit.	"I tried to quit once."
A low quit rate.	"I've tried 3 times to quit".
Recurrent drug cravings.	"I've got to have a cigarette!"
A persistent desire for the drug.	"Where can I smoke?"
Tolerance, more drug is needed to satisfy increasing cravings.	"I tried a low tar cigarette, but I just smoked more."
Physical dependence.	"I can't quit."
Withdrawal symptoms.	"I was a bear when I tried to quit."

Visitors to the M. D. Anderson Cancer Center in Houston, a smoke-free hospital, can observe another characteristic of nicotine addiction. In the evenings, patients gather in the parking garage for a smoke. Some are pulling chemotherapy IV pumps behind them. You might see the classic picture of someone smoking through a hole in their throat called a "stoma." They continue to smoke despite having their cancerous larynx removed. This is further testimony to the power of nicotine addiction.

Smokers Surveyed About Quitting

Many smokers have made the decision to quit but have failed to succeed. About 50% of smokers say they believe that smoking would be very difficult to quit, and up to 70% fail when they try. In a poll of smokers, conducted in March 1994, 70% said they wanted to quit. Of those that wanted to quit, 48% have tried one or more times but failed. A desire to quit, and one or more unsuccessful attempts to quit, are characteristic of nicotine addiction.

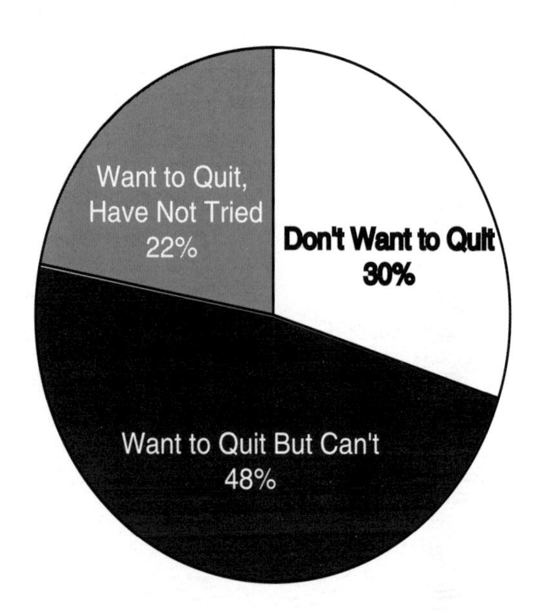

Quit Rates

The quit rate per year for nicotine is 2.5%. In contrast, the quit rate for heroin or cocaine is 30%. The 1988 Surgeon General's report indicates that nicotine is as difficult to quit as heroin or cocaine. Dr. Victor J. DeNoble, Ph.D., a former Philip Morris researcher, found that nicotine addiction was "on a level comparable to cocaine."

"Nicotine addicts often compare quitting smoking to the loss of a mother, or the loss of best friend," says Dr. Lynn Kozlowski, M.D., of the Addiction Research Foundation. This point was illustrated when a retired businesswoman, and a smoker for 40 years suffering from emphysema, was asked about her thoughts on quitting. She candidly said, "I can't quit smoking.... Smoking is my...best friend." Her best friend is killing her.

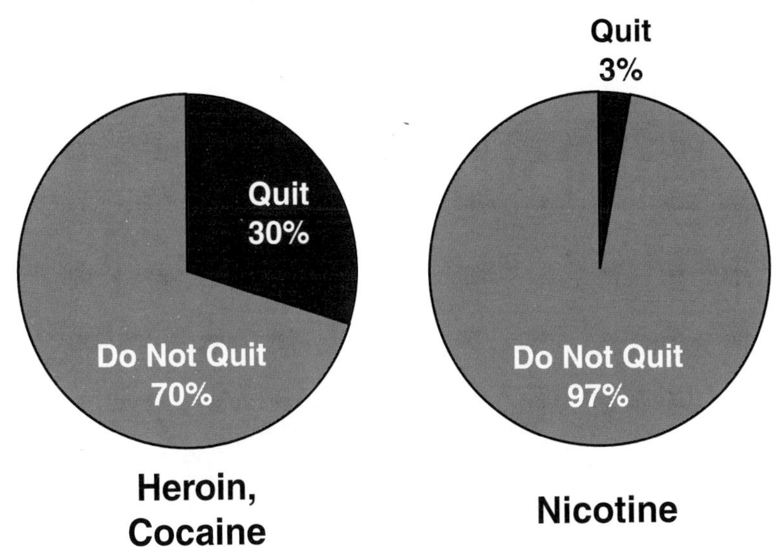

Nicotine Withdrawal

"The torture being beyond human power to bear."

- Sigmund Freud

Sigmund Freud said it well when he described his personal feelings during nicotine withdrawal. To avoid the negative effects of withdrawal, nicotine takes over the brain and controls the smoker by compelling them to smoke. When the lack of nicotine causes withdrawal symptoms, nicotine controls a smoker's behavior even more.

More than half of smokers say they experience craving when they have not smoked. Some smokers can't sleep all night without smoking. This is the face of nicotine addiction, smoking to avoid withdrawal symptoms. These are:

- Craving Nicotine
- Irritability
- Frustration or Anger
- Anxiety
- Difficulty Concentrating
- Restlessness
- Decreased Heart Rate
- Increased Appetite

FDA Declares Nicotine is Addictive

On August 2, 1994, an advisory panel to the Food and Drug Administration declared nicotine to be addictive. Testimony was heard that as few as five cigarettes a day can cause addiction in some people.

Nicotine Addiction in Children

More teens are smoking every day. There were approximately 2.6 million children between the ages of 12 and 17 addicted to nicotine in 1989. In 1993, that number had grown to over three million. Not only are more smoking, but they are starting younger. Smoking increased 30% in the 13 to 14 year group, between 1991 and 1994.

Survey of Teens	
Tried to quit, but can't.	57% to 75%
Regret they ever started smoking.	70%

"Wouldn't it be great, even if a teenager did experiment with smoking, there wouldn't be enough nicotine in a cigarette to addict him?"

—Dr. David Kessler, Commissioner of the FDA.

Five Cigarettes: Hooked for Life

"There is evidence that it is easier to become addicted to nicotine than heroin or cocaine," explains Dr. John Slade, M.D., a Robert Wood Johnson Medical School physician and drug researcher. First time smokers usually go through a sequence of decisions before their first cigarette. For those that decide to try smoking, after smoking four or five consecutive cigarettes, they have a 94% chance of becoming a long-term nicotine addict. Of the 3,000 teens that start smoking every day, nine of every ten will become addicted and half will smoke for 20 years.

Smokeless Tobacco and Nicotine Addiction

Smokeless tobacco in the form of snuff and chewing tobacco (spit tobacco), are ways other than smoking to self-administer nicotine. The average amount of nicotine delivered is 3.6 mg., in snuff and 4.6 mg. in chewing tobacco. See appendix D for the nicotine concentrations of some brands of smokeless tobacco.

Teens can begin a life of smoking by using smokeless tobacco first. They start before they have a clue to why they should not. When kids chew tobacco, they get hooked on nicotine. Once they become addicted to nicotine, they are more likely to start smoking cigarettes. Whether smoked or chewed, the nicotine equivalent of five cigarettes will give a child a 94% chance of becoming a nicotine addict. Furthermore, nicotine is the gateway drug to other drugs of abuse, such as cocaine or amphetamines.

Another danger signal is that smokeless tobacco sales are on the rise. From 1981 to 1991, U.S. Tobacco Company's sales of smokeless tobacco increased 50%. Most of the new smokeless tobacco users are under 19 years old.

In a recent survey of high school students in Iowa, 15% of the boys reported using smokeless tobacco, and 24% said they smoke. Consider these recent U.S. statistics:

- **65% of those that try snuff are under 12 years old.**
- **One in four smokeless tobacco users are under 19 years old.**
- **One million adolescents use smokeless tobacco.**

Smokeless Tobacco is NOT a Safe Alternative

Contrary to the beliefs of some wellmeaning health care professionals, smokeless tobacco is not a safe or a reasonable alternative to smoking, nor is it an aid to smoking cessation. The American Dental Association's Council on Access, Prevention, and Interprofessional Relations says, "Promotion of smokeless tobacco use for any reason sends an improper public health message." The only safe alternative for a smoker is to quit, with or without the aid of safe nicotine substitutions such as gum, patch or nasal spray, used under the supervision of a physician or tobacco cessation professional. Tobacco in any form and any amount is a health hazard to humans.

Nicotine: The Gateway Drug

The Gateway Drug Theory says a presumed gateway drug makes its users more likely to experiment with other drugs such as cocaine, heroin and alcohol. It is important to note, that recent data lends scientific plausibility to classify nicotine as a gateway drug. If only ten percent of teen smokers go on to abuse other drugs like cocaine and heroin, we have a serious public health problem confronting the nation. Consider that 20% of students graduating from high school today are nicotine addicted. A survey done by Parents Resource Institute for Drug Education (PRIDE) in 1995, shows that both nicotine and drug use has increased among high school students from 1991 to 1995. This trend supports the notion that nicotine is a gateway drug.

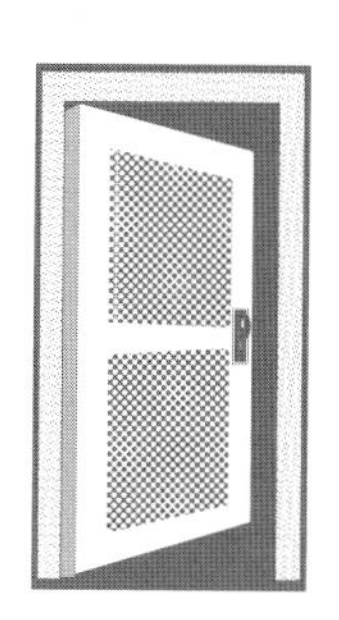

Percent Using	1991	1995	% Change
Cigarettes	35%	44%	Up 26%
Marijuana	17%	28%	Up 65%
Cocaine	3.4%	4.5%	Up 32%
Alcohol	52%	54%	Up 4%

NICOTINE: The DRUG

"Nicotine is an addictive drug—it is a settled issue."

- John Slade, M.D., Robert Wood Johnson Medical School

Drug: Any chemical agent that affects living processes.

Nicotine clearly fits the definition of a drug. The life processes of smokers are dramatically affected by nicotine. However, it is not "dope," the slang name for a narcotic. On the other hand, it is an addictive drug. Nicotine is the drug responsible for the continuation of smoking.

The tobacco industry often describes nicotine using the same lingo a doctor would use to describe a drug. A Philip

Morris company official wrote:

> "Think of the cigarette pack as a storage container for a day's supply of nicotine. Think of the cigarette as a dispenser for a dose unit of nicotine. Think of a puff of smoke as the vehicle of nicotine."

Other than for cessation of smoking, nicotine has no established therapeutic use. Nicotine gum, tablets, nasal spray, and skin patches have proven useful for the relief of nicotine withdrawal symptoms. Although it is not used as a medicine, nicotine's toxicity and presence in tobacco give it "A considerable measure of medical importance," according to the authors of *The Pharmacological Basis of Therapeutics.*

Nicotine, when smoked,

reaches the brain in eight seconds.

Heroin by injection , takes twice as long.

As cigarette smoke is inhaled into the lungs, the small airways quickly absorb nicotine. From the lung, it is rapidly delivered to the blood stream. From a practical point of view, inhaling smoke from a cigarette is a more efficient way of administering nicotine than by intravenous injection. On the other hand, cigar and pipe smoke do not have to inhaled to be equally effective in entering the blood stream. Cigars and pipe tobacco, as well as smokeless tobacco have additives that allow nicotine to pass easily through the lining of the mouth. From there, nicotine is rapidly delivered to the blood steam. Consequently, the Food and Drug Administration (FDA) classifies cigarettes as "drug delivery devices," like a syringe, pill, or inhaler. The FDA is not alone — Philip Morris, in a 1992 memo, refers to a cigarette as "nicotine delivery device."

The first time smoker may feel sick, nauseated and dizzy. It's natures way of telling them not to smoke it. Tolerance develops rapidly to some of the merely unpleasant effects of nicotine, such as nausea, vomiting, dizziness and depression. But tolerance does not develop to the resulting increase in heart rate and blood pressure. The lack of tolerance to these effects is the reason why smokers are more susceptible to heart attacks.

Nicotine disappears from the body rapidly — taking as little as 30 minutes for half of the nicotine in the body to disappear (The half-life of nicotine ranges from 30 to 240 minutes). Therefore, smokers need to feed their habit as often as every 30 minutes to maintain the amount of nicotine they crave. Unfortunately, the harmful chemicals in tobacco smoke do not disappear from the body so quickly. Some can stay for long periods of time, maybe even years.

The reinforcing property of nicotine causes the body to crave the drug's effects. The reinforcing effects are increased alertness, relaxing of muscles, facilitation of attention, and a decrease in appetite and irritability. It can also cause mood changes. "Nicotine is about five to ten times more effective than amphetamines in producing mood changes," explains pharmacologist Dr. Jack Henningfield, of the National Institute on Drug Abuse. Dr. Henningfield also says that the relaxation and stress relieving properties that smokers experience is not due to nicotine. "One of the misconceptions is that nicotine relieves stress," he says. It is more likely that, because of nicotine's short duration of action, the smoker begins to experience withdrawal symptoms within 30 minutes of the last cigarette, which include irritability, frustration, anxiety and anger. When the person smokes again, nicotine reverses the withdrawal symptoms and the person is left with a feeling of relaxation.

The Dose

A person who smokes two packs a day will self-administer about 14,000 doses of nicotine a year. Like a narcotic, nicotine is a subtle destroyer of the human spirit. It makes smokers slaves to the cigarette. They will continue this high rate of smoking despite their knowledge of its health risks.

Smokers Take 14,000 Doses of Nicotine a Year

The amount of nicotine in a cigarette is measured two ways. The amount of nicotine in the tobacco, is the nicotine concentration or strength. Cigarettes are sold in different nicotine concentrations, ranging from 1.5 to 2.5%, (about 8 to 9 mg. each).

The amount the smoker actually receives is the nicotine yield, delivery, or dose. Measuring the nicotine yield is not as straight forward as it should be. The FTC measures the amount of nicotine in cigarettes using a mechanical smoking machine. The nicotine yield is measured, not the concentration in the whole cigarette. If there are air holes in the cigarette, as low tar cigarettes have, it tricks the FTC smoking machine. The machine has no fingers, and it leaves the air holes open, drawing in mostly air. For the most part, regardless of the FTC nicotine yield, all cigarettes deliver about the same amount of nicotine to the smoker.

"...Cigarettes deliver a nice jolt of nicotine."

-Addsion Yeaman, Brown & Williamson Tobacco Co, 1963

The average nicotine delivered in 1950 was 2.7 mg. Today the average yield is 1.0 mg. (0.3mg to 3.2 mg.). Although the nicotine yield has decreased from the past, it has always been high enough to maintain addiction.

The dose of nicotine a smoker receives from a cigarette largely depends on the brand smoked, and the manner, or intensity the smoker uses. They easiest way to maintain the nicotine a smoker craves is to smoke a maximum yield nicotine cigarette brand, such as Camel, Winston and Marlboro.

Even when smokers switch to so-called "low tar-low nicotine" cigarettes, they can change the way they smoke in order to get the same amount of nicotine as they were getting from a maximum yield nicotine cigarette. One way is to take deeper puffs more often. Normally a smoker receives only ten percent of the nicotine in a cigarette, but intensive smoking can increase the yield to 40%.

Another method to increase nicotine yield is to block the air holes in ventilated cigarettes. Air holes in ventilated cigarettes let more air into the draw. If they are left open, the smoke contains 90% fresh air and only ten percent tobacco smoke. The air holes are near the filter where a smoker holds the cigarette. Fingers block the air holes and the smoker gets a full blast of smoke and nicotine. These are common, self-learned effective methods of self-administration of the drug nicotine to maintain adequate levels the brain needs and has become accustomed to.

"Nicotine is not only a very fine drug, but the techniques of administration by smoking has distinct psychological advantages. Smoking is a habit of addiction."

-Sir Charles Ellis, Scientific Advisor, B.A.T.,
(Brown & Williamson Tobacco Co)

"Free" Nicotine

The practice of freebasing crack cocaine became widespread in recent years because it works as quickly as an intravenous injection. Crack is smoked in a pipe-like apparatus and it is more potent and addictive than powered cocaine.

Nicotine, like crack, is also smoked as a freebase, or free nicotine form. The free form of nicotine is more rapidly absorbed, and has a greater impact on the brain. Dr. Henningfield says, "The cigarette is essentially the crack cocaine form of nicotine delivery." The free nicotine yield is increased by adding impact boosters to the tobacco. Impact boosters, such as ammonia, convert normal "bound" nicotine to free nicotine. According to research done at B.A.T., in 1967, free nicotine is "a better gauge of the strength of the tobacco product." Consequently, there are 46 million Americans who 'freebase' nicotine on a regular basis.

"The cigarette is essentially the crack cocaine form of nicotine."

Supercharging

From a practical point of view, ammonia "supercharges" tobacco without having to "spike" or add nicotine. Supercharging increases the dose of nicotine in pipe tobacco and cigars by enhancing free nicotine absorption. Marlboro is one cigarette that is supercharged with ammonia, and consequently has a very high free nicotine yield.

Cigars are Supercharged

Contrary to popular opinion, cigar and pipe smokers can become nicotine dependent even when they don't inhale. Free nicotine is more easily absorbed by the lining of the mouth and throat. Cigars are heavily supercharged with ammonia, and consequently deliver the nicotine impact of about five cigarettes. Furthermore, a cigar smoker can get enough nicotine from one or two cigars a day to become addicted, according to Dr. Henningfield. Smoking as infrequently as a few cigars a month may produce cravings, which puts the cigar smoker at risk of becoming addicted.

A New Nicotine Delivery Device: Eclipse

R. J. Reynolds (RJR) spent $1 billion to develop and test market a nicotine delivery system in 1988, called Premier. It consisted of an aluminum cylinder, some charcoal, and a bit of tobacco. The tube held glycerin beads containing nicotine. One would light the "nicotine pipe" and inhale free nicotine carried by the heated glycerin vapor. Premier was withdrawn from the market in 1989 because it bombed in test markets. It would not stay lit easy, and consumers rejected it.

In 1996, RJR began test marketing a similar nicotine delivery device called Eclipse. Eclipse is similar to Premier in that it has a carbon tip that is lit. Eclipse is different in that it contains a small amount of tobacco, and no nicotine beads. The hazards of Eclipse are discussed in chapter nine. Smoking is a way to self-administer nicotine, and these low-smoke free nicotine deliver devices get right to the heart of the matter.

Nicotine Targets the Brain

Brown & Williamson Tobacco Co. (B.A.T.) researchers were writing about how nicotine stimulates the brain as early as 1962: "The hypothalamo-pituitary stimulation of nicotine is the beneficial mechanism which makes people smoke." It was not until recently however, that the pharmacological basis of how nicotine works on the brain was discovered. In 1995, the journal of *Science* published research showing evidence of nicotine receptors (nicotinic acetylcholine receptors) in the reward system of the brain called the limbic system.

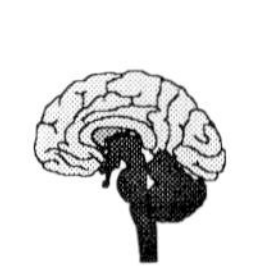

Neurotransmitters are chemicals that brain cells use to communicate with each other. They act on small "on-off switches" on brain cells called receptors. Nicotine increases the flow of the neurotransmitter glutamate in the limbic system, which indicates that the reward center has been stimulated. Dr. Lorna W. Role, a cell biologist research author at Columbia University in New York, says that a faster flow of glutamate "is like turning up the volume on a radio." Nicotine stimulates the reward system, telling the person "That was good, do it again."

"Nicotine commandeers the normal pathways of reward," explains Dr. John Dani, a researcher at Baylor College of Medicine in Houston. It commands you to repeat the action, to keep the nicotine flowing into the bloodstream. "Nicotine tells you to keep on smoking." Nicotine becomes the dangling carrot, and the smoker makes constant effort to get it.

When one continues smoking, the balance of neurotransmitters in the brain begins to change, and the brain becomes accustomed to it. The brain tries to return to normal and modifies enzymes to compensate. For the brain to then work properly, it must have a constant supply of nicotine. This unconscious desire explains the addiction of the individual to nicotine. Tobacco company researchers at B.A.T. in 1962 concluded: "A body left in this unbalanced status craves for renewed drug intake [nicotine] in order to restore the physiological equilibrium."

To restore the balance in the brain, a regular smoker may need nicotine as often as every thirty minutes. Nicotine addiction requires the highest frequently of administration, far exceeding the demands of a cocaine, alcohol, or heroin addiction.

Nicotine is administered by the user more times per day than any other drug of abuse!

The Nicotine-Dopamine Reward System

One of the three main divisions of the brain is the brain stem. It is responsible for controlling breathing, heart rate, gastrointestinal functions, eye movement, equilibrium, and body movement. The brain stem is further divided into three major parts, one being the midbrain (or mesencephalon). A collection of parts within the midbrain called the limbic system, controls emotions, pleasure and reward. The limbic system (mesolimbic dopamine system) is the reward center of the brain. The reward center encourages basic drives required for survival, such as eating, and reproducing. Not only does it reward for survival, but it is also called the addiction center because it provides the reward that reinforces the use of drugs.

Neurotransmitters are chemicals used by cells to communicate with one another. Nicotine affects the amount of neurotransmitters in the brain, such as dopamine, acetylcholine, and glutamate. Stimulation of the mesolimbic system with nicotine will increase dopamine and glutamate.

The mesolimbic system, the reward-addiction center of the brain, is primarily regulated by the neurotransmitter dopamine. The mesolimbic system is where a class of anti-depressants, called monoamine oxidase inhibitors, act to prevent the breakdown of the neurotransmitters serotonin, dopamine, phenethylamine, and norepinephrine. Nicotine works in a similar way on dopamine, which profoundly effects the reward-addiction center.

Recent evidence from scientists at Brookhaven National Laboratory says that nicotine decreases the level of Monoamine Oxidase B (MOA B). MOA B is an enzyme that breaks down dopamine. Smokers have 40% less MOA B in their brain. By preventing the natural breakdown of dopamine, a corresponding increase in dopamine occurs, which in turn stimulates the reward-addiction center. Therefore, using tobacco increases nicotine levels which in turn causes an increase in dopamine. Dopamine and nicotine work together to stimulate the reward-addiction center. The pleasure is provided by dopamine, which reinforces the use of nicotine as well as other drugs of abuse such as amphetamine, alcohol, cocaine, and heroin. Nicotine has long been called the Gateway Drug, because smokers often are observed to graduate to other drugs of abuse.

The COVER UP

Science has only recently proven that nicotine is addictive, but why has it taken so long? The tobacco industry has known about the addictive properties of nicotine since 1963. Before 1994, there were only a few published reports on nicotine addiction. In 1972, Consumers Union's book Licit & Illicit Drugs, by Edward M. Brecher, contained a warning that nicotine was an addictive drug. Sixteen years later, the Surgeon General's Report of 1988 addressed nicotine addiction as a problem. Tragically, to the average American, nicotine addiction has largely gone unnoticed, and is generally misunderstood. Why has there been such a lack of publicity about nicotine dependency until 1994? The tobacco industry has concealed this information for over 30 years.

B.A.T.

As early as 1963, B.A.T. studied the nature of nicotine addiction. B.A.T. scientists reported, "Chronic intake of nicotine tends to restore the normal physiological functioning of the endocrine system, so that at ever-increasing dose levels of nicotine are necessary to maintain the desired action. This unconscious desire explains the addiction of the individual to nicotine." However, they withheld their research from the public that proved nicotine was pharmacologically addictive.

Philip Morris

On March 21, 1983, Philip Morris blocked damaging research on nicotine addiction from being published by Dr. Victor J. DeNoble, Ph.D., and Dr. Paul C. Mele, Ph.D. both Philip Morris scientists at the time. Their research would have been the first publication of its kind proving that nicotine is addictive. In the study, "lever-pressing" was established and maintained by nicotine. Rats would self-administer intravenous nicotine by pressing a lever. Self-administration is a key characteristic that established nicotine as addictive. DeNoble's publication had been accepted by the *Journal of Psychopharmacology*, but they were told by Philip Morris lawyers to withdraw it. "Do not go public with the data, and do not talk about it in public. Your work makes us look like a drug company. The company can not afford to do that work. This would not look good with the current litigation." Consequently, Dr. DeNoble's lab was shut down on April 4, 1984. DeNoble's lab animals were ordered killed, and his files destroyed. Dr. DeNoble was not fired — he quit, when the new position they offered was not Ph.D. work.

Obviously, Philip Morris management became concerned about DeNoble and Mele's findings. The timing of their discovery of the addictive properties of nicotine could have posed a legal problem for the company, because only 30 days prior, the Cipollone tobacco liability suit had been filed. Rose Cipollone, a New Jersey resident, was suing Philip Morris, Liggett Group, and Loews Corp. She smoked their cigarette brands, and claimed that it caused her lung cancer. Her attorney argued that she was addicted to nicotine and couldn't quit smoking, and was mislead by pre-1966 advertising that cigarettes were safe. Mrs. Cipollone died in 1984.

Addiction research scientists say that progress was hindered by the tobacco industry. By delaying this information, "It set the field back six years at least before work like it could be accomplished by Canadian researchers," explains Dr. Henningfield. Canadian researchers Corrigall and Coen, first published critical research on the self-administration of nicotine in rodents later in 1989.

Dr. DeNoble made another discovery that Philip Morris withheld for eleven years. He found acetaldehyde, a by-product of burning sugars in tobacco leaf, is addictive. Sugar is commonly added to tobacco. In his experiment, rats would press a bar one hundred times an hour for nicotine or acetaldehyde. When both were mixed together, the rats would press the bar five hundred times an hour. This data demonstrated that it is plausible that acetaldehyde adds to nicotine addiction. The possible link of acetaldehyde to tobacco addiction was unknown until then.

Philip Morris' Position

Philip Morris maintains that DeNoble's work on nicotine addiction was published. However, in was not published in the *Journal of Psychopharmacology*, or any other peer reviewed journal as an article. It was however, published as an "abstract." Abstracts are brief summaries giving no details of the methods used or the results. Also, abstracts are usually printed only in trade publications that are not widely read. Most scientists agree that DeNoble's research was "buried."

The Industries Position on Nicotine Addiction

Since 1963, internal tobacco company memos openly state that nicotine is addictive. Nonetheless, for decades they have publicly denied nicotine is addictive, just as their executives have denied the health hazards of smoking for over 30 years. Despite the truth, at the Congressional hearings in 1994 when all six tobacco company CEO's where asked if they thought nicotine was addictive, they all answered no.

"I do not believe that nicotine is addictive"

-Thomas Sandefur, B&W, B.A.T.
-William I. Campbell, CEO, Philip Morris Co.
-James W. Johnston, CEO, R.J. Reynolds.
-Edward Horrigan, CEO, Liggett Group Inc.
-Andrew Tisch, CEO, Lorillard Tobacco Co.
-Joseph Taddeo, CEO, U.S. Tobacco Co.
-Donald S. Johnston, CEO, American Tobacco Co.

> **"Cigarettes, like other enjoyable things—like eating Twinkies, may be habit forming"**
>
> -R. J. Reynolds CEO James W. Johnston

$50,000:
The Lifetime monetary cost of nicotine addiction.

The average smoker will spend about $50,000 buying cigarettes over 40 to 50 years. If all the smokers today continued smoking for 50 years, they would collectively spend $2.4 trillion dollars, which is about $1 million for every person in the U.S. today.

UST Mulled Over a Nicotine Candy

L. F. Bantle, Vice President of UST in 1968, expressed his ideas on the marketing direction of snuff products. He said "We must sell the use of tobacco in the mouth and appeal to young people." A top UST scientist suggested marketing a "swallowable chew: a confection with nicotine." After mulling over the idea for two years, UST decided to reject selling a sweet, edible nicotine confection.

Smokers are Victims

Treat smokers with empathy. Remember they are addicted to a drug—they are victims of lies and deception. They have been duped. Smokers should be encouraged to quit—but it is best not to criticize them. Teens should be educated on nicotine addiction and the hazards of smoking to prevent them from starting. Efforts in this area can bring the greatest reward—saving a life.

If you smoke, this book cannot tell you how to quit. It can tell you the reasons you continue to smoke from a physical perspective. The psychological addiction to smoking is a whole other body of science, another book in itself. It is much more complicated. It can't be examined under a microscope.

Ask any ex-smoker and they will tell you, though, that you have to make up your own mind to quit. Hopefully, then, this book will open your mind to the reality of a smoker's life and death. If you choose a longer, better quality of life, then quit now. Pick a date; announce it to you friends and family. Seek out a recommended cessation program. Call the American Cancer Society for help. See your physician to discuss whether a "patch" would be helpful and safe for you. Do it now—there is never a better time. Make this be the first day of the rest of your life. Join the ranks of nonsmokers, and that elite group of ex-smokers, proud to have been able and willing to cut the slavery bond to tobacco addiction. Now that you've taken this gigantic step, you'll want to reap all the benefits.

■ ■ ■ ■ ■ ■ ■ ■ ■ ■ ■ ■

The tobacco industry has been accused of manipulating nicotine in tobacco products to keep people hooked. ABC was sued by Philip Morris for reporting that they deliberately "spike" cigarettes with nicotine. Despite the outcome of the settlement, which misled the public to think that ABC was wrong, tobacco companies do manipulate nicotine yields in cigarettes. Also it is interesting to note that the remainder of ABC's *Day One* programs accusations about the industries procedures were also true, and they were not challenged. Find out next why "supercharging" may be closer to the truth than spiking.

Chapter Seven

Spiking and Supercharging

"Determine the minimum nicotine drop

to keep normal smokers hooked."

-R. A. Tamol, Philip Morris, Feb 1, 1965

Tobacco companies brag about how consistently their cigarettes are manufactured, stating "No matter when or where you buy them, they taste the same." They claim nicotine gives a cigarette taste. Despite this, they have done little research on the taste of nicotine. Instead, they researched the effects of nicotine "on the brains of smokers." Their research concluded that the effect of nicotine on the brain was more important to the smoker than flavor.

From a practical point of view, consistency in tobacco products means a brand always has the same amount of nicotine. If no discretion was used in selecting tobacco leaves and they were randomly picked for use, cigarettes wouldn't be consistent in nicotine concentration.

Therefore, the amount of nicotine must be manipulated in the manufacturing process for cigarettes to be consistent. In the same manner, pharmaceutical manufacture's must manipulate the amount of drug in pills to assure each one has the same dose. Otherwise, one pill may relieve pain, and the next one may not.

Cigarette manufactures claim they only measure nicotine concentration two times, once before processing, and again after making the cigarettes. William Campbell, CEO of Philip Morris, testified in 1964 to Congress that this was true. Manipulation implies that nicotine concentration is constantly measured throughout the manufacturing process, but they claim they don't. Instead, they claim they constantly measure and carefully regulate the amount of tar. In natural tobacco the ratio is about 70 parts nicotine to 1000 parts tar. Tar and nicotine are tied together, if one is increased the other goes up too. So from a practical point of view when they manipulate tar, they also manipulate nicotine. Despite the tar smokescreen and Mr. Campbell's testimony, Ian L. Uydess, a former Philip Morris scientists, says they "routinely targeted and adjusted" nicotine concentrations in cigarettes. Furthermore, he says that nicotine is adjusted to an "optimum range" preferred by smokers.

Manipulation assures they will reach the desired concentration of nicotine for each brand. This is a practice they have used for 40 years. Nicotine is manipulated in the cigarette manufacturing process by:

1. Blending different tobaccos.
2. Adding tobacco extract and reconstituted tobacco to cigarettes.
3. Adding "impact boosters," such as ammonia, to the tobacco which increases the yield of free nicotine, a much more potent form of the drug.

Blending Tobacco

A single tobacco crop can be called a batch. Every batch contains different amounts of nicotine. The tops of tobacco plants have higher nicotine concentrations. So different tobacco batches and tops can be mixed together to get the desired nicotine concentration in the final blend. In 1995, Rep. Henry Waxman obtained tobacco company documents which describe the method used to increase nicotine levels in low tar cigarettes through blending. William A. Farone, a former Philip Morris director of research, says they routinely manipulated nicotine concentrations by blending. For example, the nicotine concentration of a low-tar brand, Merit Ultra Light, was routinely altered by blending with nicotine-rich tobaccos.

Y-1 Tobacco

For ten years, B.A.T. secretly grew a genetically engineered high nicotine tobacco in Brazil, called Y-1. Y-1 has the highest concentration of nicotine known, 6.2 % compared to 2.5% - 3.0% in regular flue-cured tobacco.

In 1993, B.A.T. blended four million pounds of Y-1 in five of its brands: Raleigh Lights Kings Size, Viceroy King Size, Viceroy Lights King Size, Richland King Size, and Richland Lights King Size. B.A.T. says that Y-1 was a "blending tool for flavor."

Nicotine Used as an Additive

The tobacco industry lists nicotine sulfate, and tobacco extract, as two of the additives they use in the manufacturing process of cigarettes. Tobacco extract contains nicotine. This implies that nicotine, either as nicotine sulfate or tobacco extract, is added to some cigarette brands.

A small amount of nicotine is also added to tobacco in the process of applying additives. Tobacco additives can be easily applied to tobacco when dissolved in denatured alcohol. Coincidentally, pure grain alcohol is denatured with nicotine, as required by law, to make it poisonous and not drinkable. Trucking records show that in the 1980's, Philip Morris received thousands of gallons of denatured alcohol. Additives are sprayed on tobacco dissolved in this nicotine-alcohol solution, which adds a very small amount of nicotine to the tobacco. This is another method used by the tobacco industry to adjust the amount of nicotine in the cigarette.

Reconstituted Tobacco

Reconstituted tobacco is actually a cheap filler that is mixed with tobacco to: 1. Save money in the cigarettes manufacturing process, and 2. Control nicotine concentrations. RJR pioneered a two step process for making reconstituted tobacco. American Health Foundation, an independent laboratory of Valhalla, New York, analyzed two RJR cigarette brands. One contained 25% reconstituted tobacco, and the other 33%. Currently marketed RJR cigarette brands contain 22% to 33% reconstituted tobacco, and some generic brands have twice that amount.

Today, the reconstitution process is widely used in cigarette manufacturing. Philip Morris's Park 500 factory, is said to be a reconstituted tobacco facility. There are companies that specialize in reconstituting tobacco. LTR Industries, a

French subsidiary of Kimberley-Clark, advertised in trade journals "The Kimberly-Clark tobacco reconstitution process used by LTR Industries permits adjustment of nicotine to your exact requirements."

Reconstituted tobacco is made from floor sweepings, that is tobacco debris, stalks, stems, scraps, and dust. First, this tobacco waste is treated with hot water. The hot water removes all of the nicotine, and turns brown in the process. Then the remaining fibers are ground and rolled into a flat sheet.

This brown water is then percolated until it is reduced to a syrupy mixture called tobacco extract. It is very concentrated with 48% nicotine. Tobacco extract is then sprayed on the flat sheet of fibers, fortifying it with nicotine. The nicotine concentration is controlled at this point and measured with sophisticated instruments called gas chromatographs.

Tobacco extract is listed as a tobacco additive used in the cigarette manufacturing process. It contains nicotine, which the tobacco industry says adds a nicotine "kick" to the tobacco. B.A.T. internal documents show that they discussed adding a "high-nicotine tobacco extract" to their cigarettes in 1970.

Supercharging Cigarettes

Impact: Tobacco industry code for the pharmacological effect of nicotine on the smoker.

The amount of nicotine delivered to the smoker can be increased by adding "nicotine impact boosters" to the tobacco. Ammonia, and diammonium phosphate (DAP) are commonly used to boost the nicotine delivery by increasing the pH, making it more alkaline. William A. Farone said that ammonia chemistry was important to Philip Morris to "maintain adequate nicotine delivery to satisfy smokers."

It is interesting to note that impact boosters do not change the nicotine yield as measured by the FTC smoking machines. Ammonia changes the nicotine to the free form, which is more potent. The FTC method can't distinguish between nicotine and free nicotine.

For all practical purposes, ammonia supercharges the nicotine, giving it what Philip Morris describes as an enhanced "nicotine kick." Marlboro is an ammonia rich, supercharged cigarette. Ian L. Uydess says that Philip Morris clearly understood that high nicotine impact products had the best "taste," and sell the most. Philip Morris is purported to have made charts in 1973 of Marlboro sales verses free nicotine yields, demonstrating that as nicotine rose, so did sales.

The FDA Investigation on the Manipulation of Nicotine

The FDA has collected evidence showing that tobacco companies can control nicotine levels in rods, which is industry jargon for a cigarette. Some of Dr. Kessler's evidence that nicotine is manipulated is in the patents the tobacco companies own. They have developed and patented processes to increase nicotine in cigarettes.

The ratio of tar to nicotine is relatively constant in natural tobacco, with 70 parts nicotine to 1000 parts tar. High nicotine tobacco also has a high concentration of tar. However, over the last ten years, the amount of tar in cigarettes has been falling. You would then expect that the nicotine would also be falling. Instead, the amount of nicotine has been increasing! FDA measurements show the nicotine in ultra-low tar 100's is 30% higher than regular 100's. More interestingly, from 1968 to 1985 the nicotine ratio of Benson & Hedges brand moved up and down like a roller coaster while the concentration of tar remained constant.

Patents Owned by Tobacco Companies

Patented Processes	Company
Increase nicotine by adding nicotine to rod.	R. J. Reynolds
Development of new nicotine analogs.	Philip Morris
Manipulation of nicotine in the reconstitution process.	Philip Morris
Adding extra nicotine to papers, filters.	Philip Morris; R.J.Reynolds; Gallaher Ltd.
Tobacco de-nicotine process.	Brown & Williamson; R. J. Reynolds

Benson & Hedges brand: Nicotine Levels:

YEAR	Ratio: Nicotine per 1000 parts Tar
1968	67
1981	200
1983	111
1984	69
1985	58
Natural Tobacco	**70**
Philip Morris *"Optimum Ratio"*	**100**

"If there isn't manipulation," Dr. Kessler asks, "how did that happen?" "These finding lay to rest any notion that there is no manipulation and control of nicotine undertaken in the tobacco industry." Dr. Kessler feels he has shown that the tobacco industry manipulates the nicotine level in tobacco with the intention to maintain addiction, and that these findings allow the FDA to bring tobacco under its jurisdiction for regulation. On February 25, 1994, Dr. Kessler wrote the Congress:

"Evidence brought to our attention is accumulating that suggests that cigarette manufactures may intend that their product contain nicotine to satisfy an addiction on the part of some of their customers."

Summary of Methods Used to Manipulate Nicotine:

- Tobacco is blended to calibrate the nicotine concentration specification for each brand.
- Tobacco extract, fortified with nicotine, is added to reconstituted tobacco. Tobacco extract is a government-registered additive.
- Small amounts of nicotine are contained in the mixture used to apply additives to tobacco. Nicotine is a government-registered additive.
- Adding "impact boosters" to tobacco which doubles the free nicotine delivered in the smoke or chew.

Manipulating Nicotine In Smokeless Tobacco

Tobacco companies also deny they adjust the nicotine concentration in snuff, a smokeless tobacco. However, an interoffice memo submitted as evidence at the *Marsee v. United States Tobacco Company* trial in 1986, revealed that UST was carefully calibrating the concentration of nicotine in it's three brands of snuff. Furthermore, they tested and re-tested the nicotine level in each brand, to maintain the right "nicotine kick."

Supercharging Snuff

Another way UST increases the nicotine delivery in snuff is by adjusting the pH level, by increasing its alkalinity with ammonia. The more ammonia in the snuff, the more nicotine is delivered to the dippers blood stream. There is more ammonia in Copenhagen than in Skoal Bandits. Consequently Copenhagen delivers a whopping 79% of the nicotine it contains, and Skoal releases only seven percent. UST scientists admitting this said, "UST uses chemicals to change the pH of it's tobaccos, and therefore, (increases) the amount of nicotine released into the users blood." Snuff then, is supercharged the same way cigarettes are.

The Graduation Strategy

The "graduation strategy" gets starters using low strength nicotine, candy-like snuff, and later graduate to higher strength nicotine snuff. Additives, such as honey, cherry flavor, and chocolate are used in beginners' snuff. Flavors make snuff taste like candy which makes it easier for starters to become accustom to the taste of nicotine. UST once targeted young people to use Happy Days, a low strength nicotine snuff (no longer sold). Skoal Bandits is another starter product sold today which contains only 2.16% nicotine. Users eventually graduate to Copenhagen, a maximum strength nicotine snuff, with 3.2% nicotine. Advertising budgets support the graduation strategy because more is spent on starter snuff than the stronger brands. In 1984, UST spent $7.2 million on advertising starter snuff, and $2.6 million on all other brands.

The graduation strategy is still working today, and has been confirmed by two independent studies. One study, by the CDC, followed young users of Skoal. To their surprise, researchers found that 33% of the Skoal users had switched to Copenhagen within four years. Similar results were also published in 1994 by the National Institute on Drug Abuse in Tobacco Control. UST commented on the studies calling them "false and misleading."

Nicotine Concentrations in Smokeless Tobacco: Top Secret

In 1986, Congress passed a law requiring tobacco companies to disclose the amount of nicotine and additives used in smokeless tobacco to the federal government. It is important to note that the same law allows tobacco companies to keep them a secret from the public. Fortunately, independent researchers have measured nicotine in several brands of smokeless tobacco and published their findings. (See Appendix D for examples of the nicotine concentrations of smokeless tobacco.)

The Tobacco Industries Position on the Manipulation of Nicotine

On April 14, 1994, at the Congressional Hearing, the CEOs of seven major tobacco companies denied under oath, that they "spike" cigarettes with nicotine. Despite their testimony, Lorillard admitted later to the Congressmen, that the amount of nicotine in their cigarettes had increased ten percent from the amount in 1982.

Consider testimony by William K. Campbell, CEO of Philip Morris, who said "Nothing in the processing of tobacco or the manufacture of cigarettes increases the nicotine in our products above what is naturally found in the tobacco." Campbell implies that the amount of nicotine they add to tobacco does not exceed the total amount of nicotine found in natural tobacco.

Scott Ballin of the Collation on Smoking and Health, said that the evidence shows that there is a "Very calculated and intended effort by the tobacco industry to control the amount of nicotine in cigarettes."

■■■■■■■■■■■■■

Cigarette smoke contains much more than nicotine. What is in tobacco smoke that makes it so harmful? One hundred thousand chemicals in tobacco smoke make it a potent poison, and smokers inhale those chemicals fresh from the flame.

"The probabilities are that some combination of constituents of smoke will be found conducive to the onset of cancer."

Addison Yeaman, B.A.T.

Chapter Eight

The Toxic Cocktail

Tobacco smoke inhaled directly from a cigarette is called mainstream smoke. The smoke that billows from the end of a lit cigarette is called secondhand or side-stream smoke. Environmental Tobacco Smoke (ETS), is the term most often used today for secondhand smoke polluted indoor air. Non-smokers have chosen not to smoke, but when they inhale secondhand smoke, they are smoking involuntarily. Involuntary smoking is also called passive smoking.

Carcinogen: Chemicals that are known to cause cancer.

Co-carcinogens: Chemicals that work with carcinogens to increase the risk of cancer.

Mutagens: Chemicals that cause mutations in genes.

Tobacco smoke contains some 100,000 complex chemicals. Only about 4,000 have been identified and classified, and the remainder have not. The most prevalent and significant are nicotine, tar, and some 2,000 extremely toxic chemicals and gases (Appendix B). Tar contains carcinogens, mutagens, and co-carcinogens, that all can speed the process that leads to cancer. Experts say the greatest health hazards of smoking are attributed to carbon monoxide, nicotine, and tar.

Toxic Gases

Numerous gases such as carbon monoxide, carbon dioxide, ammonia, volatile nitrosamines, hydrogen cyanide, sulfur-compounds, nitrites, hydrocarbons, aldehydes and ketones are in tobacco smoke. Most of these gases are toxic and some are known carcinogens. Compared to severely polluted air, environmental tobacco smoke has 200 times more nitrogen oxides. Nitrogen oxides cause inflammation in the lungs and coughing.

Carbon Monoxide

Carbon monoxide is a toxic gas that is invisible, odorless, tasteless, and colorless. A high concentration of carbon monoxide causes central nervous system damage and death by asphyxiation. It is best known for its dangerous presence in car exhaust. If a car is left running in an enclosed garage, lethal levels of carbon monoxide can accumulate. The entire garage becomes a carbon monoxide gas chamber. Similarly, in restaurants for instance, there is no escaping the hazards of carbon monoxide in the "no-smoking section."

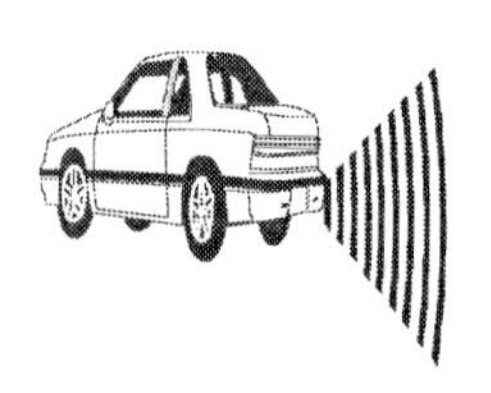

Carbon monoxide has a lethal effect on hemoglobin, the molecule in red blood cells that carry oxygen. Exposure to low levels of carbon monoxide converts normal hemoglobin to carboxyhemoglobin. When the concentration of carboxyhemoglobin in the blood reaches three to six percent, the oxygen supply to the heart muscle is greatly reduced. Susceptible people exposed to carbon monoxide can experience intensely painful angina attacks, or cardiac arrhythmia. Smokers normally have five to nine percent carboxyhemoglobin, which puts them at risk of a heart attack.

Free Radicals

Free radicals are very destructive reactive oxygen species—superoxide radicals, hydrogen peroxide, and hydroxyl radicals. When the skin is exposed to free radicals, collagen molecules cross link, causing the skin to wrinkle. Free radicals also cause damage to DNA, which can lead to cancer. They are also extremely toxic to heart muscle cells. Free radicals have been linked to premature aging and elevated cholesterol.

The body normally produces some free radicals, such as hydrogen peroxide, and hydroxyl radicals, which are used in the bodies defense mechanisms. The body also has a defense mechanism to protect itself from free radicals. The body is armed with antioxidants called free radical scavengers, which help keep free radicals in check by detoxifying them. So normally, there is a healthy balance of free radicals and antioxidants. However, the body is not equipped to handle the heavy burden of free radicals in tobacco smoke.

One puff of tobacco smoke contains 10^{16} free radicals, about 100,000,000,000,000,000 molecules.

By comparison, a normal breath contains about 10^{22} molecules of air, about 100,000,000,000,000,000,000,000 molecules.

Antioxidant vitamins, such as vitamin A (beta carotene) and vitamin E (alpha-tocopherol) are thought to provide protection from free radicals. However, research has shown that antioxidants do not protect smokers from lung cancer. The only thing a smoker can do to help protect themselves from lung cancer is to stop smoking.

Free radicals are so dangerous, that RJR is developing a cigarette they claim has less free radicals.

Tar

Tar is an innocent sounding name for the brown goo that remains in tobacco smoke after water and nicotine are removed. This dark-colored Polycyclic Aromatic Hydrocarbon (PAH) is formed when tobacco is burned. A PAH in tar called benzo-(a)-pyrene is also found in chimney soot. In 1775, a London doctor first described the association of soot to cancer of the scrotum in chimney sweeps. Another PAH, 7,12-Dimethylbenzo(a)anthracene, causes mammary tumors in animals, and is thought to play an important role in causing breast cancer in women who smoke.

Tar contains 60 documented carcinogens, including nitrosamines, metallic ions, and a radioactive compound Polonium-210. Over forty years ago researchers discovered that by rubbing tar on the skin of mice, a tumor would develop. Benzo(a)pyrene is attracted to the heart and lungs, causing damage to the DNA in those organs. PAH's also begin the process of atherosclerosis, in which fatty deposits accumulate on blood vessel walls. Tar is hazardous in very small amounts, therefore no low tar cigarette is safe.

Nitrosamines

Research has shown that nitrosamines may cause cancer. Nitrosamines achieved fame when researchers told us that flame broiled meat may cause stomach cancer. Burning meat forms nitrosamines. In the same manner, when tobacco is burned, dozens of nitrosamines are formed. The average one pack a day smoker inhales 16 micrograms of nitrosamines a day. By comparison, the typical nonsmoker absorbs only about one microgram of nitrosamines a day from food, beer, and cosmetics.

In addition to the burning process, more nitrosamines are formed during the curing and aging process of tobacco. One is attributed to a herbicide commonly sprayed on tobacco crops. Therefore curing, aging, and herbicide use makes cigarettes, as well as smokeless tobacco, rich sources of nitrosamines. Researchers reported in *The Journal of the National Cancer Institute* in 1995, the amount of nitrosamines in two UST smokeless tobacco products:

Copenhagen, snuff	**17 gm per gram**
Skoal, wintergreen snuff	**15 gm per gram**

1/3 of an ounce of snuff a day (ten grams), contains from two to ten times more nitrosamines that one pack of cigarettes.

Nitrosamines Can Cause Cancer

Nitrosamines can cause cancer if inhaled, ingested, or absorbed through the skin or mucus membranes in the mouth. Some nitrosamines concentrate in the urine, and are blamed for bladder cancer. Cancers of the lip, mouth and throat, are frequently seen in people using smokeless tobacco products. Each nitrosamines seeks it's own ground zero—causing tumors in specific body sites. Following is an example of some nitrosamines in tobacco smoke, and where they cause cancer:

Nitrosamines are Attracted to these Target Body Sites:

Tumor Site	NNK	DENA	DMNA	NNN	NPYR
Lungs	Yes	Yes	Yes	Yes	Yes
Bronchi	Yes	Yes			
Trachea	Yes	Yes		Yes	
Nasal Cavity	Yes	Yes	Yes	Yes	
Liver	Yes	Yes	Yes		Yes
Stomach		Yes			
Esophagus		Yes		Yes	
Skin	Yes	Yes			
Breast		**Yes**			
Kidney		Yes	Yes		
Bile Duct			Yes		
Inner Ear					Yes
Testis					Yes
Blood (Leukemia)					Yes

NNK = 4-(*N*-methyl-*N*-nitrosamino)-1-(3-pyridyl)-1-butanone
DENA = Diethylnitrosamine
DMNA = Dimethylnitrosamine
NNN = N-nitrosonornicotine
NPYR = N-nitrosopyrrolidine

NNK

The nitrosamine NNK is a very aggressive and dangerous carcinogen. It preys on the lungs, nasal cavity, liver, and trachea. Applied to skin, swallowed, or injected, NNK causes cancer in animals. As if NNK wasn't enough, there are forty-two more nitrosamines in tar.

46 million Americans inhale 43 nitrosamines into their lungs point blank.

The body turns most of NNK into NNAL—another powerful lung carcinogen. An enzyme normally detoxifies NNAL into harmless compounds. African-Americans lack the enzyme that detoxifies NNAL, and therefore, have about 35% more NNAL. This is why they have a high rate of lung cancer.

Tobacco is Radioactive !

Polonium-210, the radioactive element discovered by Marie Curie in 1898, occurs naturally in soil and in tobacco. Only a small sample of polonium will cause the air to glow. The concentration of polonium-210 in tobacco varies, depending on the area grown, and by the method used to cure it.

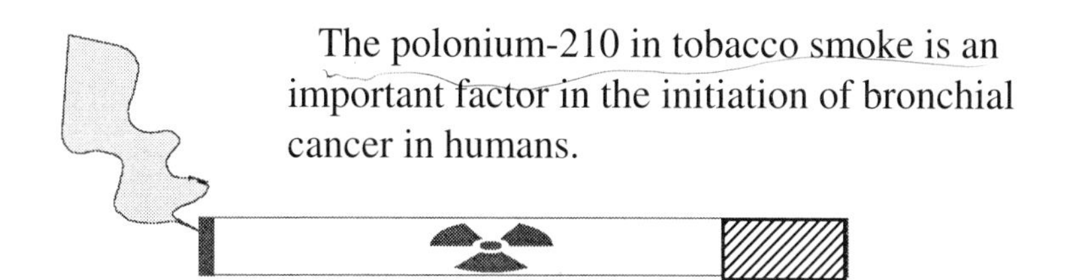

The polonium-210 in tobacco smoke is an important factor in the initiation of bronchial cancer in humans.

Polonium-210 concentrates heavily in smoker's lungs, liver, and blood. The body can't rid itself of polonium. 138.4 days are required for half of an amount of polonium to decay away naturally (half-life of 138.4 days). Biopsies done on smokers reveal polonium-210 in the lungs (lung parenchyma, peri bronchial lymph nodes, and bronchial epithelium), and in the bones in concentrations twice that of nonsmokers. Furthermore, the average smoker has six times more polonium-210 in their urine than nonsmokers. This may be the cause of the high incidence of bladder cancer in smokers.

Benzene

Gasoline and tobacco smoke both contain benzene —a carcinogenic, noxious chemical. Smokers inhale about ten times more benzene (about 2 mg. daily) than nonsmokers. Benzene exposure is suspected to be a cause of bladder cancer and leukemia.

Despite Mass Poisonings—No Regulation

Carcinogens that are one thousand times less potent than nitrosamines are prohibited by law from use in everything from food to pesticides. Yet the carcinogens in tobacco smoke are not prohibited, because the tobacco industry enjoys unique freedoms from government regulations. The tobacco industry is not accountable to the Consumer Product Safety Commission, the Environmental Protection Agency (EPA) or The Occupational Safety and Health Administration (OSHA). The tobacco lobby has successfully fought against tobacco control regulations that would protect people from these dangerous carcinogens.

Similarly, the additives used in tobacco are not required to be tested for safety as additives in food and drugs must be. The tobacco industry's freedom from being required to test the safety of additives, threatens the health of all, smokers and nonsmokers alike.

No testing — no regulations —

means no safety.

700 Untested Additives

The Federal Government is supposed to protect the public and our environment from exposure to toxic substances. It is forbidden by law to dump hazardous chemicals in landfills or waterways. Yet the same government allows some of those same toxic substances to be added to tobacco, which in turn are inhaled or chewed by millions of people. Politically speaking, the Federal Government protects tobacco companies, not the public.

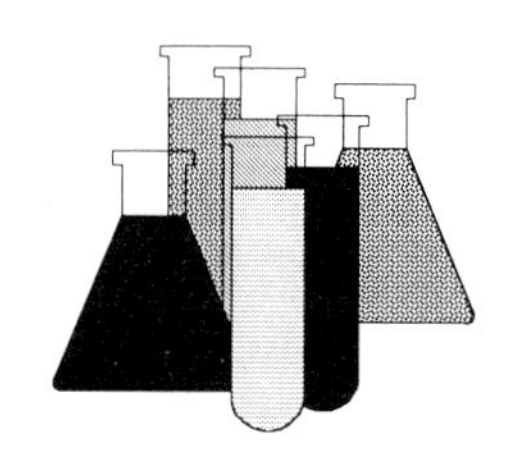

In the past, the tobacco industry has secretly used over 2,000 chemical additives in manufacturing cigarettes and other tobacco products. Even asbestos was once used in Kent micronite filters. *The Cigarette Labeling and Advertising Act* of 1985, requires tobacco companies to disclose to the government what additives they use, and at the same time conceal them from the public. Today, the tobacco industry still uses about 700 additives, but none are listed on any tobacco product.

Additives are used to flavor and process tobacco. Moistening agents are used such as glycerin, propylene glycol, and diethylene glycol. Some commonly used flavoring agents are honey, sugar, rum, licorice, chocolate, prune, vanilla, peach, and coumarin. It is important to note that coumarin was banned as a food additive in 1954 because it causes liver damage and cancer. Despite this knowledge, B.A.T. continued to use coumarin until the 1990's.

The *599* List

On April 13, 1994, one day before Congressional hearings on smoking, and 11 years after the *Cigarette Labeling and Advertising Act* was passed, tobacco companies finally disclosed to Congress a list of 599 chemical additives used in tobacco processing. According to one member of Congress, some of the additives they use were omitted from the list. The Federal Government allows the tobacco companies to suppress the list from the public. The 599 List contains no information on how much, in what combination, or what brands contain the additives.

The same month, some of chemical additives on the 599 List were made public. On April 8, 1994, National Public Radio's Rebecca Pearl named thirteen chemical additives on the 599 List. Her report is summarized in the chart on the following page. It is important to note that the FDA does not allow any of these 13 additives in food. Why then does Congress allow them in tobacco?

Top Secret: The Toxic Five

The industry maintains that the additives are not harmful, but five of the 13 additives are on the US Government's hazardous chemical list. The toxic five are regulated by the EPA who forbids discarding them in land fills. You can't bury them, but you can smoke them. The tobacco industry is not accountable to the EPA for cigarette additives.

No regulations — No safety

From a practical point of view, smokers "inject" toxic chemical additives into their blood. Rep. Ron Wideman (Oregon) says: "Some of the additives in cigarettes are so toxic they cannot be dumped in land fills by EPA laws. These toxins are delivered directly to lungs by a "drug delivery device (cigarette)."

Additives	Properties	EPA Hazardous Chemical List
1. Nicotine sulfate	Addictive drug; Toxin	
2. Di-n-hexyl ether	Enhances combustion; gasoline additive	
3. Dehydroxy-metho-puro lactone	Flavor	
4.Mega stigma trianone	Untested food additive	
5.Maltatol	Artificial sweetener; Not FDA approved	
6. Tobacco extract	Contains nicotine, and carcinogens	
7. Ammonia	Toxic irritant; "Impact booster"- Releases free nicotine.	
8 Angelica oil root extract	Carcinogen; Toxin	Toxin
9. Sclareol	Toxin; Pro-convulsant; Causes convulsions in animals	Toxin
10. Guranic acid	Liver toxin	Toxin
11.Ethyl Furoid, (2-furoate)	Liver toxin; Biological warfare agent.	Toxin
12.Methaprine	Insecticide; Toxin	Toxin
13. Freon-11, (no longer used)	Chloroflurohydrocarbon; When burned, forms phosgene, a suffocating and highly poisonous war gas.	

Sclareol

1-Naphthalene propropanol, α-ethenyldecahydro-2-hydroxy-α-2, 5, 5, 8 a-c pentamethyl-,[1-R-(1α (R+1, 2β, 4β, 4aβ, 8aα)]

Sclareol, one of the toxic five, is listed by the EPA as a hazardous toxin. This chemical, which causes convulsions, has raised concern with many physicians. "I will evaluate long term smokers differently now, especially those that suffer convulsions," says Dr. Berry Rumack, M.D. of the University. of Colorado School of Medicine. Dr. Rumack said, "We have removed chemicals (such as the toxic five) from the food chain. It is inconceivable we allow known toxic chemicals to be delivered to citizens, when we could have easily terminated such exposure."

46 Million Smokers are a Walking Toxic Dump

Angelica Oil Root

Angelica oil root extract is another one of the toxic five. The EPA Toxic Substance Control Act lists angelica oil as a known carcinogen, and a moderate toxin (#2). When angelica oil is burned, it produces an acrid, irritating smoke.

Tobacco company's representatives quickly point out that some of the chemicals are used as a food additives. But burning changes chemicals and questions arise about their safety. Dr. Lawrence Fisher, the Director of Environmental Toxicology at Michigan State said "What I am concerned about is what do these chemicals become after they are burned—they could become a problem." None of the additives have been tested for safety after burning in cigarettes. Instead, they have been kept secret by Congress and the tobacco industry.

Studies have not been done on the safety of the 700 tobacco additives alone, or in combination with the other 4,000 chemicals found in burning tobacco.

Some chemicals become more toxic when they are combined with other chemicals. With over 4,000 chemicals in tobacco smoke, the potential for that happening is great. Dr. Berry Rumack, said "We do not know the effect of these additives in combination on humans."

Tobacco companies use additives that are known carcinogens in the processing of tobacco. The quantities are relatively small and their hazardous effects are probably minuscule compared to the 60 carcinogens already in tobacco. Adding one more can be compared to dipping a bullet into rat poison before it is fired into the brain of a victim. "The additives are of little concern," says Louis Sullivan of the Department of Health and Human Services. "To make a big deal about the additives, would divert the public's concern about the more serious tobacco hazards."

The Tobacco Industries Position on Additives

The industry maintains that the chemical additives are not harmful. A tobacco company toxicology consultant, John Fraulley, Willimgton, Delaware, said regarding the additives, "I have tested them, they are safe at levels in tobacco." When questioned about the safety of the additives in combination, especially over the life of the smoker, he said that in his opinion, continuous exposure in combination is not more toxic. On the other hand, Dr. Fraulley has never reported testing them in combination.

Components of Environmental Tobacco Smoke (ETS)

The same 4,000 chemicals, gases and toxins, and chemical additives that are in mainstream smoke are also in secondhand tobacco smoke. The same chemicals in mainstream smoke that cause heart disease, nicotine, carbon monoxide and PAH's such as, benzo[a]pyrene, benzene, formaldehyde and toluene are in secondhand smoke, but slightly less concentrated.

However, there are some important differences in the two kinds of tobacco smoke. The most startling difference is that secondhand smoke is more of a health hazard than mainstream smoke. The temperature of the burn makes the difference. When a smoker draws in a puff of a lighted cigarette, they are fueling the fire with oxygen which increases the temperature of the burn 200° to 300° C. Between puffs, secondhand smoke is smoldering at a lower temperature, and at slightly increased alkaline conditions. The result is that secondhand smoke has more ammonia, less oxygen, and greater concentrations of nitrosamines. One potent nitrosamine, DMNA, is up to 100 times more concentrated in secondhand smoke. Despite a dilution effect, ETS contains higher concentrations of carcinogens. Therefore, the EPA classifies tobacco smoke as a human Group-A carcinogen, in the same class as radon, asbestos, arsenic, and benzene.

The White Serpent is a Class A Carcinogen!

Another major difference is the particle size. ETS particles are smaller than mainstream smoke. These very small particles, 0.01-1.0 mM (about the size of a yeast cell), reach deeper into the lungs, making it almost impossible for the lungs to remove them. Particles less than 1.0 mM are considered very dangerous and are known to cause death and disease. Small particles are especially dangerous to children with asthma and the elderly with emphysema. ETS particles are so small they pass through ordinary air filters. The only effective way to remove tobacco smoke particles is with a High Efficiency Particulate Air (HEPA) filter.

The most important differences between environmental .obacco smoke and mainstream smoke are listed in the chart below.

MAINSTREAM SMOKE	ENVIRONMENTAL TOBACCO SMOKE
More Cyanide	More Concentrated Nitrosamines
More Concentrated	Less Oxygen
Particle size, 0.1-1.0 mM	More Carbon Monoxide
	More benzo[a]pyrene
	Particle Size Smaller, 0.01-1.0 mM

ETS: The Invisible Killer — Any Amount is Harmful

Common sense says that if mainstream smoke is harmful, secondhand smoke is harmful. A poison is a poison, even in small amounts. For the nonsmoker, it is important to note that research shows that nonsmokers are harmed more by tobacco smoke than smokers.

There is no safe amount of a carcinogen, below which it does not increase the risk of cancer. Similarly, there is no safe number of cigarettes below which there is no risk to the smoker. This has been proven in so called "Dose Response" studies. The same applies to tobacco smoke. No amount of cigarette smoke is safe—very little can be harmful and can cause cancer.

The Hazards of ETS is a Recently Discovered Phenomenon

In 1971, the U.S. Surgeon General first linked secondhand smoke to disease. In 1976-1977, a group of investigators published information on the significance of glycoproteins in tobacco smoke. During the aging process of tobacco, the sugar and the proteins in the leaves combine to form glycoproteins. Glycoproteins are known to be the cause of allergic reactions, and blood clots. In 1977, Brown & Williamson researchers reproduced those early experiments on glycoproteins, and confirmed they are a health hazard. That information, as well other data on toxins and carcinogens they identified in secondhand smoke were not disclosed to the public. The significance of that work and what B.A.T may have known about it was not fully realized until 1996. Investigators at the Pickower Institute in Manhasset, NY, reported that they suspected glycoproteins, called Advanced Glycation Endproducts (AGEs), were responsible for hardening of the arteries (arteriosclerosis).

■ ■ ■ ■ ■ ■ ■ ■ ■ ■ ■ ■ ■

Smokers are a walking toxic dump—cigarette smoke is poisonous. How bad for you health is smoking? How do the odds of dying from smoking compare to the odds of winning a lottery? Are your chances better to die from: 1) an automobile accident, 2) a gun shot, or 3) from smoking? Are smokers more likely to die from a heart attack or from lung cancer? Does smoking only cause lung cancer, or does it cause other cancers as well? The cruel, horror story unfolds.

Smoking kills the equivalent number of people that would fill three jumbo jets every day.

Chapter Nine

Disease and Death

Smoking is Harmful —

Compared to What?

Most people know that smoking is harmful, but according to the Federal Trade Commission, they do not know how harmful. Visual imagery in cigarette advertisements associate smoking with healthy activities. Experts say that is one reason most people underestimate the real health hazards of smoking. When people learn the truth about the hazards of smoking, they become much more concerned.

"Someone has to win."

- Hopeful lottery player.

There is no safe number of cigarettes one can smoke without increasing the risk of lung cancer—one cigarette a day will increase the risk. A smoker's risk of lung cancer is one in 1,000. Their odds of getting lung cancer is about seventeen thousand times better than winning a lottery. When compared to being struck by lightning, or getting killed in an automobile accident, the risks of lung cancer is higher. Still, most smokers do not think they will get cancer. To find out how smoking compares to other preventable deaths and injury, check the chart below:

Preventable Death or Accident	Risk Factor: One in
Nuclear Reactor Close to Home, Cancer	100,000,000
Struck by Lightning	600,000
Pedestrian hit by car, Fatality	40,000
Injured at work	5,000
Auto Collision; Fatality	5,000
Cancer from Smoking	3

Anyone who reads the newspaper, or watches the evening news knows that numerous people are killed every day by gun shots, drugs and car wrecks. But the average person would be surprised to know that more Americans have been killed by tobacco than by World Wars I & II, the Vietnam War, AIDS, heroin and cocaine combined.

In 1990, smoking was responsible for 38% of all preventable deaths, making it the number one cause.

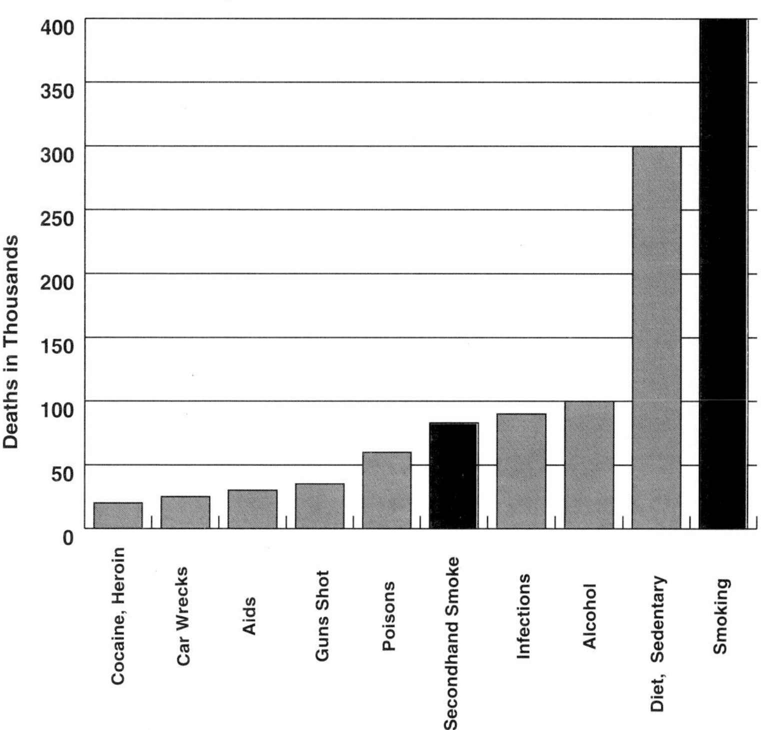

Preventable deaths caused by narcotics, cocaine and heroin, are the tenth cause of preventable deaths. Newt Gingrich, Speaker of the United States House of Representatives, expressed his misunderstanding of the magnitude of tobacco deaths when he responded to the FDA's announcement to regulate nicotine in 1995. Bewildered and hostile, he accused the FDA of "picking a brand new fight when we haven't won the far more serious fights about crack and cocaine and heroin." Contrary to Gingrich's statement, cigarettes kill 26 times more people than illegal drugs.

Mortality from Smoking

One Smoker Dies Every 73 Seconds from Smoking Related Diseases

One out of every five deaths is caused by smoking. In 1993, 46 million Americans smoked, about 25% of all adults. Smoking related diseases will kill 36% to 40% of smokers. Some 434,000 Americans are killed annually, about the same number of people as live in Albuquerque, New Mexico.

Smokers that Die from Smoking Related Disease

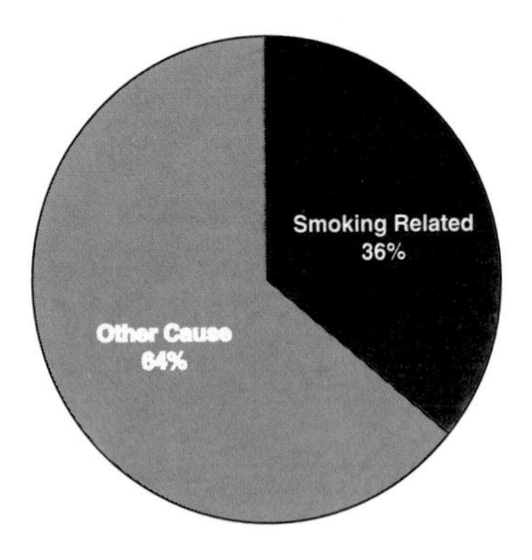

Smokers have a Shorter Life Span

The typical smoker averages 30 cigarettes a day. Over 50 years, they will smoke one half million cigarettes. This constant burden of toxins reduces their life expectancy by about 15 to 20 years. People are starting to smoke younger, and they are dying younger than the smokers who started smoking in their 20's or 30's. A smoker that starts in adolescence has a 50% chance of dying prematurely from smoking.

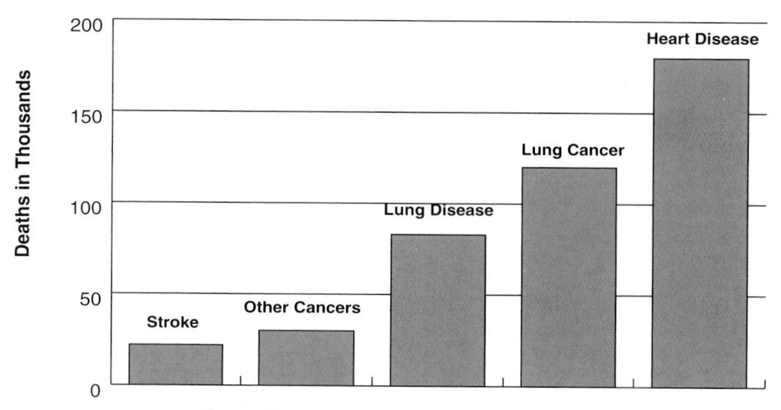

Cardiovascular Deaths

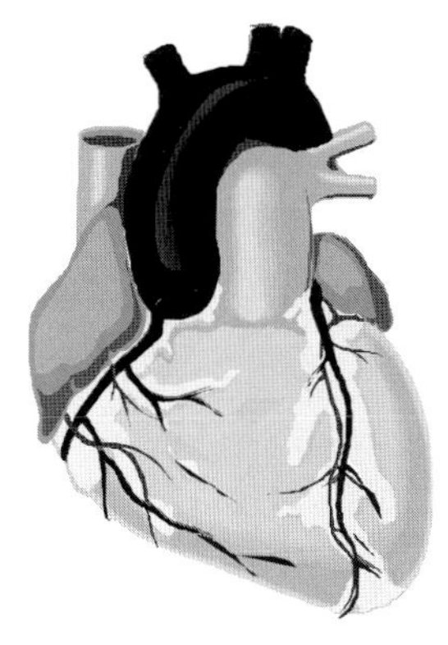

The number one killer of smokers is heart disease. Researchers estimate that 30% to 40% of the 717,700 cardiovascular deaths a year are caused by smoking. Contrary to the belief of most Americans, heart disease attributed to voluntary and involuntary smoking has a larger impact on public health than lung cancer.

For years it was thought that a smokers risk of dying from heart disease was about three times higher than a nonsmoker. However, that view has changed since new evidence was reported in the *British Medical Journal* in 1995 that says the risk is much higher.

In one of the most comprehensive studies ever done on smoking and heart disease, researchers at the John Radcliffe Hospital in Oxford studied over 13,926 survivors of heart attacks. When researchers divided the patients into groups by age, they found something startling. Among the youngest age group studied, 30-49 years, smokers had five times the rate of nonfatal heart attacks as nonsmokers. In that age group, 80%

of the heart attacks were caused by smoking. This study shows that smoking causes many more heart attacks in smokers under 49 years old than formerly believed. Dr. R. Peto, an investigator at Radcliffe, said "In the United States smoking is causing 40,000 heart attacks a year in people in their 30's and 40's." A study in Finland in 1996, confirmed Peto's conclusion. Researchers at the University of Tromso found that the risk of heart attacks among smokers was highest in the 45 years old and younger age group. Furthermore, the risk was higher among women (risk 710 times higher than a nonsmoker) than among men (230 times).

Smoking causes ischemic heart disease and arteriosclerosis. Ischemic heart disease is a result of obstructed arteries of the heart. Arteriosclerosis causes blood vessels to thicken and harden. The major complications of those diseases are chest pain (angina pectoris), heart attack, and sudden cardiac death. Smoking increases the risk of dying of cardiovascular diseases 1.9 to 2.8 times in men, and from 1.7 to 3.0 times in women. Ischemic heart disease killed 99,000 smokers in 1990.

Several studies show that smoking and a high fat diet further increases the risk of heart disease. Smoking and eating saturated fats lowers the good cholesterol, HDL. Low levels of HDL causes coronary arteries to become blocked (atherosclerosis). The combination of risk factors increases the risk of dying of atherosclerosis four times in men, and three times in women.

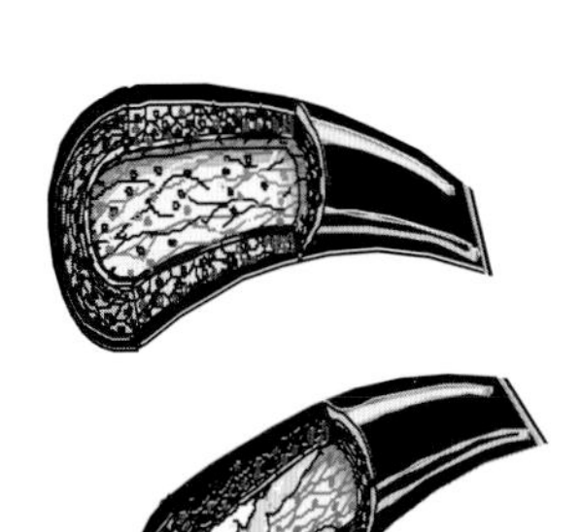

Tobacco use also damages peripheral blood vessels. Buerger's diseases, which is not uncommon in smokers, constricts the blood vessels of the legs, causing constriction, pain, and gangrene.

Carbon monoxide is one culprit in tobacco smoke that cause heart disease. Carbon monoxide reduces the amount of oxygen in the blood, and starves the heart of oxygen. This is true for smokers and nonsmokers that breathe secondhand smoke. Documents from B.A.T. written in 1974, allege that scientist funded by the Tobacco Research Council reported carbon monoxide as a key factor in cigarette related heart attacks. This was not made public until 1994. These observations are similar to the asbestos industry, which withheld health hazard information from the public, and eventually led to their downfall.

Cigar Smoking Causes Heart Attacks

A 12 year study of cigar smokers was done by the National Health Screening Service of Norway. The relative risk of heart attack for cigar smokers was the same as those that smoked 20 or more cigarettes a day, (280% higher that nonsmokers). Cigar smoking increases the risk of a heart attack, even if it is not inhaled. Tar.and nicotine are absorbed into the blood stream and both are carried to the heart. Nicotine is another culprit in tobacco that causes heart disease.

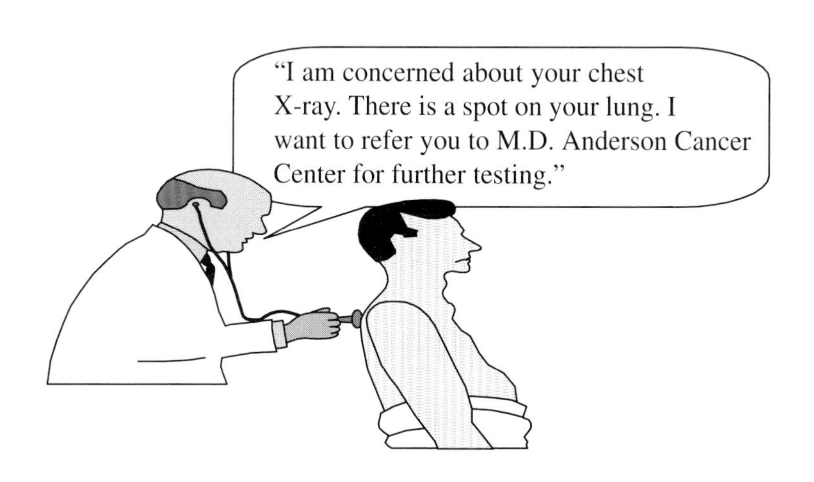

Smoking Causes Cancer

A smoker is more likely to hear these dreaded words than a nonsmoker. Dr. Charles A. Le Maistre M.D. at the M.D. Anderson Cancer Center, calls the alarming cancer deaths from smoking "One of the cruelest epidemics in U.S. history." Thirty percent of all cancer deaths are related to smoking. The risk of all cancers for smokers is about 50% to 200% higher than nonsmokers.

Smoking is the Cause of 30% of all Cancer Deaths

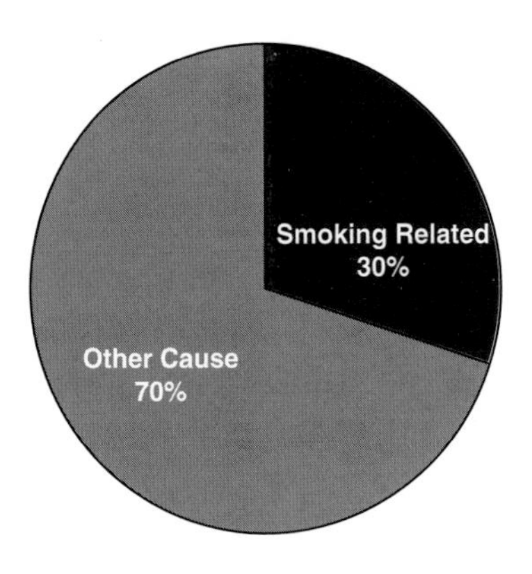

Latency Period

Cancers do not happen overnight. The latency period, the time from exposure to a carcinogen to tumor formation, is usually years. Lung cancer has a latency period of eight to 26 years. Bladder cancer has a latency period of 40 years. Other forms of cancer can take as little as one year to develop.

How Smoking Causes Cancer

The carcinogens in tobacco smoke triggers a cascade of events that lead to cancer. The are two stages in the formation of a cancerous tumors—initiation and promotion.

Initiation

Initiation, the first stage, starts with damages to a cell's DNA, the basic material of inheritance of all living things. Initiation can be caused by tar. If the damage is to some important genes that protect from cancer, or to an oncogene, it can result in uncontrolled cell growth. Uncontrolled growth of cells is the hallmark of cancer.

Smoking Kills the Guardian Angel Gene

One of the bodies defense mechanisms against cancer is the tumor suppressor gene p53, often called our "guardian angel gene." If the guardian angel gene is damaged or destroyed, initiation occurs more easily and increases the risk of tumor formation. Carcinogens in tobacco smoke destroy the guardian angel gene's ability to protect from cancer. This is especially important in head and neck cancers attributed to smoking.

Carcinogens Damage DNA

Carcinogens in tobacco smoke can stick to DNA. These dangerous chemicals cause damage to the DNA called adducts. Benzo(a)pyrene, a PAH combustion by-product found in tar, causes DNA adducts in the cells of the heart, lung, liver, skin, kidney, and spleen. Another PAH is attracted to breast tissue where it can damage the breast cancer genes BRCA one and two.

Higher numbers of adducts are found in the DNA of smokers, as well as nonsmokers who are exposed to environmental tobacco smoke. It is a simple formula—the more tobacco smoke a person inhales, the more adducts they will have in their DNA. As the DNA adducts accumulate, it puts them at a higher risk of cancer.

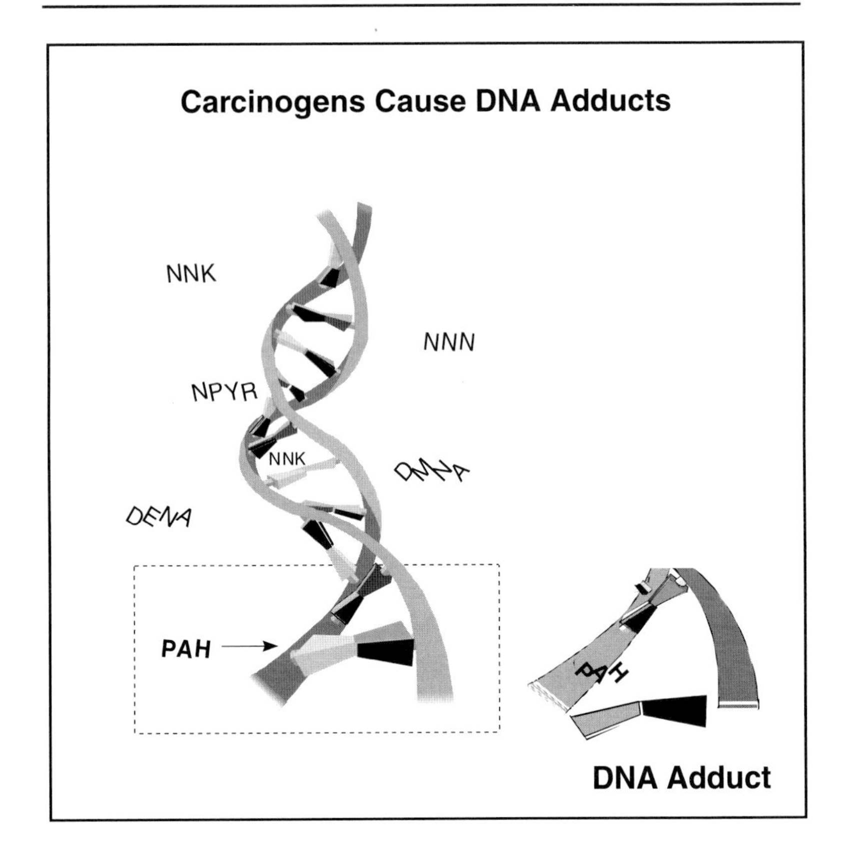

Carcinogens Cause DNA Adducts

Promotion

Lung cancer begins when a normal cell in the lung-bronchial lining converts to a malignant cell. This process, called promotion, causes the conversion of normal cells to cancerous, malignant cells. Chemicals called promoters start this process. Promoters, like phenol are in the gas phase of tobacco smoke.

If a smoker quits before age 50, they will have half the risk of dying in the next 15 years than those that continue. This is because their exposure to harmful promoters in tobacco smoke diminishes when they stop smoking. This is why a smoker's risk of lung cancer is reduced after they quit.

Co-carcinogens

Co-carcinogens are chemicals that increase the potency of carcinogens. Co-carcinogens, such as catechol, are in tobacco smoke. Diabolically, co-carcinogens activate the 60 carcinogens in tobacco smoke to multiply the risk of developing a tumor.

Alcohol and Smoking — A Dangerous Combination

Two carcinogens acting together can cause more damage than the sum of their effects acting alone. This is called the synergistic effect (1+1=3). Synergism is seen with tobacco smoke and asbestos exposure, which increases the risk of lung cancer. Alcohol and smoking also act together synergistically to increase the risk of cancer of the mouth, esophagus, and larynx. "Carcinogenic synergism" applies to cigarette and cigar smokers who also drink alcohol.

Lung Cancer

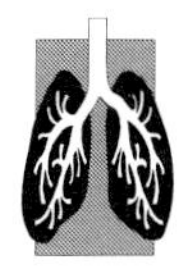

Researchers at Thomas Jefferson University discovered the human gene that is responsible for lung cancer in smokers, called FHIT. Dr. Carlo Croce, Thomas Jefferson University, the lead investigator of the study published in *Cell*, says that one or more of the 60 carcinogens in tobacco smoke may damage the FHIT gene, which then initiates lung cancer. FHIT seems to be responsible for at least two kinds of lung cancers, small cell and non-small cell tumors.

Since the first U.S. Surgeon General's report on smoking and cancer in 1950, over two million people have died from lung cancer, about the same number of people that live in Atlanta, Georgia. In 1991, there were 161,000 new cases, and 143,000 deaths attributed to smoking. Estimates for 1996 have risen to 177,000 new cases, and 158,700 deaths.

Lung Cancer Death Rate in U.S.

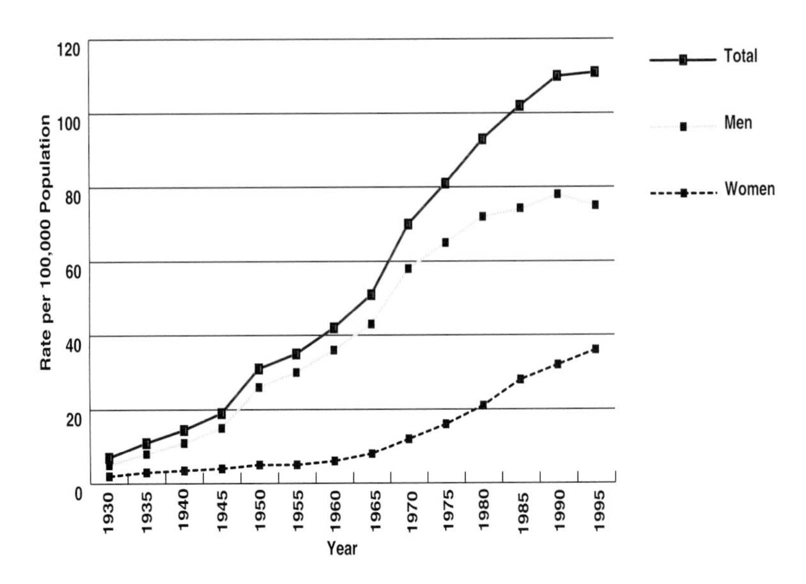

Smoking is responsible for 87% to 90% of all lung cancers. Lung cancer is the number two killer of smokers, and it is one of the most lethal kinds of cancer. Few if any are cured, and the prognosis is poor for most, with only ten to 20% surviving longer than three years. Smoking increases the risk of dying of lung cancer 22 times in men, and 12 times in women.

Percent of Lung Cancers Caused by Smoking

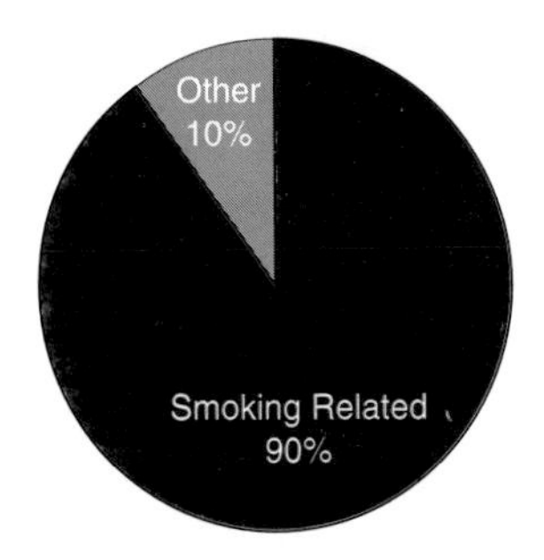

Lung Cancer Starts When You Are Young

The younger a person is when they start smoking, the higher their risk of lung cancer, and smokers are starting younger every year. The risk of dying from lung cancer is highest in those that start smoking before age 15. Today, cancer specialists are seeing new lung cancer patients as young as 30. Lung cancer is no longer an exclusive disease of the very old.

Researchers at the University of Utah, found that men who start smoking before age 19, have twice the risk of lung cancer than those that start after age 19. Women who start smoking before age 25, have three times the risk. Lung cancer takes about 20 years to develop. If you start smoking before age 19, you are more likely to die from lung cancer. If you start smoking in your 30's, you are more likely to die from a heart attack.

Smoking Kills one of every four smokers that start as adults.

Smoking Kills one of every three smokers that start as teens.

Research has shown that young smokers with no symptoms can still have lung damage. Pathologists performing autopsies on smokers have reported observing lung damage in young smokers who had no symptoms. The smokers studied were all under 29 years old, yet each had lung damage, an accumulation of inflammatory cells, edema, fibrosis, and epithelial hyperplasia. This unusual kind of lung damage is called the "precursor of emphysema."

No Genetic Protection for Smokers

"My Grandmother smoked for 60 years and she didn't die of lung cancer. I smoke, but I'm not going to get cancer because I have good genes."

-A misinformed smoker

A recent study of 681 pairs of male twins in the United States challenges the misconception that genes make some smokers resistant to lung cancer. Both pairs of twins in the study smoked the same amount. Identical twins have identical genes. If lung cancer runs in families, both of the smoking twins would have the same risk of lung cancer.

Researchers discovered however, that if one brother got lung cancer, the other brother did not. Each brother had a different risk of lung cancer, even though they had identical genes and both smoked. The study showed that lung cancer caused by smoking does not run in families.

Laryngeal, Oral, and Esophageal Cancer

Some 81% of laryngeal, and 92% of oral cancer deaths are caused by smoking. Nicotine is caustic to the mouth, pharynx, esophagus and stomach. The risk of cancer of the throat, and larynx is 27 times higher in male smokers than non-smokers. The risk is six times higher for women smokers. In 1991, 9,000 oral and laryngeal cancer deaths were attributed to smoking. In 1996, an estimated 8,260 will die from oral cancers (lip, tongue, mouth and pharynx), and 4, 250 from cancer of the larynx.

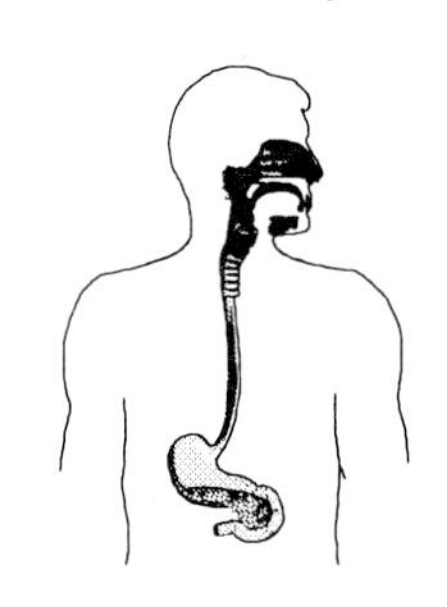

Smoking is the cause of an alarming increase in esophageal cancer. An estimated 11,200 Americans will die of esophageal cancer in 1996. Some 80% of esophageal cancer deaths are caused by smoking. For smokers, the risk is ten times higher for men, and eight times higher for women.

Cancer of the Bladder

Recent estimates state that up to 60% of bladder cancers are related to smoking. Damage to the DNA in bladder cells, especially mutations in the guardian angel gene, have been linked to bladder cancer. Tobacco use destroys the guardian angle gene, which increases a smokers risk of bladder cancer. In 1996, an estimated 11,700 people will die of bladder cancer.

Other Cancers Associated with Smoking

There is also a relationship between smoking and developing other cancers, such as leukemia and multiple myeloma. In addition, smoking is a cause of cancer of the pancreas, kidney, stomach, cervix, and endometrium, which kills 31,600 people a year.

Smoking is a contributory cause of the following carcinomas:

Types of Cancers Caused by Smoking	Annual Number	Increased Risk of Death
Bladder and Kidney	7,000	140% -300%
Pancreatic	8,000	210% -230%
Blood: Leukemia	3,600	
Stomach	2,800	
Cervical	1,400	210%
Other	8,800	

Stroke

Stroke is the fifth largest killer of tobacco users. The smoker has a one and a half to three times higher risk of stroke than a nonsmoker. In combination with high blood pressure, a smoker has ten to 20 times increased risk. In 1990, 23,281 American smokers died of cerebrovascular diseases.

Lung Diseases Caused by Smoking

Smokers are more susceptible to lung infections than nonsmokers. Tobacco smoke toxins reduce immunoglobulins and natural killer cells. The relative risk of death from pneumonia, influenza, and other respiratory diseases is about 400% higher in smokers. Heavy smokers are chronically ill with, what doctors describe as, "chronic inflammatory disorder of the lower airways." A Philip Morris scientist discovered the nitrosamines in tobacco smoke inhibits the lungs healing ability.

Emphysema and Chronic Bronchitis

Two diseases of the lungs that result from cigarette smoke injury are emphysema and chronic bronchitis, called Chronic Obstructive Pulmonary Diseases (COPD). Smoking is the leading cause of COPD in the U.S., causing 84% of COPD deaths in men, and 79% in women. In 1991, the fourth leading cause of death was COPD, with 90,000 Americans dead from the disease. Emphysema affects about 20% of heavy smokers, making it the number three killer of smokers.

When a smoker becomes breathless and can't easily exhale, they have emphysema. Their lungs become over distended. Smoking has damaged the tiny air sacks called alveoli, and they develop a barrel chest, and hold their shoulders high. To avoid exertion, they walk slowly. Their speech is labored, and they can speak only in short phrases between their futile attempts at taking in air. Laughing is avoided because it sets off violent spasms of the bronchus, causing their face to turn blue from lack of oxygen.

The destruction is irreversible, and progresses with time. Death from emphysema is described as "wreaked with suffering," like being slowly suffocated. "There are severe quality of life issues with this illness," says Dr. Brad Rodu of the University of Alabama.

Smokers Cough

The hallmarks of chronic bronchitis are smokers cough, and excessive mucus production. When smokers cough in the morning, the spasm can be as violent as the Heimlich Maneuver clearing a lodged oyster from the airway.

Over time, the smoker's airway becomes a smoke charred chimney. The goblet cells over produce mucus. Cilia, the little hairs that rid the airway of tiny particles, no longer function.

Inflammation increases and causes more damage. A fibrotic, inflammatory lung disorder, called eosinophilic granuloma, starts destroying the lungs. All of these conditions further increase the risk of lung cancer.

The Real Picture of a Smoker: The Sick and Dying

The true picture of a smoker is not the healthy smiling athletes portrayed in tobacco advertisements. If we had windows in our chests, with our lungs clearly visible to others, no one would smoke.

Cigar Smoking and Cancer

While an epidemic of teen smoking rages in this country, some of the parents of these children are caught up in an epidemic of their own – the cigar fad. Like their teen counterparts, ten million adult cigarophiles think that cigar smoking is harmless. Despite their false sense of safety, The CDC says cigar smokers die of cancer and cardiovascular diseases at a rate 34% higher than nonsmokers. Medical authorities, like Dr. Michael J. Thun of the American Cancer Society, says "Cigar smokers have a 2.5 times higher rate of lung cancer than lifelong nonsmokers." They also have higher "risks from cancer of the larynx, mouth and esophagus." In 1992, the EPA published data on cigar smokers indicating their relative risk of lung cancer ranged from 1.0 to 9.2, (risk is up to 920 percent higher than a nonsmoker) with the risk increasing with the number of cigars smoked. Cigar smoking increases the risk of emphysema five times, and the risk of stroke three times higher that nonsmokers.

From a practical point of view, cigar smoking is essentially the same as using snuff with the same potential for addiction but with greater health risks. The juices formed in the mouth of the cigar smoker consists of saliva, tobacco leaf residue, tar, ammonia, nicotine, and tobacco smoke rich in carcinogens. This brown, carcinogenic, foul-smelling spittle baths the tender mucus membranes where it is absorbed into the blood vessels and is then swallowed. The carcinogens start the process of cancer by changing normal cells to abnormal or atypical cells. When examined, doctors find atypical cells in the larynx of 99% of cigar smokers.

What makes cigar smoking more of a health hazard than smokeless tobacco is that it is burned like a cigarette. Incinerating tobacco produces more carcinogens in its thick plume of noxious smoke. Even though most cigar smokers claim they do not inhale, they can't avoid inhaling some of the smoke. Furthermore, if they smoke indoors, they inhale their own secondhand smoke. Both contribute to a higher risk of lung cancer. The CDC says that a five cigar a day smoker has three times the risk of lung cancer than a nonsmoker. Compared to the price of a cigar, this is a heavy price to pay to make them think they look like a successful big wheel.

Many well meaning people, some doctors even call cigar smoking the lesser evil when compared to smoking. This may be true statistically, because most cigar smokers only smoke a few per day or week. However, as with any tobacco product, there is a definite dose response relationship, meaning that the more you smoke, the higher your risk for disease and death. There are health hazards with any amount of tobacco use, whether it be smokeless, cigarettes, pipes or cigars. The only way to be 100% risk free is to be 100% tobacco free.

Like the cigarette industry, cigar advertising and promotions use celebrities to glamorize cigar smoking. Demi Moore, Jack Nicholson, Bill Cosby, Whoopi Goldberg, Linda Evangelista, Jim Belushi, and Rush Limbaugh are among those that are irresponsibly helping to promote this new anti-health craze. On the contrary, David Letterman has publicly announced that cigars are a health hazard and that he is attempting to quit his 20 a day addiction.

Celebrities and models, both men and women, are frequently seen flaunting their "torches of success" on the cover of *Cigar Aficionado,* a new cigar publication. Arnold Schwarzenegger, a former pro-health figure, is one striking example. How does a parent tell their child smoking is bad when the child sees their hero Arnold smoking a cigar? This magazine glorifies the invisible drug, and is notoriously credited with starting the cigar fad. Readers are mislead into believing that cigar smoking is safe because you don't inhale. As the magazines go, one by one from the newsstand, one smoker is buried every 73 seconds in the cemetery.

The Good News about Quitting:

The Health Effects Can be Reversible

Smokers need not despair! Despite the difficulties of quitting, two million smokers are able to do so each year. The risk of cancer and heart disease can be reduced after quitting. Good things start happening to your body after you quit smoking:

20 Minutes	· Blood pressure and heart rate drops
8 Hours	· Oxygen level in blood returns to normal
24 Hours	· Risk of heart attack drops.
48 Hours	· Smell and taste returns to normal.
2 Weeks	· Lung function increases 30%.
1 Month	· Cilia grows back in lungs.
1 Year	· Risk of heart disease reduced 50%.
5 Years	· Lung cancer risk reduced 50%.
5-15 Years	· Risk of stroke reduced to same as nonsmoker
10 Years	· Lung cancer risk same as nonsmoker; · Risk of other cancers reduced.
15 Years	· Risk of heart disease reduced to same as nonsmoker.

Fatalist Smokers say — "Everybody's Gotta Die"

No one can seriously claim that if you don't smoke you will live forever. However, there is one thing you can be sure of: if you smoke, you will suffer more and die sooner, and the quality of life in your final years may be so miserable, that death will be welcome. Cancer and emphysema are painful and slow deaths. Pick your poison – pick your torture: smoking will bring the Grim Reaper before you are ready to go.

The Hazards of Smokeless Tobacco

Contrary to the opinion of most smokeless tobacco users, snuff and chewing tobacco are very harmful and can be addictive. Although there is no smoke, the juices contain nicotine and some 11 carcinogens, which are absorbed by the lining of the mouth. Smokeless tobacco users can become addicted to nicotine in the same way smokers do, and they share the same risk of cardiovascular diseases.

The juice from tobacco contains potent carcinogens, about ten times more than in cigarette smoke. Some brands have nitrosamines in extraordinarily high amounts, up to 20,000 times more than foods like bacon and beer. Carcinogens like NNK are linked to a high incidence of cancer of the mouth, gum, lip, tongue, salivary gland, and pharynx, larynx. Using smokeless tobacco increases the risk of dying of cancer of the lip, mouth, and pharynx 27.5 times in men. Oral cancer is lethal, killing 48% in less than five years. Smokeless tobacco damages the gums and can lead to tooth loss. It causes a decrease in gingival blood flow, which leads to ischemia, necrosis (dead tissue), gingival recession, soft tissue alterations and thick white patches of precancerous lesions called leukoplakia.

One study of high school smokeless tobacco users found 50% had leukoplakia. Over a five year period, five percent of these lesions will become malignant.

A Safer Cigarette?
It's a Contradiction of Terms!

Eclipse has a carbon tip that is lit and cooks the tobacco rather than burning it. However, the tip of Eclipse contains a small amount of tobacco that does burn. So for the first puff or two, Eclipse is no different from a regular cigarette. The smoker inhales tar, carcinogens, carbon monoxide and nicotine. Furthermore, secondhand smoke is released as usual.

However, after the first two inhalations, the remaining reconstituted tobacco, which is treated with glycerin, does not burn. The tobacco is heated by the carbon tip which vaporizes the glycerin. Glycerin vapor then carries tar, and substantial amounts of nicotine and carbon monoxide to the smokers lungs. In is important to note that Eclipse carries the same risk of nicotine addiction as a regular cigarette.

RJR claims that secondhand smoke is reduced 90%, and it is not as dirty and smelly as a traditional cigarette. They also claim that less tar and smoke is delivered to the smoker. They also claim every hazard is lower except one for one, Eclipse delivers 52% more carbon monoxide than a regular ultra low-tar cigarette. Without saying it, RJR infers that Eclipse is safer. However, the health hazards of Eclipse have not been evaluated by qualified independent scientists not associated with or funded by the tobacco industry. Furthermore, the FDA has not had the opportunity to review RJR's data. Doctor Stanton Glantz, University of California–San Francisco, says, "When you look at history, distrusting the tobacco companies has been a prudent strategy." After all, RJR is the same company that compared smoking with eating a Twinkie.

The burning question is: "How much of the harmful chemicals are reduced by heating tobacco instead of incinerating it?" There is no reliable data available. One can only speculate that Eclipse is less hazardous than a regular cigarette. However, one thing is for certain, Eclipse does increase the risk of heart attacks, cancer, emphysema, stroke, and all the other diseases associated with smoking. No one knows exactly how much of a health risk comes from smoking Eclipse. Research can answer the health risk question, but John Hughes, professor of psychiatry at the University of Vermont, says "I think those studies would take at least a year."

So, for the most part, the jury is still out on the health hazards of Eclipse. However, we know that there is no such thing as a safe cigarette, so that holds true for Eclipse as well. Furthermore, there are some risks to the nonsmoker from the reduced amount of passive smoke emitted from Eclipse. The accumulative risks are proportional to the number smoked, the size of the room, the amount of ventilation, and the time of exposure.

It is also important to note that the Eclipse nicotine delivery devices do not burn down to a butt like cigarettes. It looks like a un-smoked cigarette when it is discarded. Smokers should be cautioned not to leave these discarded devices where children or pets could eat them. They are as lethal as a cigarette if swallowed.

Furthermore, another ugly picture will change. Lets say one of every four smokers litter, using the Earth as their ashtray. The number of butts thrown on the ground every day, during the average three hours a day spent outdoors or in a car, is 35 million butts. If Eclipse gets ten percent of the cigarette market, the number of Eclipse devices that will accumulate on the ground every year, is 1.3 billion – litter that looks like a whole cigarette.

Death and Destruction from Fires Caused by Smokers

In 1991, 2,300 people died in fires caused by careless smokers, almost 50% of all deaths caused by burns. Another 5,000 were badly burned. The same year, 187,000 fires were started by careless smokers, which caused $552 million in property damages. In May 1996, five fraternity members at the University of North Carolina died in a fire caused by a careless smoker who flipped a cigarette into a pile of trash.

A lighted cigarette is a serious fire hazard. Unlike barbecue charcoal that needs attention to stay lit, an unattended cigarette will burn continuously to the filter. On the other hand, untreated, natural tobacco cigarettes will not stay lighted, and the smoker must constantly relight them. Long ago, tobacco companies recognized this inconvenience and corrected the problem with additives, the same additives used in gasoline. Therefore today, cigarettes don't burn out on their own, they stay lit. With a minority of smokers carelessly flipping 35 million lit cigarettes butts in all directions every day, fires are bound to happen.

Cold Opinions

At the Congressional hearing in 1994, Congressmen stated that smoking kills 434,000 Americans every year. James Johnston, CEO of RJR, disputed the figures saying they were "computer generated." Every day, there are 1,178 computer generated deaths from smoking. Do the families of the victims of smoking understand this point of view?

■ ■ ■ ■ ■ ■ ■ ■ ■ ■ ■ ■ ■

There are special hazards for women who smoke. Smoking during pregnancy also affects the unborn fetus. Find out why 3,700 infants are dying needlessly every year.

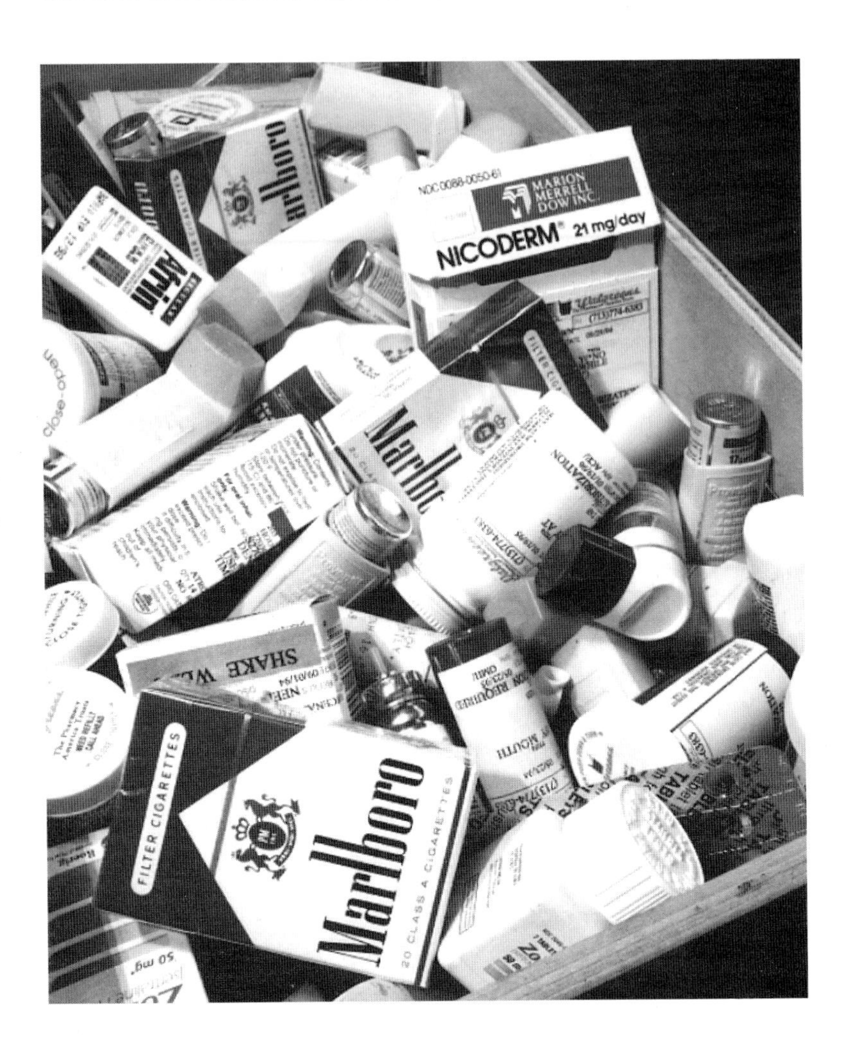

The contents of this drawer depicts the struggle of a smoker with chronic bronchitis. DMR started smoking at age 16. After several unsuccessful attempts to quit, he died of a sudden heart attack at the age of 48.

Chapter Ten

Women and Infant Victims

Smoking holds special health risks for women and their unborn children. Every year, 125,000 American women die from tobacco related diseases, and to make matters worse, women are starting to smoke at a faster rate. In 1993, 22.5% of women smoked, about 22 million. In the near future, more women will die from tobacco related diseases than men.

More Women are Dying from Tobacco Related Ilness

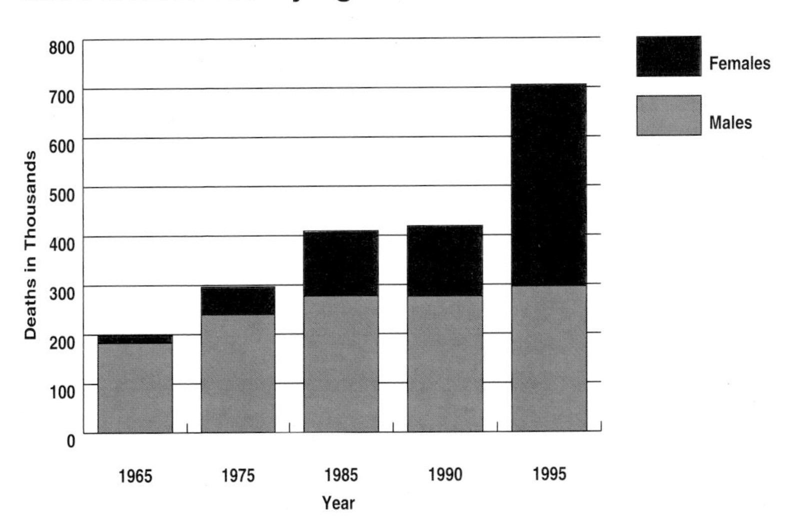

The increase in women smoking is blamed largely on tobacco advertising that specifically targets them. One of the most recent promotion themes is "It's a woman thing." The majority of women smokers are from lower socioeconomic status, and 87% start before they are 18 years old. The CDC says 73% of women smokers want to quit.

Heart Disease

Although deaths from heart disease are declining in the US, it kills 3.7 times more women than lung cancer and breast cancer combined. According to the CDC and the Nurses' Health Study, women who smoke at least one pack a day, have six times the risk of a heart attack as women who do not. Women who smoke and use oral contraceptives face even a greater risk, about ten times higher. Some 61, 000 American women died from heart disease caused by smoking in 1990.

Female smokers also have a higher risk of heart attacks than male smokers. Researchers in Norway reported in 1996 that among middle aged smokers over 45, women had a relative risk of 3.3, almost twice that of men who smoke with a relative risk of 1.9. More striking, the overall risk was higher among that group of smokers age 35 to 44. The relative risk was 7.1 in women, and 2.3 in men. The Copenhagen City Heart Study also found that smoking had a larger impact on the heart health of women. The study found a relative risk of 9.4 for women smokers, and a rate of 2.9 for men smokers.

Lung Cancer

Lung cancer is now the number one cancer killer of both men and women. The incidence of lung cancer in women surpassed breast cancer in 1987. Women who smoke have two to three times the risk of lung cancer as women who do not. An estimated 64,300 American women will die from lung cancer in 1996 alone.

Breast Cancer

Breast cancer will claim about 44,300 women in 1996. Women who smoke two packs a day have a 25% to 75% higher risk of dying from breast cancer than women who don't. A number of researchers have tried in the past to find a solid link between smoking and breast cancer. In 1996, because of a more accurate experimental method, a casual link between smoking and breast cancer was established.

In 1996, Dr. Alfredo Morabia, a member of a research team at the University Hospital in Geneva, first reported a clear cause-effect relationship between smoking and breast cancer. Dr. Morabia's data shows that 20 or more cigarettes a day will increase the risk of breast cancer up to 4.6 times (460%). Smoking as few as ten cigarettes a day will more that double her risk, to 2.7 (270%). The authors of the study stated that the increased risk is biologically plausible. The carcinogens in tobacco smoke (mainstream and secondhand) such as DENA, which are known to cause breast cancer in animals, may actually concentrate in the mammary ducts for long periods of time. Carcinogens stored there have ample time to mutate the breast cancer genes BRCA 1 and 2. Dr. Morabia's data indicates that 30% of all breast cancers are caused by smoking.

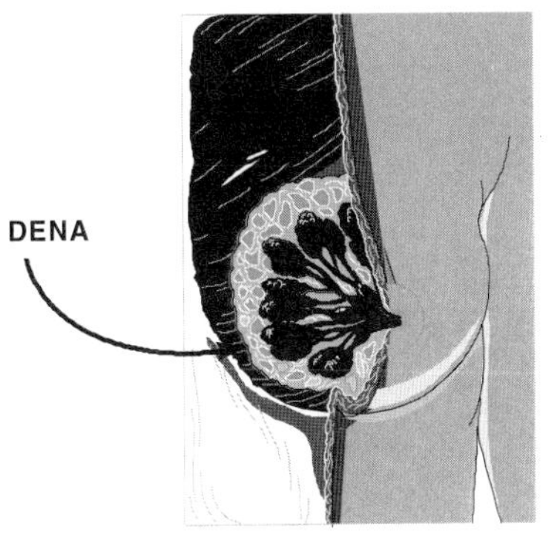

Osteoporosis

Women who smoke are at a higher risk for osteoporosis. This degenerative disease causes the bones to become less dense, and more fragile with age. Women that smoke one pack of cigarettes a day from adulthood to menopause, will have five to ten percent less bone density that a nonsmoker.

Older women who have low bone density are more likely to suffer bone fractures. Cigarette smoking may also reduce bone strength, which can lead to spinal deformity. These circumstances are compounded by the fact that older women who smoke are weaker and have poorer balance, and have an increased risk of fracturing the vertebra, forearm or hip.

Smoking Causes "*SMOKERS FACE*"

Smoking also causes a cosmetic ugliness that can be especially dreadful for women, "smokers face." Constant puckering of the mouth to draw in smoke causes deep creases in the skin radiating around the lips. After years of smoking, these unnatural creases become permanently visible "smoker's wrinkles."

Dr. Jeffrey B. Smith, a dermatologist at the University of South Florida, says that smoking reduces circulation in the skin, and it causes elastin fibers in the skin to thicken, and reduces the formation of collagen. And if that was not enough, free radicals in tobacco smoke further damage the skin. The result is a wrinkled, flaccid, dry, shriveled, gray face. This makes smokers look decades older. Dr. Smith also says that these effects increase the smokers risk of skin cancer, both squamous cell carcinoma and melanoma.

If you have just started smoking, take this test. Go to a mirror and take a deep drag from a cigarette. Look closely at the lines radiating around your lips, and think about freezing like that. If you smoke for years and then quit, you may save yourself from a heart attack or cancer, but the wrinkles are permanent.

Maternal Smoking During Pregnancy

Prenatal Smoking

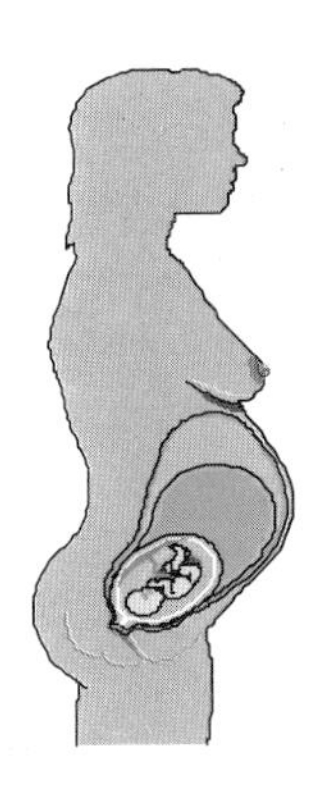

Some one million unborn children every year are exposed to tobacco smoke because their mothers' smoke. In 1991, a survey of women who smoke, revealed 28% were pregnant. As bad as cocaine is for a fetus, smoking cigarettes may be worse. "If you smoke", says Dr. Gileon Koren of the University of Toronto, "your baby smokes with you." Smoking raises the risk of prenatal death, a few weeks before and after birth, by 20% to 40%.

Maternal smoking during pregnancy causes 141,000 fetuses to die in miscarriages annually. Smoking also increases the risk of tubal pregnancies, placenta previa, and premature placental separation. It is also blamed for premature births, which is the third largest cause of infant mortality. Annually, about 61,000 babies weighing less than 5 lb. 9 oz. are born to mothers who smoke.

Maternal smoking during pregnancy is also responsible for a risk of mental development problems, such as speech, language, intelligence, behavior and attention span. An estimated 30% of all mentally retarded children can be attributed to mothers smoking during pregnancy. Researchers at Emory University reported in *Pediatrics*, that they found a link in maternal smoking and giving birth to a mentally retarded child. As few as five cigarettes a week increases the risk of a retarded child by 50% to 60%. Those that smoked at least one pack a day had the highest increase risk, which rose to 75%. The authors concluded that maternal smoking may be a preventable cause of mental retardation.

Mothers who smoke during pregnancy deprive the fetus of oxygen and nutrients. The nicotine chokes the placenta. Carbon monoxide causes oxygen starvation. The toxins in tobacco smoke flow from the mother's blood into the fetus, where it can damage delicate fetal cells. It has been linked to twice the risk of having an infant born without one or both kidneys, or with kidneys that do not function because of its size or shape. Maternal smoking is also the cause of Sudden Infant Death Syndrome (SIDS).

Maternal smoking during pregnancy has very severe consequences for the infant, but it may surprise you that it also has severe consequences for the mother. Researchers in Finland found that pregnant mothers who smoke die at a rate 2.3 times higher than women smokers that are not pregnant. These women suffered a high incidence of death from heart disease, and cancer of the breast, esophagus, trachea, bronchus and lung.

■■■■■■■■■■■■

You may be saying to yourself now, "This is easy. I am never going to smoke—period!," or "I am going to quit smoking today!" Despite these smart decisions, today your health is still at risk from tobacco smoke. Environmental tobacco smoke invades your personal breathing space—and your children's breathing space. How could a child smoke the equivalent of 90 packs of cigarettes before they are five years old?

Chapter Eleven

The White Serpent

Fred never smoked, but tobacco smoke killed him. It was New Year's Eve on a smoky dance floor in New Orleans. Fred was having a grand time dancing with Gloria, his wife of thirty-five years. Fred did not know that his heart was not getting enough oxygen because of the carbon monoxide in the air. A sudden heart attack, caused by environmental tobacco smoke, robbed him of his life.

Environmental Tobacco Smoke: a Major Indoor Air Pollutant

We are bombarded every day by hundreds of chemicals, both natural and manmade, from indoor and outdoor air pollution, pesticides and herbicides in our food and chemical pollutants in our water. The crop yields required to provide us with an adequate food supply are dependent upon the use of chemicals. Outdoor air pollution, is largely a product of technology, transportation and industrialization. There are no easy solutions to many of these problems, but as individuals we can take measures to limit our exposure to some of the chemicals in our environment. We can drink filtered or bottled water, and eat organic fruit and vegetables. We can stay indoors during air pollution alerts.

On the other hand, indoor air quality is more important to our health than outdoor pollution, simply because we spend 80%-90% of our time indoors, either at home, work or in public buildings. Indoor air pollution comes from radon, cleaning chemicals, lead, pesticides, asbestos, carbon monoxide, bio-contaminants such as pest feces and mildew, solvents, and most important, environmental tobacco smoke. ETS accounts for 85% of all indoor pollution.

We can improve the air quality in our homes by reducing the sources of contamination, improving ventilation and using air filters. And most importantly, we can prohibit smoking.

On the other hand, the government must take responsibility to protect the public from unsafe air in public buildings and in the workplace. The highest priority should be to limit exposure to contaminants that are dangerous health hazards, are manmade and don't occur naturally, and are not byproducts of an essential process.

The White Serpent

ETS fits these characteristics: it has the greatest potential to harm human health and cause death, is man made and not naturally occurring, and is not a byproduct of an essential process. The source of ETS, smoking, is not essential to life, and is easy to control. It serves no useful purpose except to satisfy smokers' cravings for nicotine and to quench the insatiable thirst of the tobacco industry for profit. More importantly, there's new shocking evidence that ETS is more harmful to nonsmokers than smokers. Despite a wise decision not to smoke, tobacco smoke may still kill you or your children.

The White Serpent can be Cloaked: Invisible and Odorless!

Secondhand smoke is generally not difficult to see or smell. The air in most bars is thick with a putrid cloud from burning tobacco. White serpents wind their way towards the ceiling, leaving no doubt that you are in nothing less than a gas chamber. However, in buildings where smokers and nonsmokers are separated, the ventilation may be good enough to diffuse the visible white cloud of poison from the room. You may be in a restaurant trying to enjoy a meal, and after a few minutes you can't smell tobacco smoke any longer. Both not seeing or smelling misleads you into thinking you are out of danger, but beware — the white serpent is merely cloaked and damages your health with every breath.

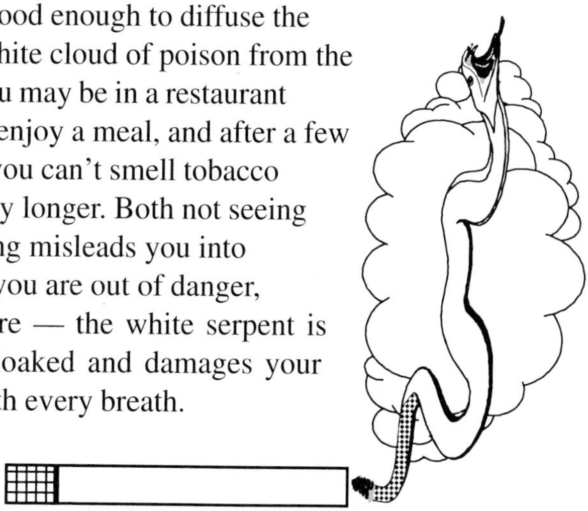

If you see and smell tobacco smoke when you first enter a room, but after a few minutes you can't, has the white serpent disappeared? No! Carbon monoxide, and other gases in tobacco smoke are invisible like air or radiation. Even if you can't see smoke, it could be present.

The reason the smell seems to vanish is because the sense of smell quickly adapts to an odorous atmosphere. In the first few seconds, the nose adapts about 50%. You experience olfactory adaptation every day. When you first apply a perfume or cologne in the morning, it smells strong. But after a few minutes you can't smell it as much. You eventually think the scent has disappeared, but friends ask you all day "what is that fragrance you are wearing?" You have adapted to the fragrance, and can not smell it any longer. In the same manner, you adapt to the smell of tobacco smoke.

Passive Smoking Kills One Nonsmoker Every 6 ½ minutes

In the scientific literature, there are wide ranges of estimated deaths attributed to the cumulative effects of exposure to secondhand smoke. Ischemic heart disease deaths range from 30,000 to 60,000 annually, but the mean of 45,000 is quoted most often. The EPA estimates that there are 3,000 lung cancers attributable to ETS exposure annually. However, other estimates for lung cancer are as high as 8,400. ETS is responsible for 11,000-12,200 other cancer deaths. Also 20,000 deaths from atherosclerosis are attributed to ETS. 3,700 infants die from SIDS and respiratory diseases because their mothers smoke. Considering all of these causes of death attributed to the cumulative effects of secondhand smoke, a more suitable figure is 82,700 deaths in the U.S. every year:

Heart Attacks, Ischemic Heart Disease	**45,000**
Atherosclerosis	**20,000**
Other Cancers	**11,000**
Infant Deaths	**3,700**
Lung Cancer	**3,000**
Total Annual Deaths from ETS	**82,700**

How Many Americans are Exposed to EnvironmentalTobacco Smoke?

Unfortunately, today we can't totally avoid secondhand smoke. The average nonsmoking adult is exposed to ETS in public buildings, restaurants, workplaces, social settings, cars, and at home when visitors and spouses smoke. In a 1983 survey, 63.3% of nonsmoking adults said they were exposed to secondhand tobacco smoke, 34.5% for ten hours a week, and 15.9 % at least 40 hours a week. A 1995 study published in the *Journal of the American Medical Society,* reported that 37% of nonsmoking adults surveyed say they are exposed to ETS at home or work. Even more alarming, of those nonsmokers surveyed, 87.9% tested positive for components of carcinogenic tobacco smoke in their blood. More than half did not know they were exposed to dangerous levels of ETS.

From a 1992 EPA report, others have reported that 50% to 75% of nonsmoking adults tested were positive for cotinine, a breakdown product of nicotine. That means up to 94.5 million people are exposed to ETS. Therefore, a conservative estimate of nonsmokers exposed to secondhand smoke, at home, at work, and in public buildings, is about 75% (50%-75%), or some 94.5 million. The bottom line for all nonsmokers, including ten million children exposed to ETS, is 104.5 million people.

104.5 Million Nonsmokers are at Risk of Death and Disease Caused by Passive Smoking

Over 104.5 million nonsmokers are regularly exposed to ETS, and most are not aware they have been exposed, or that they are at a higher risk of disease. Despite this high rate of exposure of secondhand tobacco smoke, only 46 million (25%) of Americans smoke.

Detecting Secondhand Smoke in the Blood of Nonsmokers

Cotinine- A breakdown product of nicotine. A biomarker for exposure to secondhand smoke.

NNK, nicotine, and cotinine are biological markers used to detect exposure to tobacco smoke. Cotinine and nicotine concentrate in blood, hair, and urine of people, after exposure to ETS. Nonsmoking family members that live with a smoker have cotinine in their urine. Nicotine and cotinine have also been detected in the hair of mothers and their babies. Children's health problems directly correlate with an increase in cotinine levels in their blood. The National Health and Nutrition Examination Survey, concluded that 91.7% of the U.S. population age four and older have cotinine detectable in their urine.

How Much Secondhand Smoke are Nonsmokers Exposed to?

In 1994, an important study was published on occupational exposures to tobacco smoke. The lead investigator was Dr. S. K. Hammond, of the University of California, Berkeley (UCB). Dr. Hammond's group investigated 25 workplaces, offices, and manufacturing areas. They compared tobacco smoke levels according to the company's smoking policies: no policy, smoking restricted, smoking not allowed.

Smoking Policy in Effect	**Nicotine levels, mg/cubic M (median)**	
	OFFICES	**SHOPS**
Smoking Allowed	8.6	2.3
Smoking Restricted	1.3	0.7
Smoking Not Allowed	0.3	0.2

The risk assessments for lung cancer was called a significant risk where nicotine levels exceeded 6.8 mg/M. There was a significant risk for lung cancer at 50% of the offices tested. In offices where smoking was allowed, the mean nicotine exposure was 8.6 mg/M.

In shops where smoking was allowed, the mean nicotine exposure was 2.3 mg/M. In 12% of the shop workstations the risk was significant. In the remaining shops, the risk assessments for lung cancer, was called a risk of obvious concern. Workers exposed to this level of tobacco smoke for 40 years will have a lung cancer risk of three in 10,000.

In a study done by Dr. Michael Siegel, at UCB in 1993, nicotine levels were measured in offices, bars, homes and restaurants.

The table below summarizes Dr. Siegel's findings:

Site	Nicotine, mg/cubic M median (range)	Risk Assessment (Median)
Bars	19.7 (75-1320)	significant risk
Restaurants	6.5 (3.4-34)	significant risk
Offices	4.1 (0.8-22)	obvious concern
Homes	4.3 (1.6-21)	obvious concern

One Cigarette Equivalent—The amount of secondhand smoke a nonsmoker inhales that is equal to the risk of smoking one cigarette.

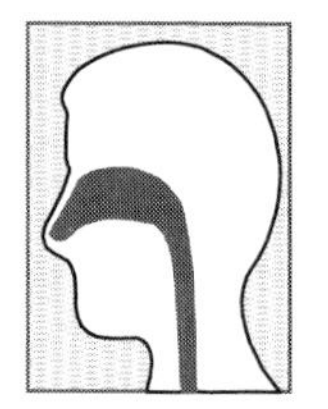

Nicotine is not the risk factor, but it is a direct gauge of how much tobacco smoke is in the air. Dr. Siegel's group measured nicotine in the air to estimate the hazards from tobacco smoke's 2, 000 toxic chemicals. Then to evaluate the risk, the researchers converted the nicotine levels to cigarette equivalents. One cigarette equivalent is the amount of tobacco smoke exposure equal to smoking one cigarette. The cigarette equivalents could not be measured for all 60 carcinogens in secondhand smoke. So the cigarette equivalent risk for only three carcinogens were calculated for offices, shops and restaurants.

Carcinogens Measured in ETS	Cigarette Equivalents, One Month		
	Shop	**Open Offices**	**Restaurant**
Benzene	3	15	8
4-aminobiphenyl	14	64	34
N-Nitrosodimethylamine	46	220	116
Cigarette equivalents	63	299	158
Packs per Month	**3.1**	**14.9**	**7.9**

The carcinogen specific cigarette equivalent risk for lung cancer, was calculated based on a 40 hour work week for a period of one month. The cigarette equivalent for an office worker was 15 packs, for a shop worker three packs, and for a restaurant worker eight packs. Occupational exposure to tobacco smoke presents a substantial risk to workers where smoking is allowed. On the average, smoke levels were equal to or higher than smoke levels in the homes of people who smoke.

ETS is an Occupational Hazard — Restaurant and Bar Workers

"When I get home from work, my clothes and hair smell bad like a dirty ashtray. I blow brown stuff out of my nose all night. I cough more than I used to."

-a bartender

An 18 year old waitress dressed in her seafood restaurant uniform sits uncomfortably in her allergy doctor's waiting room. Her breathing is labored—she is having an asthma attack. She had to leave work because her boss required her to work in the smoking section. Short of breath, and short on time before she was out of a job, she anxiously asks her doctor to convince her supervisor to move her to the nonsmoking section.

Seventy-five million restaurant and bar workers in the U.S. are at a very high risk for smoking related disease from ETS. These smoky places are an "occupational health hazard." The employees have higher rates of heart attacks, and lung cancer. The risk of lung cancer for nonsmoking restaurant workers is equal to smoking eight packs of cigarettes per month.

Years of breathing secondhand tobacco smoke will shorten their lives and lower their quality of life in later years. Most restaurant workers do not know about the hazards of ETS. They can't speak out as a group because they are not organized. It's the restaurant owners who are organized.

Many restaurant associations receive funds from the tobacco industry, and violently oppose any smoking restrictions. Restaurants for a Sensible Voluntary Policy, a Los

Angeles group, is funded by the Tobacco Institute. In early 1994, the Texas Restaurant Association, and the New York State Restaurant Association both spoke out against a smoking ban in restaurants.

Some 15 million food service workers, and 60 million bar workers need Federal Government protection from the hazards of environmental tobacco smoke in their work place. Restaurants and bars must be included in national legislation to ban smoking in public places to protect the people who work in them.

Snake Pit on Wheels —

Place a child into an enclosed four cubic yard space

and smoke one cigarette every 30 minutes.

This is what a typical car trip is like for ten million children that ride in a car with a parent that smokes, and the white serpent. It is like being in a snake pit on wheels. The interior space of the average automobile is only about four cubic yards. Investigators measured the concentration of NNK in cars with one person smoking. ETS levels were three times higher in cars than in restaurants, and 15 times higher that in homes.

Another study published in JAMA in 1996, measured nicotine levels in cars and buildings. The lead researcher, Dr. Pirkle, found the level of ETS in a car was six times higher than in a home with one or more smokers:

Site	Nicotine Levels, in mg/M^3
Homes	7-14
Indoor Public Places	1-10
Offices	8
Cars	7-83
Restaurants	6.5

Recent medical studies have established the risk of lung cancer from ETS is equal to smoking one cigarette for every two and a half hours of exposure. The average smoker will smoke one cigarette every 30 minutes. A child riding in a car that is forced to breathe secondhand smoke will smoke the equivalent of two cigarettes every five hours of car travel. The cumulative risk of a child in a car for 30 minutes a day, five days a week, would be equal to smoking about 12 packs of cigarettes by age five.

If the parent smokes at home, that adds another 90 packs. Studies have shown that the risk of lung cancer for people living with smokers is 30%. Therefore, by the time a child that is exposed in the home and car reaches their fifth birthday, their cumulative health risk would be about the same as if they had smoked 102 packs of cigarettes. Unfortunately, these unwilling child smoking victims number over ten million.

Parents who smoke routinely in the family car and at home with their children, make them inhale the equivalent of 102 packs of cigarettes by the age of five.

Is this Child Endangerment?

"While deliberate violence and abuse

are very serious concerns,

cigarettes kill many more children".

-Dr. DiFranza, U. of Massachusetts

Today there are no state laws on the books that protect children from injury from secondhand smoke. Dr. DiFranza says "Smoking should be banned wherever children are present." If children, especially those with asthma, are continually exposed to ETS in the home despite a doctors advice, then this should be treated as child neglect or abuse in custody cases.

Secondhand Tobacco Smoke is More than an Irritation — It's a Murder Weapon

Environmental tobacco smoke was once thought of as just an annoyance, an irritation to nonsmokers and allergy sufferers. The reason for this misunderstanding is because prior to

1986 there was scant published scientific evidence that secondhand smoke was harmful. The Surgeon General's Report of 1982 stated: "Involuntary smoking may pose a carcinogenic risk to the nonsmoker." However, it was not until 1986 that the Surgeon General concluded that secondhand smoke was the cause of lung cancer and other diseases. However, over the last five years, the body of research on the toxicity and carcinogenicity of environmental tobacco smoke has grown significantly. The data is not the only thing that has increased. The body of medical evidence available today says the health risks from ETS exposure is higher that previously thought. More interesting, like active smoking, the biggest risk of dying from ETS is not from lung cancer, but from a heart attack. Prolonged exposure to secondhand smoke is the fifth largest cause of preventable deaths in the United States.

The cumulative effects of exposure to secondhand smoke takes its toll on the health of nonsmokers. Consequently, nonsmokers have more asthma, allergy symptoms, flu, pneumonia, emphysema, cancer, low birth weight babies, SIDS, arteriosclerosis and heart attacks. The effect of ETS is so severe, it kills about 83,000 people annually. In the same manner, one in eight children, about ten million are exposed to significant amounts of ETS in and outside of the home, killing 3, 700 under one year old annually.

The Lungs Soak Up ETS Carcinogens in the Air Like a Sponge

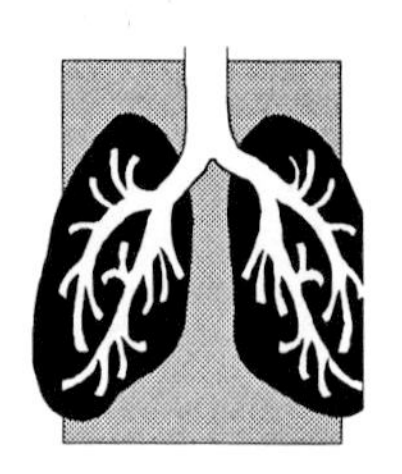

As you inhale tobacco smoke, the lungs work like a "sponge." They soak up secondhand tobacco smoke, and squeeze the chemicals out directly into the blood. Air samples from places where smoking is allowed, such as bars and restaurants, contain 60 carcinogens like NNK in the air. As you would expect, nonsmokers that breathe tobacco smoke have NNK in their urine. NNK in smoke is inhaled into the lungs, passes into the blood, circulates throughout the body, and passes through the kidneys into the urine.

Cardiovascular Hazards of ETS

"Environmental tobacco smoke is a major preventable cause of cardiovascular disease and death"

-Council on Cardiopulmonary and Critical Care,
American Heart Association, August 1992.

Ischemic Heart Disease- restricted blood flow to the heart muscle due to obstructed coronary arteries.

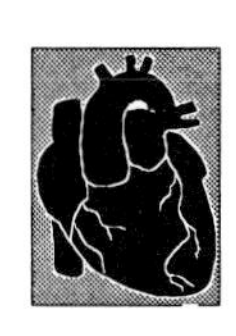

Ischemic heart disease is the largest cause of death from exposure to environmental tobacco smoke, which kills an estimated 45,000 (30,000 to 60,000) Americans annually. Another 180,000 have nonfatal heart attacks. Also, some 20,000 die from atherosclerosis attributed to the cumulative effects of ETS.

Tobacco smoke causes both short term and long term toxic damage to the heart. Short term damage occurs quickly. Secondhand smoke increases heart rate and blood pressure. It causes blood platelets to clot faster, which increases the risk of a thrombus and causes heart arterial damage. The carbon monoxide in ETS puts the nonsmoker into a state of hypoxia, or oxygen deficiency, which can quickly reduce the ability of the blood to carry oxygen to the heart. Just 20 minutes of exposure to ETS can increase the risk of a heart attack.

The long term, cumulative effects of secondhand smoke can also increase the risk of a heart attack later in life. The relative risk of a heart attack for nonsmokers living with a smoker is about 1.20 to 2.11 times higher. In a recent study of almost one half million spouses married to smokers, published in the *American Heart Journal* in 1996, found they had 20% higher rates of heart disease.

Passive smoking raises blood cholesterol, increases LDL, the bad cholesterol, and decreases HDL, the good cholesterol. This increases the risk of arteriosclerosis. The toxins in ETS damage the coronary arteries, causing them to constrict, and progress the development of atherosclerosis. Researchers at the Nelson Institute of Environmental Medicine in New York, have identified one component of environmental tobacco smoke (1, 3 butadiene), that is most responsible for the development of arteriosclerosis.

A recent study reported in the *New England Journal of Medicine*, showed that secondhand smoke can damage children's arteries too. Nonsmokers as young as 15 years old showed early stages of atherosclerosis after chronic exposure to passive smoke. These same changes to the artery walls have also been observed in the umbilical arteries of newborn infants whose mothers were exposed to secondhand smoke.

Environmental Tobacco Smoke Causes Cancer

Water is harmless in the amounts we normally drink. But if you drink an extremely large amount of water, several gallons of water at one time, you may die. So water is safe up to a "threshold dose" of a gallon or more at one time. This is the principal behind so called "dose response" studies. You increase the dose of a drug until you find the minimum amount (threshold dose) that will cause an effect. On the contrary, there is no threshold dose for a carcinogen to cause cancer.

Exposure to the Smallest Possible Amount of ETS Increases the Risk of Cancer

Exposure to very small amounts of a carcinogen will increase the risk of cancer. This has been proven in dose-response studies. Similarly, there is no threshold dose for inhaled tobacco smoke – any amount will increase the risk of cancer. Similarly, there is no number of cigarettes or cigars that is safe. Any number of cigarettes or cigars will present some risk of cancer to the smoker.

Most cancers have a latency period of years before tumors develop. Exposure to small amounts over a long period of time is the classic carcinogen exposure pattern that predicts cancer. Nonsmokers exposure to ETS typically fits this classic pattern. The cumulative effects of frequent, tiny exposures of secondhand tobacco smoke will increase the risk of lung cancer. Today we know there is a strong association of exposure to ETS with developing squamous-cell and small-cell carcinomas of the lung.

CAUTION: ETS is a <u>Class A</u> Carcinogen!

Lung Cancer

In 1987, an assessment of secondhand tobacco smoke and lung cancer was done by the International Agency for Research on Cancer (IARC). The IARC committee concluded that "passive smoking gives rise to some risk of lung cancer."

The 1992 EPA Report on Secondhand Smoke and Lung Cancer

Five years prior to the EPA report, there were only 13 published reports on the risks of lung cancer caused by exposure to secondhand smoke. However, those 13 studies were convincing enough for the medical community to declare that secondhand smoke presented a risk of lung cancer to nonsmokers. The EPA added another 30 studies to that body of evidence in 1992.

In 1992, an outside panel of scientist convened by the EPA, determined that ETS is a cause of lung cancer, and results in about 3,000 deaths each year. A nonsmoking female married to a smoker had an relative risk 1.19 times higher (19% risk) that those married to nonsmokers.

The EPA Data: Statistical Significance

Some critics have tried to disqualify the EPA data by stating that it was not statistically significant. That usually means that the results were no different from random chance. Furthermore, data that may not be statistically significant, can still be very good data. However, of the 17 studies done on the risk of high concentrations of secondhand smoke, nine were statistically significant. Of the 24 studies that showed an increase risk of lung cancer to nonsmoking women living with a smokers, nine were statistically significant. 14 studies showed a critical piece of evidence — a dose-response curve. That means the risk of lung cancer increases proportionally to increases in exposure to ETS. Of these 14 studies, ten were statistically significant. In a final summary analysis of the data, called a meta-analysis, the EPA calculated the increased risk of lung cancer for a woman living with a smoker was 1.19 or 19%.

To put this in perspective, a relative risk of only 20% will increase the lifelong risk of lung cancer to one in 1000, which is 100 times more that the risk of exposure to 20 years of asbestos. Consequently the EPA classified tobacco smoke as a human (Group A) carcinogen, in the same group as radon, asbestos, arsenic, and benzene.

The Risk of Lung Cancer from Environmental Tobacco Smoke is 100 times higher that the effect of 20 years of exposure to chrysotile asbestos.

Several studies done since the EPA report, concluded that ETS is a risk factor for lung cancer in nonsmokers. Three studies of some 1,300 nonsmoking women who were exposed to ETS at home, were found to have an increased relative risks of 130% to 240% for lung cancer.

The next time you enter a restaurant and you choose to sit in the nonsmoking section your health is still at risk. If the restaurant allows smoking, and if smoking is not limited to an isolated room with a separate ventilation system, you will be in the 100 Times More Hazardous than Asbestos Section. Do you prefer a serving of White Serpent with your meal?

The Risk of Secondhand Smoke to Nonsmoking Spouses

Nonsmoking women married to smokers have a higher risk of lung cancer. The relative risk of lung cancer to non-smokers living with a smoker is 130% to 240%. Those who were also exposed to ETS during childhood, have the highest relative risk of 325%. Other studies found that many of these women have precancerous lesions in their lungs.

Breast and Other Cancers

Secondhand smoke causes about 11,000-12,200 cancers other than lung annually, including breast, brain, cervical, sinus, leukemia, endocrine glands, and thyroid. Smoking is a known cause of breast cancer, but it may surprise you that secondhand smoke is one too. Recent data from University Hospital in Geneva says the cumulative effects of secondhand smoke could be responsible for up to 20% of breast cancers today. This means women who live with a smoker, or who work in a restaurant, have three times the risk of breast cancer as women not exposed to ETS. Secondhand smoke is inhaled, enters the blood and circulates through almost every tissue in the body, including the breasts. Once in the breast tissue it accumulates and is stored for months or years.

The 60 chemicals that cause or promote cancer bathe the breast cells, and attack and damage the "breast cancer gene." After the DNA damage is done, and the breast cancer gene is mutated, a breast tumor starts growing.

Secondhand smoke should be treated like the deadly enemy that it is to women. It may not be the only cause of breast cancer, but it is a significant cause.

Other Diseases and Deaths Associated with ETS

The World Health Organization, the EPA, and the U.S. Surgeon General have determined that environmental tobacco smoke causes numerous respiratory diseases, such as:

- Pneumonia
- Bronchiolitis
- Tracheitis
- Middle Ear Infections
- Asthma attacks (1,000,000 a year)
- Bronchitis and emphysema (300,000 a year)

The Effect of Secondhand Smoke on Children

"I see many children with asthma attacks. The parents often smoke at home. The doctor usually orders the parents not to smoke at home around the child. Unfortunately, the child is repeatedly taken back to the emergency room, because the parents do not comply with the doctors' orders. Nicotine addiction continues their smoking at home, despite damage to their children's health."

-Emergency room nurse, Texas Children's Hospital

Prenatal and postnatal exposure to environmental tobacco smoke is devastating to children's health. About 22% of babies born to nonsmoking mothers are exposed to secondhand smoke inhaled by their mothers before they are born. A fetus is at particular risk to the potent noxious carcinogens in ETS. Carcinogens circulate through unborn children, causing DNA adducts, which increase the risk of cancer.

Carcinogens in Mothers and Their Babies

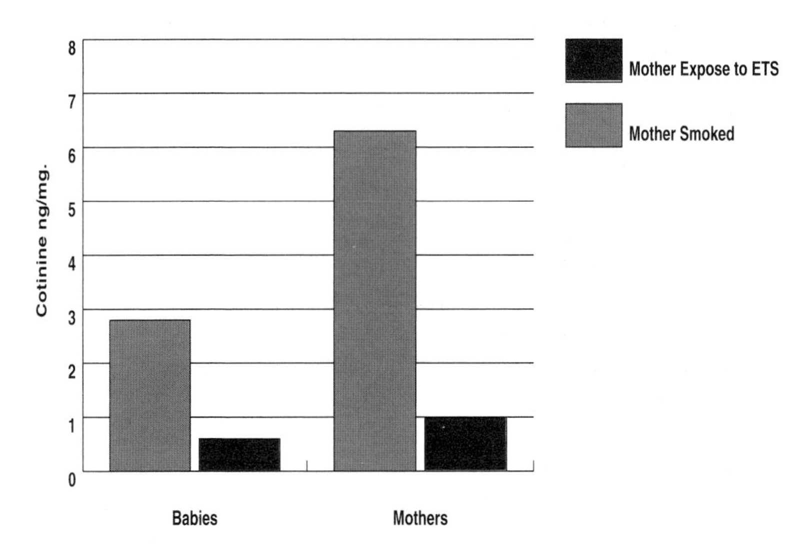

Postnatal Secondhand Smoke Exposure Kills Babies Before Their First Birthday

Each year 1,900 to 5,600 babies in the U.S. die within the first year of life because their mother's smoke. Some 1,200 to 3,700 of these infants die from SIDS, the second largest cause of infant death in America. The average risk of an infant dying of SIDS is threefold higher among mothers that smoke, and the risk increases with the number of cigarettes smoked.

The National Health Interview Survey on Child Health in 1988 found 42% of children under five, and 56% to 70% of all children are exposed to secondhand smoke at home from one or more family members.

Today, about ten million children, under the age of six in the U.S., are exposed to tobacco smoke in public places, the home, and in automobiles, annually causing:

- Two million doctors visits for coughs.
- 2.2 million cases of otitis media, middle ear infections.
- 165,000 tympanotomy tube operations.
- 150,000-300,000 cases of respiratory infections in babies.
- Three million lower respiratory tract infections in children.
- 15,000 hospitalizations for lower respiratory tract infections.
- 35% more influenza.

- In children under five, 436,000 bronchitis, and 190,000 pneumonia.
- 26,000 new cases of asthma.
- 529,000 doctors office visits for asthma.
- 26,000 newborn admissions to intensive care units.
- 1,900 deaths from Sudden Infant Death Syndrome, SIDS.
- Increased risk of brain tumors.

The 2,000 toxic chemicals in tobacco smoke have adverse effects on children's developing lungs. Research shows that children exposed to tobacco smoke for five years have a ten percent decrease in lung function growth. Children with underdeveloped lung function have more frequent respiratory infections, and are two times more likely to develop asthma. One study of asthmatic children who lived with a parent that smoked found the children's lung function was compromised, and there was a direct correlation of the child's cotinine level with asthma attacks.

Some 4.8 million children in the U.S. have asthma. The number of new cases of asthma are on the rise and so is the death rate. Among children four years old and younger, asthma deaths increased almost two fold from 1980 to 1993. They also were 56% more hospital admissions. Children exposed to secondhand smoke make one half million doctors office visits annually for asthma attacks. Environmental tobacco smoke acts as a trigger of asthma, causing inflammation, excess mucus, bronchial constriction, wheezing, coughing and difficulty in breathing.

Hazards of ETS Greater for Nonsmokers

"The biochemistry of ETS in passive smokers is different than in active smokers, rendering the passive smokers more sensitive to the toxins in ETS."

-Dr. Stanton A. Glantz, UCSF

Common sense says that if mainstream smoke is harmful, secondhand smoke is harmful. A poison is a poison, even in small amounts. What makes ETS even more dangerous, is that damage to the body accumulates with each additional exposure. It is especially important to note that nonsmokers are more harmed by secondhand tobacco smoke than smokers.

Smokers all have an equally high risk of cancer largely, because there is no genetic difference that would protection one over another. In contrast to smokers, some nonsmokers have a higher risk of cancer and other diseases attributed to the cumulative effects of secondhand smoke. The difference is in their metabolism of carcinogens, and it is genetic.

Recent research shows that there is a genetic difference in some people's ability to metabolize carcinogens in tobacco smoke. Nonsmokers that metabolize carcinogens slowly have more adducts in their DNA than nonsmokers that metabolize them quickly. This suggests that some unlucky nonsmokers that metabolize carcinogens slowly, have a higher risk of cancer and disease than those that metabolize faster. Furthermore, the cumulative effects of ETS increases their risk of lung cancer more than it would a smoker.

While some people may metabolize carcinogens faster, it does not eliminate their risk of getting cancer. Smokers of 20 or more cigarettes a day have the same risk of getting cancer no matter if they are fast or slow metabolizers. In this aspect, all smokers are unlucky.

The Tobacco Industries Position on the Dangers of ETS Exposure

The tobacco industry has lied to us for over 30 years about the hazards of smoking and nicotine addiction. They have shown a total lack of concern that their product kills 434,000 people a year. Why should they be concerned if it kills another 83,000 nonsmokers? Now the tobacco industry has embarked on another massive propaganda campaign of lies and deception, using junk science to sell the public that ETS is harmless. The tobacco industry carefully guards its profits and smoking bans decrease profits because it causes smokers to smoke fewer cigarettes. For them, when it comes to a choice between profit or saving lives, let the massacre go on. Everyone is damaged by secondhand tobacco smoke, and above all, children suffer the most.

The Tobacco Companies Can Not be Trusted with Our Children

RJ Reynolds Propaganda

RJR placed full-page advertisements in newspapers across the country in 1995 claiming that the harm from exposure to secondhand smoke in the work place was "very little." "The tobacco industry say work exposures (to ETS) are trivial compared to home exposures (of ETS)," says Dr. Hammond, of UCB. Referring to his study published in *Journal of the American Medical Association* he said "This paper says that is clearly not true."

Approximate Risk of ETS, Equivalent to Number of Cigarettes Smoked per Month.

	Cigarette Equivalents per month	
Place of Exposure to ETS	**RJR Advertisement**	**UC-Berkeley Data**
Living at home with smoker	1.5	158
Food service employee	2.0	298
Office Exposure	1.25	158

The data in the RJR ads was cited by Larry C. Holcomb, and done by Healthy Building International (HBI), Fairfax, VA. That research was partially funded by the Tobacco Institute. The estimates are lower than those established in the literature by objective scientists from UCB, Dr. Hammond and Dr. Siegel, who are not funded by the tobacco industry.

HBI is touted as an independent research firm. They measured tobacco smoke levels in the typical workplace. A summary of HBI's data published in *Environment International*, was used in testimony 129 times in OSHA hearings, Congressional subcommittee hearings, in the California legislature, and in law suits, to show secondhand smoke is not a hazard to nonsmokers in the workplace. What HBI did not reveal was their multimillion dollar research was paid for by the Tobacco Institute and the Center for Indoor Air Research

(CIAR), both which are tobacco industry funded organizations.

Why are RJR's Reported Numbers So Low?

One reason that RJR's data is so low, is because some of the HBI data was allegedly faked. Three former employees of HBI say that 25% of the data they collected for the research was altered. Smoke levels were reported lower than actually measured in the offices. One technician reported that a superior cut the measurements of the smoke he actually measured in half.

Several other methods were used to distort the measurements, both up and down. One HBI technician was told to measure ETS in buildings where no one was smoking. 20% of the rooms measured were reported smaller than they actually were. One room was reported as three times larger than it actually was, consequently the concentration of smoke reported was three times less that it actually was. Some data looked as if it was arbitrarily fabricated. A room in the Tobacco Institute measured zero for tobacco smoke, despite four people smoking there.

Dr. Stanton A. Glantz, M.D., UC, San Francisco, says "If this data is fraudulent, it throws into question all their assertions." The tobacco industry claims ETS is harmless. In February of 1996, a federal grand jury was investigating secondhand smoke and the relationship between HBI and the tobacco industry. Prosecutors are charging that HBI violated the law by failing to disclose that their research was paid for by the Tobacco Institute, and that HBI had allegedly falsified the data. Even more interesting, the law firm Covington & Burling allegedly made payments to HBI for the Tobacco Institute. If this is true, it is another example of how the tobacco industry uses "attorney-client privilege" to cover-up the industries activities and sponsorship of research.

Philip Morris Propaganda

More recently, Philip Morris has become concerned that the growing tobacco control movement in Europe will decrease cigarette sales there. The European public is becoming more aware that secondhand smoke kills people. Philip Morris has placed full page ads claiming the hazards of secondhand smoke is as dangerous as eating cookies and milk.

■ ■ ■ ■ ■ ■ ■ ■ ■ ■ ■ ■

Tobacco companies need to counter the hazardous health effects of tobacco use and of ETS. They had no problem cranking out junk data to support their own claims, but that presented them again with another problem. They would do research proving smoking kills people, secondhand smoke kills people, and nicotine is addictive. However, they had to keep all unfavorable research data confidential and hidden from court orders. For this trick, they turn to the lawyers.

Chapter Twelve
Checkbook Research

"The only scientist in the world who takes a position opposing the fifty-thousand published articles on the dangers of smoking are those in the employ of the tobacco industry."

-C. Everett Koop M.D., former U.S. Surgeon General

The Council for Tobacco Research

"CTR, Public Relations Masquerading as Science."

-Rep. Henry Waxman, 1994.

The tobacco industry created and funded an alleged nonprofit research group in 1954, called the Council for Tobacco Research, (CTR) of New York (originally named the Tobacco Industry Research Committee). The industry announced they would study "all phases of tobacco use and health." An aggressive campaign was started to promote the perceived benefits of tobacco. Since CTR was formed, it has spent $100 million on junk research. Today, it has a budget of $19.5 million a year.

The tobacco industry has benefited from CTR's help with lawsuits. Vast world data bases are searched to find expert witnesses that will testify that there are other causes of lung cancer than smoking. These scientist and doctors have been selected to serve as industry witnesses in lawsuits and in the legislative investigations.

CTR is not all science — it is part public relations. One of the earliest public relations efforts of CTR was to bring to the attention of the public that, "There is no conclusive proof that cigarette smoking is a cause of lung cancer or other problems of human health." The public relations firm Hill & Knowlton (Hill & Knowlton no longer represent any tobacco firms), was heavily involved in those promotions. They published newsletters with grossly misleading titles such as, "Lung Cancer Found in Nonsmoking Nuns."

CTR moved into funding "special project" research in 1960, because they found a "political need for research." Special projects were designed to help defend the tobacco industry in court, but no attempt was every made by CTR to disclose that intention. They attracted noted scientists who wanted grant money.

They also claimed that a board of independent scientists would award special project grants, rather than the tobacco companies. However, the Council put together a grant task force made up of lawyers, not doctors. CTR used an outside Missouri law firm as the funding arm for its research. The CTR structure was not a typical grantor-grantee relationship. It was an attorney-client relationship, scientists being the clients. This was a very clever strategy that would allow CTR to bury research that was damaging. This strategy would also prevent their researchers from testifying in court, and protect all documents from discovery. Currently, there are over 1,500 potentially damaging CTR documents sealed and protected under "client-attorney" protection.

In 1972, Dr. Hugh Fudenberg was given a CTR grant to look for hereditary risks that may make some people more susceptible to emphysema. His first results showed that about ten percent of people may be at a higher risk, and he wanted to warn these people not to smoke. His research was cut off immediately by CTR. CTR's lawyers usually steered research in the direction of results that were favorable to the industry.

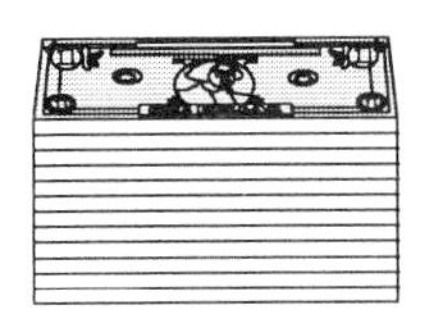

CTR supported James F. Smith, a University of Tennessee researcher, who concluded smokeless tobacco use did not cause cancer. Dr. Smith's studies were used as evidence in a liability trial in 1986 over the oral cancer death of an Oklahoma boy who used snuff. His CTR supported research helped win the case for U.S. Tobacco.

Carl Seltzer, has received over $1.0 million from CTR. Mr. Seltzer, a smoker since the age of ten, was touted as "expert in smoking and heart disease" from Harvard. The real Mr. Seltzer is a child obesity specialist at the Harvard School of Public Health. Seltzer disputed the Framingham Heart Study's conclusion that smoking causes heart disease. He was also sent to Australia and New Zealand to push the tobacco companies position.

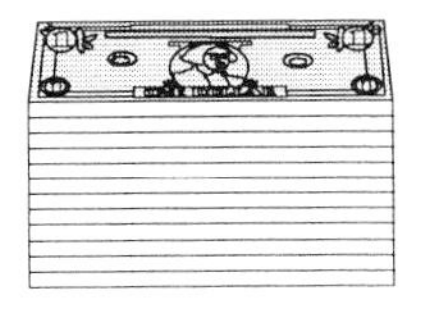

Theodor Sterling, received $5.2 million to dispute research linking smoking to lung cancer and other lung diseases.

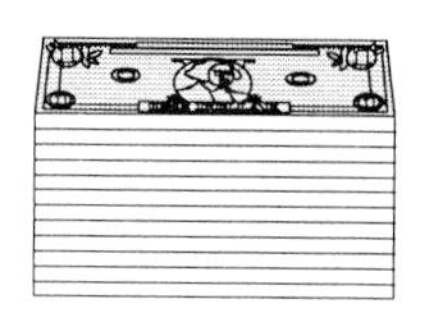

Domingo Aviado, is another recipient of "special projects" grants from CTR, totaling $476,00 over a four year period from 1979-1983. Mr. Aviado, an alleged pharmacologist born in the Philippines, was another CTR puppet that testified on behalf of the tobacco industry. In 1990 he testified before a panel in the Philippines who were working to place warning labels on cigarettes similar to those in the U.S. Aviado testified that smoking was not the cause of heart disease, but it was instead diet, nutrition, gender and air pollution.

Another way to look for researchers susceptible to being seduced with grant money, is to look for the post-doctoral. Young investigators want to make a name for themselves, and need grant money to get a start. Some need it just to stay afloat in academia. Grant money is difficult to find when you have published little. A pharmacologist, who did research for CTR from 1979-1981, said "It was early in my career and it got me started with a laboratory."

Lucrative "Junk" Science — Checkbook Research

Year Two, 1964-1965: Death toll: 394,000.

The Lawyers Behind CTR

For those that have seen the movie "The Firm", the law firm depicted in the film would look like a copy shop compared to the opulence of Shook, Hardy & Bacon. They have 50 attorneys and other specialists totally devoted to tobacco defense. Shook-Hardy has managed CTR's special projects funding, as well as shielding the tobacco industry from legal liability for 40 years. Shook-Hardy has become the tobacco industry's chief legal muscle. Today they primarily work for Philip Morris, B.A.T., and Lorillard Tobacco Co. and have won almost every tobacco death liability law suit every filed.

CTR Now Under Federal Investigation

Seven U.S. congressmen asked Attorney General Janet Reno in 1994 to investigate CTR for fraud, and surprisingly named the firm Shook-Hardy as a target for the investigation. Federal prosecutors in early 1996 were investigating CTR to determine if they lied to the government when they applied for their nonprofit status. Furthermore, they are looking into an allegation of fraud: that CTR was hiding research findings on the hazards of smoking since 1954.

The alleged scam on the America public worked this way. CTR sponsored research they speculated would be favorable to their cause. CTR wanted sympathetic data, that is data that would show smoking was not harmful, or that something else like coffee caused lung cancer. However, most of their research concluded what everyone else's did: smoking caused cancer, heart disease, and nicotine was addictive. Dorothy Cohen, who helped write CTR annual research reports said:

"When CTR researchers found out that cigarettes were bad and it was better not to smoke, we didn't publicize that."

If the research proved what everyone else did, that smoking causes lung cancer, or that nicotine was addictive, the data was turned over to Shook-Hardy. There the papers were secure, on a restricted "tobacco" floor, with walls of reinforced concrete, and with the security equal to the Pentagon. Documents like these were safe from subpoenas because Shook-Hardy protected them under the attorney-client privilege.

Some of the documents from the tobacco floor of Shook-Hardy may soon be made public. In May of 1996, a federal judge ordered 33 RJR documents held in attorney-client protection to be produced for inspection.

Tobacco Symposia

Symposia are conferences at which topics are discussed by various speakers, and are usually designed to educate audiences, and provide a format for scientific discussion and debate. Normally, in the world of science and medicine, symposiums are well-balanced and treat the subjects objectively, and fairly. Speakers are usually credible, world experts in their field.

Pharmaceutical companies commonly use symposiums to promote their products. The question that often arises: Is it science or is it promotion? Disguising promotion as science is considered unethical and deceptive in the pharmaceutical industry. The FDA insists on fair balance at pharmaceutical industry sponsored symposiums.

Tobacco symposiums are billed as "the consensus of scientific experts," a gathering "of leading experts from around the world." The question is, are these symposiums well balanced and do they treat the subjects objectively, and fairly? A high number, 78%, of symposium articles fail to disclose the source of funding, hiding the fact that the author has ties to the tobacco industry. This suggests that the majority of speakers at tobacco industry symposium are connected to the tobacco industry. Why else would speakers funded by the tobacco industry openly disagree with research performed by credible scientists and published in peer reviewed journals.

72% of Tobacco Sponsored Symposium Articles Claim that ETS is Not Harmful

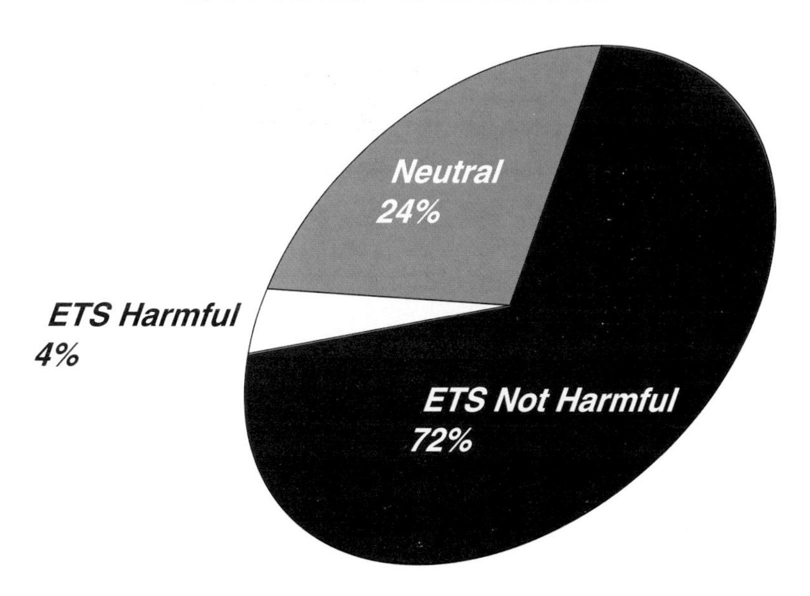

Symposiums are often accompanied by a publication of articles, and abstracts of talks given. Analysis of symposium articles sponsored by the tobacco industry suggest that they are not balanced or fair and most present ETS as not harmful. This kind of misrepresentation gives the nonsmoker a false sense of security about the safety of ETS.

Articles claiming ETS is not harmful often appear in non-peer reviewed journals. That means these articles are not scrutinized by an editorial board of independent peer experts for good scientific methods and sound conclusions. These non-peer reviewed journals, or so called "throwaway journals," publish articles that almost always support the tobacco industries position. On the other hand, articles sponsored by the tobacco industry that appear in peer reviewed journals, only agree with their position 13% of the time.

87% of Articles in Peer Reviewed Journals

Say ETS is Harmful

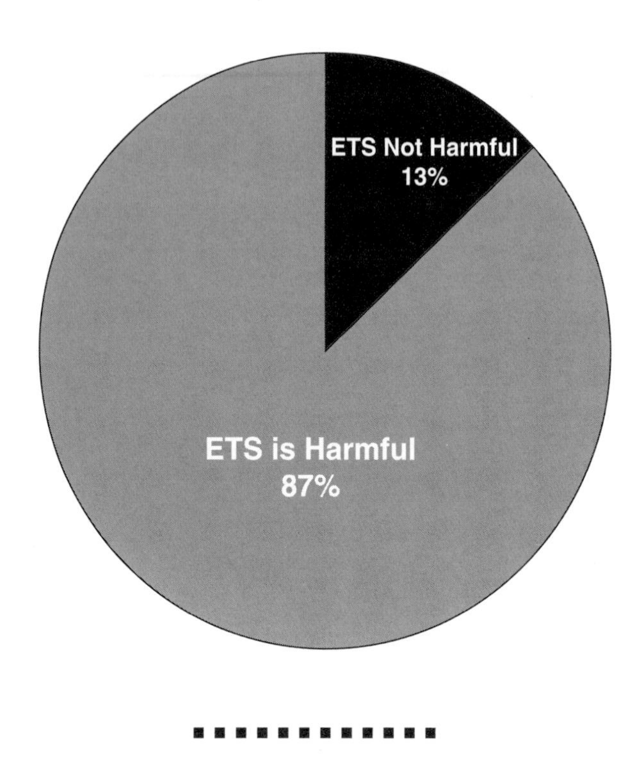

The most important duty of government is to protect the heath and safety of the public. Since the 1964 Surgeon General's report, what action has Congress taken to stop deaths from tobacco that continues at the rate of one every 73 seconds? What have they done to protect the public from the harmful effects of environmental tobacco smoke which kills one nonsmoker every 6 ½ minutes? What have they done to stop children from starting to smoke at the rate of one every 29 seconds? Why have there been more tobacco control legislative losses than gains? Find out where the root of all evil is firmly planted.

Chapter Thirteen

Gains and Losses

The Surgeon General's first report on Smoking Hazards in 1964 was a bombshell—the action Congress took was a dud. Thirty years later, tobacco related deaths in the United States have passed the ten million mark. Along the way, there have been more tobacco control legislative losses than wins.

The Cigarette Labeling and Advertising Act of 1965

The year following the Surgeon General's first Report on Smoking and Health in 1964, Congress enacted the *Cigarette Labeling and Advertising Act*, which authorized the Federal Trade Commission (FTC) to require warnings on all cigarette packages. The tobacco lobbyist, and obliging members of Congress with their hands out, were successful in weakening the FTC's proposal for a strongly worded warning. The FTC wanted to include the words "causes death from cancer and other diseases." Instead, the health warning was softened to simply read "Caution: Cigarette Smoking May be Hazardous to Your Health."

The FTC proposal was also weakened in a way that still has a devastating effect today on the Government's ability to provide health information to consumers about smoking. The act contained a preemption that prevented state governments, the FTC, FDA, or any other federal agency from requiring additional health warnings on the package:

> No statement relating to smoking and health, other than the statement required by [the Act], shall be required on any cigarette package.

It is important to note that the FDA requires health warnings and product information to be part of the package for all medications and medical devices. The information the tobacco industry persuaded Congress to withhold from the public can be found in a sample tobacco product information insert in appendix F.

In 1970 Congress amended the Act to include slightly tougher language:

> "The Surgeon General has determined that
>
> Cigarette Smoking is Dangerous to Your Health."

When Congress addressed advertising of smokeless tobacco products, they took the withholding of health information a step further. The Smokeless Act withholds health information not only from the package, but also from all smokeless advertising:

"No statement relating to the use of smokeless tobacco products and health, other than the statements required by [the Act], shall be required by any Federal agency to appear on any package or on in any advertisement (unless it is a billboard) of a smokeless tobacco product."

Year Seven, 1964-1970: Death Toll: 1,534,000.

The Comprehensive Smoking Education Act

Nineteen years following the original legislation, Congress again amended the *Cigarette Labeling and Advertising Act* in 1984. The new amendment required warnings on all cigarette advertisements and packaging. The language of the four new warnings was stronger, and must appear on a four month rotational basis.

SURGEON GENERAL'S WARNING:
Smoking by pregnant women may result in fetal injury, premature birth, and low birth weight.

SURGEON GENERAL'S WARNING:
Cigarette smoke contains carbon monoxide.

SURGEON GENERAL'S WARNING:
Smoking causes lung cancer, heart disease, emphysema, and may complicate pregnancy.

SURGEON GENERAL'S WARNING:
Quitting smoking now greatly reduces serious risks to your health.

Tobacco Industry Secret Becomes Government Secret

When Congress amended the Cigarette Labeling and Advertising Act in 1984, the tobacco industry was upset with the new health warnings. They agreed to it on one condition: that the government allow them to keep the additives they put in tobacco a secret, and not be disclosed to the public. The tobacco industry argued that additives were a 'trade secret,' and should be protected as a baker would a cake recipe. The Government accepted the deal.

Today, the list is in a safe at the CDC in Atlanta. The list can be reviewed, discussed, and acted upon by only one Health and Human Services person, the list keeper. Other authorized personnel can look at it, but first they must sign an agreement not to disclose the list. Congress has made disclosure of the list a felony, punishable with fines, imprisonment, and loss of job.

The list keeper has never raised concerns about the additives because qualified people are not allowed to discuss or report on them. This is another example of how the tobacco industry manipulates our government to the detriment of the public's health. Michael Erickson, Office on Smoking and Health, says that "Secrecy of the list has inhibited research on the safety of the 700 additives."

Walter Merryman, President of the Tobacco Institute, disagrees. He says that secrecy is not a problem, claiming that if there was a question about the additives, the list keeper never took any action. The list keeper has the option to report to Congress if there is cause of concern about the additives. No reports or action has ever been taken. Therefore, the Tobacco Institute assumes that this matter has no merit.

Questions remain about the list keeper. Who is it? Is he or she a scientist qualified to evaluate the hazards of the additives? Meanwhile, the list is kept under lock and key.

The FTC Investigates Tobacco Advertising

The Federal Trade Commission was formed in 1938 to regulate consumer products and services. The Senate Commerce Committee, who has responsibility over FTC, gave it the power to hold hearings, perform investigations, to subpoena documents, make rules, and to issue "cease and desist" orders. Violations were punishable with civil penalties up to $10,000 a day fine.

In 1976, Michael Pertschuk, Director of the FTC, made this statement regarding cigarette advertising, "the promotion of a hazardous product is an unfair practice." Under Section 5 of the FTC act, Pertschuk started investigating the unfair advertising practices of six tobacco companies.

All records, written and electronic, were subpoenaed. The subpoena was fought in court for two years. Finally in January 1979, a US District court ordered the six companies and 12 advertising agencies to hand over the documents.

For five years the FTC investigated the advertising of cigarettes. They concluded the tobacco industry had withheld information and failed to warn the public about the hazards of smoking and nicotine dependency.

The FTC concluded:

- Cigarette smoking was more dangerous than previously believed.
- Cigarette advertising contained no health information.
- Most Americans knew little or nothing about the specific health hazards of smoking.
- Americans were unable to assess the health risks of smoking for themselves.
- The current health warnings are rarely noticed and not effective.

Tobacco Friends in Congress Cripple the FTC

In 1980, Senator Wendle Ford of Kentucky tried to neutralize the Federal Trade Commission in an effort to make them lay off the tobacco industry. The FTC was portrayed as thugs and bullies. Ford was successful in weakening the FTC by deleting "unfair" from the FTC act, and eliminating the power to subpoena. That means the FTC can't investigate unfair tobacco advertising, and can't subpoena tobacco company documents to use as evidence. Even more disturbing, the new rules applies to not only tobacco companies, but all businesses. On February 7, 1980, Ford's FTC bill, was passed by the Senate, 77 to 13. The controlling influence: the tobacco states' senators and other senators that received tobacco money.

Year Seventeen, 1964-1980: Death toll: 4,565,000.

The Department of Health, Education and Welfare Investigates Tobacco Promotion to Children

In December 1976, President-elect Jimmy Carter, told Joseph Califano that in his job as Secretary of Health Education and Welfare he was to focus on preventative care. Califano began a major smoking prevention and cessation campaign.

In 1979, he commissioned a survey on teenage smoking. Califano found that four million teens were smoking, and they smoked the most heavily advertised brand—Marlboro. He wrote to the presidents of tobacco companies asking them to use ten percent of their advertising budget for antismoking ads for teens.

Here are excerpts from their responses to Califano's plea:

George Weissman, Chairman of Philip Morris:

"Advertising is not effective in altering the behavior of teenagers in regard to the use of cigarettes."

William Hobbs, R.J. Reynolds, Chief Executive Officer,

"Advertising played no part in encouraging teenagers to smoke," therefore he had "no responsibility to urge them not to smoke."

Raymond J. Mulligan, Liggett Group, President,

"The mothers and the father of this nation, whether smokers or non smokers, should continue to have the freedom of choice in the education and training of their children."

Curtis Judge, Lorillard Tobacco, (Loews) President,

"We no longer give away free samples at college campuses." This was offered as evidence that they do not promote to children.

C. I. McCarty, Brown & Williamson (B.A.T.):

Expressed no concern about addicting children and teenagers, but he was concerned about "the possible antitrust aspects of a public service effort to encourage children not to smoke."

The fact gathering on tobacco promotion shocked Califano and his staff. They realized tobacco advertising targeted children. Califano tried to get a $2 million budget for smoking education and prevention programs in schools, but was stopped by Representative William Natcher of Kentucky with the help of tobacco lobbying and cash contributions. Later in 1979, under political pressure from the tobacco zealots in Congress, Carter fired Califano.

Califano Reflects on 1979

Reflecting on 1979, Califano testified at the Congressional hearing in 1994. "If they had known that the tobacco industry had been concealing information on the addictive nature of nicotine (since 1963), they would have declared nicotine addictive in the 1979 Surgeon General's report." He feels that in 1979 the government also could have had the muscle to regulate tobacco as a habit forming drug. Califano, speaking for himself, President Jimmy Carter, and the Surgeon General Julius Richmond, said

"We were victims of the concealment and disinformation

campaign by the tobacco companies."

Mark Hatfield Tries to End the Tobacco Subsidy Program, 1981

In 1981, Senator Mark Hatfield tried to abolish the tobacco subsidy program by introducing a bill. He said, "Let the tobacco farmer stand on his own feet as we are asking the welfare recipients and the poor and the needy and the minorities...." Hatfield's bill was defeated by 53 to 42. The tobacco zealots were still in control of Congress.

'No-Net-Cost' to Taxpayers Provision - The $224 million Hoax

Until 1982, tobacco subsidies were "nonrecourse" loans, meaning tobacco farmers did not have to pay it back. On July 20, 1982, a new law called the *"No-Net-Cost" Tobacco Program Act* was put in effect making the farmers pay back the loans through assessments. It is important to note that taxpayers pay $16 million annually just to run the tobacco support program, totalling more than $224 million since 1982. Over $224 million in taxes have been taken out of our paychecks for a tobacco subsidy they call "no-net-cost to taxpayers."

Richard Durbin Tries to End the Tobacco Subsidy Program, 1995

Why should the government and taxpayers support a product that is a threat to health? That is what Representative Richard J. Durbin (D-IL) asked the House Appropriations Committee. The committee was to vote on an amendment he introduced to end the 50 year tobacco subsidy. On June 27, 1995, he said:

"Tobacco is unlike any other crop subsidized by the United States Department of Agriculture. Tobacco, when used as directed, will kill you. Why, in God's name, when we are talking about cutting Medicaid and education and are still subsidizing the production and the manufacture of tobacco?"

Rep. Durbin's statement was received with laughs and jeers from tobacco state representatives present, such as W. G. Hefner, (D-NC), Charles H. Taylor (R-NC), and Harold Rogers (R-KY). "It's an economic argument," said Hefner, who has received $69,600 from the tobacco industry since 1985.

Durbin's amendment to end the tobacco subsidy failed, 30 to 17. The tight coil of the tobacco cartel once again choked Congress into submission.

Year Thirty-two, 1964-1995: Death Toll: over 10 million.

1996 Farm Bill Kills Food Crop Subsidies — Tobacco Subsidies Live On

Since the 1930's, the government has operated farm subsidy programs. Basic crops like corn, wheat, cotton, peanuts and rice, as well as milk, are included in the subsidy program. In February 1996, the House and Senate passed a major Federal Farms Program overhaul, which ends the subsidies over the next seven years. On the contrary, just a year earlier, Congress voted down ending tobacco subsidies.

OSHA Fails to Take Action on Secondhand Smoke Exposure in the Workplace

The Federal Government protects the public from drunk drivers, deadly plagues, defective products, dangerous toys, unsafe food and terrorist attacks. One of its agencies, The Occupational Safety and Health Administration (OSHA), protects workers from exposure to hazardous substances, such as radiation, asbestos, and air pollution. Yet, OSHA has neglected to protect workers from environmental tobacco smoke in the workplace. In March of 1994, OSHA simply advised a ban on smoking in all workplaces.

OSHA's 1994 Advisory Statement on ETS

- Officially classified ETS as a potential occupational carcinogen.
- Advised reducing exposure to ETS in the workplace by using all available preventive measures.

Smoking in the workplace is a public health concern for 110 million workers as well as customers. OSHA's plan to eliminate ETS in the workplace would save American businesses an estimated $8.4 billion annually in increased productivity. Unfortunately, OSHA has taken no action on ETS in the workplace. The Coalition on Smoking OR Health, stated in a January 1994 report that:

"OSHA has announced no action to protect workers from environmental tobacco smoke in the workplace in spite of its advice and notice of the health risks of ETS."

Action on Smoking and Health (ASH) took OSHA to court over the matter. In 1996 a United States Court of Appeals ordered OSHA to stop the unreasonable delay in issuing a national workplace smoking rule. OSHA responded by saying they were too busy, but they may get around to it in ten years.

Using the Court System as a Weapon

California has some of the best smoke free laws in the country. Proposition 99 enacted in 1988 is responsible for a 30% reduction in smoking there. In San Francisco, a new smoke free ordinance was due to go in effect in January 1995. Unfortunately it was held up in court, by Philip Morris who filed a law suit to overturn the ordinance.

"We will consider challenging other restrictive smoking city ordinances around the country."

-Steve Parish, General Council, Philip Morris

Philip Morris is doing what ever it takes to fight for smokers to continue smoking in public, and they are using our courts as their weapon. As a result, public health remains in jeopardy. Philip Morris' lawsuit also increase court costs that taxpayers must pay.

Those that Speak Out Against Them Get Sued

When ABC's *Day One* reported that the tobacco industry 'spikes' cigarettes with nicotine, Philip Morris filed a $10 billion suit against ABC claiming defamation. Murry Bring, VP for Philip Morris, says ABC has "Poisoned the well of public opinion of them and the tobacco industry." The dispute was finally settled in 1995, and ABC retracted their claim that Philip Morris "spiked" cigarettes with nicotine. However, their claim that they manipulated nicotine to keep smokers hooked was unchallenged.

This lawsuit has had an intimidating influence on the media since the settlement. CBS's *60 Minutes* and *The New York Times* both stopped stories on the tobacco industry for a period of time. In November 1995, CBS announced they were killing a *60 Minutes* interview of a former B.A.T. executive, Jeffrey Wigand. Laurence Tisch, Chairman and CEO of CBS Inc., is the largest shareholder of CBS through his family owned Loews Corp. Loews also owns Lorillard Tobacco Co.

RJR stopped an antismoking advertisement in California with the threat of a libel lawsuit in 1994. The California health department said only two of 22 television stations quit running their 30 second advertisement, despite the RJR's "strong-arm tactic."

Back to the Nicotine-Free-for-all 50's

In an effort to turn back the clock to the "nicotine-free-for-all fifties," Philip Morris is using a new weapon—the voting booth. Philip Morris put a new proposal on the California ballot, that would stymie nonsmoking efforts.

Philip Morris called it *The Tobacco Control Act,* otherwise known as Proposition 188. The "act" would have replaced 270 local tough nonsmoking laws with one weak state law. Business owners would then have the option to allow smoking on an individual basis.

Philip Morris was charged with misleading the public by Secretary of State officials, who began investigating the petition campaign as deceptive. Lee Stitzenberger, a consultant for Philip Morris said "We are seeking uniformity and to provide fairness for both smokers and nonsmokers." Does Mr. Stitzenberger mean that, in all fairness, nonsmokers should get lung disease, heart attacks and die prematurely from cancer as uniformly as smokers do?

Philip Morris spent $8 million on proposition 188. Despite all this, 71% voted against the initiative, strongly rejecting Philip Morris' bogus plan.

■■■■■■■■■■■■■

The tobacco cartel has been very successful in warding off tobacco control regulations for over 30 years. What are the forces used that have protected the machine that has killed ten million people? Who are their allies? Why does Congress side with the cartel on most issues? You may be surprised to find that in Congress today, the majority does not rule — tobacco does.

Chapter Fourteen

The Cartel's Frontline Weapon

Balance of Power is in Favor of the Few

Tobacco companies represent the interests of only one of every four people, the smokers. Despite being outnumbered by 135 million adults that do not smoke, the tobacco industry is the dominant force in all tobacco and health issues. The tobacco cartel's power is out of balance in Congress. Their death grip is motivated by profit, maintained with payoffs, and driven by nicotine addiction.

"There's virtually no limit on the amount

of money we will spend."

-Philip Morris spokesperson Karen Daragan.

One Thousand Times NO!

Tobacco is grown only in a few states. In 1980, it was grown in only 51 of 531 congressional districts. However, Congress' voting record does not fairly represent the majority. The tobacco industry lobbying has been successful in thwarting over 1,000 tobacco restrictions since the first Surgeon General's report on Smoking and Health in 1964.

"Until we reform the campaign finance system, tobacco money will continue to block such attempts to enact sound health system reform, promote the public health, and protect our children and teens from the tobacco industry."

-Joseph A. Califano, Jr., Columbia University, Center on Addiction and Substance Abuse

Tobacco Zealots Lobby Activities

Tobacco Political Action Committees (PAC's) gave political parties and individual members of Congress, over $20 million from January 1986 to December 1995.

Over $11 million went directly to individuals, and almost $9 million in soft money went to political committees. Ann McBride, of Common Cause, alarmed about the soft contributions said, "These huge unlimited contributions represent the most corrupting money in American politics today." Soft money contributions influence tobacco policy in Congress, and squash the majority's voice. These "unrestricted" contributions have killed bills to end tobacco subsidies, smoking in public, and now threaten the ability of the FDA to

Tobacco's Contributions to Congress
January 1986 to December 1995

	Contributions		
Company	**PAC**	**Soft Money**	**Total**
Philip Morris	$ 3,680,128	$ 2,844,426	$ 6,524,554
RJ Reynolds	$ 3,356,888	$ 2,595,912	$ 5,952,800
US Tobacco	$ 2,042,475	$ 1,250,535	$ 3,293,010
Brown & Williamson, B.A.T.	$ 659,667	$ 562,000	$ 1,221,667
Lorillard	$ 209,300	$ 303,500	$ 512,800
Pinkerton Tobacco	$ 274,987	$ 15,000	$ 289,987
American Tobacco	$ 68,350	$ 51,000	$ 119,350
Universal Leaf Tobacco	$ 28,302	$ 15,000	$ 43,302
The Tobacco Institute	$ 886,763	$ 860,554	$ 1,747,317
Smokeless Tobacco Council	$ 199,000	$ 394,867	$ 593,867
Cigar Association of America	$ 60,650	$ 10,000	$ 70,650
American Wholesale Marketers	$ 148,075	$ 7,000	$ 155,075
Total	$ 11,614,585	$ 8,909,794	$ 20,524,379

prevent teens from starting to smoke. They have also made a mockery of the 1994 Congressional investigation into the tobacco industry. House Representative Linda Smith, R-Washington, says, "Our political system is in reality a few people in D.C. with big checkbooks controlling America's future." Until PAC money is out of Congress, there will be no faith in our Government.

How the Tobacco Industry Bought Congress:

The New Tobacco Party

During the Congressional hearings, investigating the deceptive business practices of the tobacco industry in May of 1994, tobacco lobbyists began silent, one on one meetings with members of congress. Large contributions were made to the Republican members. Some contributions went to the members' of Congress' favorite charities. Bob Dole's wife, Elizabeth Dole, is the top executive of the American Red Cross. In 1995, RJR, Philip Morris and B.A.T, gave the Red Cross $265, 530. House Rep. Tony Hall (Ohio) had the swing vote on the House Rules Committee. He had the power to decide if tobacco control amendments would get to the House floor. Hall received a contribution from the tobacco lobbyists for his Hunger Institute.

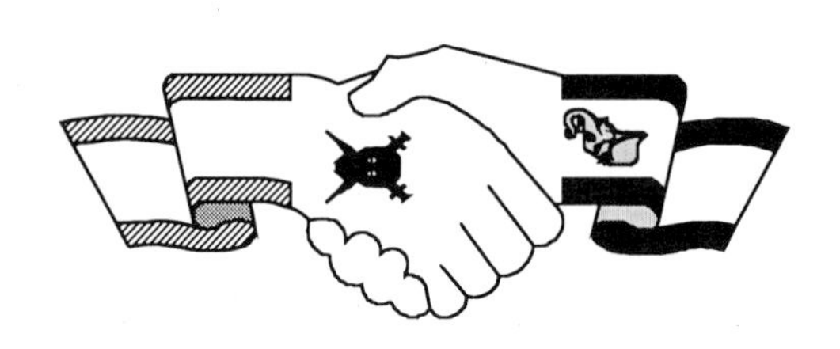

Following the hearings in 1994, the Republicans launched a crusade for a "Contract with America." A hidden element of the contract was a secret handshake with the tobacco companies. It is no coincidence that government laws and policies protect the tobacco industry. The tobacco cartel was the second biggest contributor to the GOP campaign in 1994. In first half of 1995, they gave the GOP a record $2 million. By blocking new government regulations, the tobacco cartel is the biggest winner, and the losers are the 434,000 Americans that die every year from smoking.

Until 1995, the cartel was nonpartisan, being careful not to align themselves with any particular party. They give money to either side, receiving legislative protection in return. In 1995, they gave the Republican party ten times more than the Democratic party. Furthermore, their strategy is to get Bob Dole into the White House. Bob Dole has taken over $330,000 from the tobacco industry. Is the Republican party becoming the tobacco party? As shocking as it sounds, that is becoming a reality. The Texas Democratic chairman, Bill White, said in June 1996, that the party will no longer accept contributions from the tobacco industry.

Congress is protecting the cartel's invisible drug pipeline. This means nonsmokers will continue to have to breathe tobacco smoke in public places. Nonsmokers will continue to pay the health care costs that are attributed to smoking. Cartoon advertising will continue to seduce children into nicotine addiction. All in all business as usual.

Tobacco interests were some of the top contributors during the 1994 GOP campaign. Philip Morris gave $190,750, The Tobacco Institute gave $171,027, and RJR Nabisco gave $130,252 to GOP congressional campaign committees.

A Record $ 2.4 million went to GOP in 1995

When the FDA turned up the heat in 1995, the "soft money" started pouring into the Republican party. Tobacco companies gave $2.4 million to the Republican National Committee. The first half of 1995, another $413,300 went directly to individual Republican Congressional representatives, and $154,950 went to Democratic committees.

Tobacco Company Contributors
Republican Party 1995

Philip Morris	$975,149
RJ Reynolds	$696,450
B.A.T	$260,000
Other	$468,400

Meet the Tobacco Zealots in Congress Today

Meet the top recipients of tobacco money in the House and Senate. Meet the top 35 House representatives who have collectively taken over $1.8 million in tobacco money from January 1986 to December 1995:

House Representatives, Top Tobacco PAC Recipients

Thomas J. Bliley Jr.	R-Virginia	$ 126,976
Charlie Rose	D-N. Carolina	$ 104,800
Lewis F. Payne Jr.	D-Virginia	$ 92,899
Rick Boucher	D-Virginia	$ 75,350
Jim Bunning	R-Kentucky	$ 72,450

Bill G. Hefner	D-N. Carolina	$ 70,350
Richard A. Gephardt	D-Missouri	$ 67,258
John D. Dingell	D-Mississippi	$ 64,500
Bart Gordon	D-Tennessee	$ 63,500
Howard Coble	R-N. Carolina	$ 61,892
Bob Clement	D-Tennessee	$ 55,300
David E. Bonior	D-Michigan	$ 53,800
Newt Gingrich	R-Georgia	$ 53,750
Vic Fazio	D-California	$ 52,050
Tom DeLay	R-Texas	$ 49,450
Dan Schaefer	R-Colorado	$ 49,150
Gary A. Franks	R-Connecticut	$ 48,100
Charles B. Rangel	D-New York	$ 47,950
Edolphus Towns	D-New York	$ 47,180
Norman Sisisky	D-Virginia	$ 44,750
Jack Fields	R-Texas	$ 44,450
Michael Bilirakis	R- Florida	$ 43,950
Sam M. Gibbons	D-Florida	$ 43,750
Thomas Manton	D-New York	$ 43,587
Cass Ballenger	R-N. Carolina	$ 39,900
Billy Tauzin	R- Louisiana	$ 38,800
Harold Rogers	R-Kentucky	$ 37,200
Charles Taylor	R-N. Carolina	$ 32,700
Herbert Bateman	R-Virginia	$ 32,330
John Boehner	R- Ohio	$ 31,506
Steny Hoyer	D-Maryland	$ 31,300
E. Clay Shaw	R- Florida	$ 31,300
James Quillen	R-Tennessee	$ 29,550
Jim Chapman	D-Texas	$ 29,400
Barbara Kennelly	D- Connecticut	$ 29,150

Listed below are the top 38 Senators who have collectively taken over $1.3 million in tobacco money from January 1986 to December 1995:

U.S. Senators, Top Tobacco PAC Recipients

Jesse Helms	R-N. Carolina	$	77,000
Wendel Ford	D-Kentucky	$	76,057
Mitch McConnell	R-Kentucky	$	67,500
Daniel Coats	R- Indiana	$	58,500
Trent Lott	R-Mississippi	$	53,200
Ernest Hollings	D-S. Carolina	$	52,796
Kay Bailey Hutchison	R-Texas	$	45,923
Conrad Burns	R-Montana	$	45,750
Charles Robb	D-Virginia	$	41,000
Christopher Bond	R- Missouri	$	40,500
Kent Conrad	D- N. Dakota	$	40,000
Lauch Faircloth	R-N. Carolina	$	39,250
Bob Dole *	R- Kansas	$	38,400
Hank Brown	R- Colorado	$	36,250
John Warner	R-Virginia	$	35,000
Richard Shelby	R-Alabama	$	35,000
Al D' Amato	R- New York	$	34,800
Thad Cochran	R-Mississippi	$	34,450
John Breaux	D-Louisiana	$	34,400
Fred Thompson	R-Tennessee	$	33,500

Christopher Dodd	D-Connecticut	$ 33,499
Mike DeWine	R- Ohio	$ 33,000
Connie Mack	R- Flordia	$ 32,200
Pete Domenici	R-N. Mexico	$ 32,000
Phil Gramm	R-Texas	$ 31,100
Don Nickles	R-Oklahoma	$ 30,786
Larry Pressler	R- S. Dakota	$ 30,500
Bob Kerrey	D-Nebraska	$ 26,500
Byron Dorgan	D-N. Dakota	$ 26,000
John McCain	R-Arizona	$ 24,500
Rick Santorum	R-Pennsylvania	$ 24,000
James Inhofe	R-Oklahoma	$ 21,500
Robert Smith	R-N.Hampshire	$ 21,300
Craig Thomas	R- Wyoming	$ 21,000
Larry Craig	R- Idaho	$ 20,800
Thomas Daschle	D-S. Dakota	$ 20,500
Charles Grassley	R-Iowa	$ 20,500
Frank Murkowski	R-Alaska	$ 20,500

* Bob Dole has taken a total of over $330,000 from tobacco interests during his political career.

It is important to note that these are just the top tobacco money recipients, there are too many to list them all.

"The money that the tobacco industry donates to members of Congress ensures that the tobacco industry will retain its strong influence in the federal tobacco policy process."

-Public Citizen's Health Research Group

Influence Peddling

Tobacco PAC money not only buys access to the politicians, but it buys their votes as well. Representative Linda Smith, who wants to ban PACs, says "Every night, members go across the street to these fund-raisers, where lobbyists buy access."

What would one of these parties look like? One can only speculate, but open bribery is probably not the fare. An incumbent is probably first approached by a lobbyist on a personal level. The conversation would then drift to an issue, say the FDA regulation of tobacco. The clever lobbyist will probe with questions to ascertain if the member is undecided on the issue. If not, a hint will be made that the lobbyist is considering making a donation to his campaign fund. An amount is not immediately discussed, but it looks promising enough for the member to meet the lobbyist at some other time for dinner. At dinner, following drinks and an appetizer, the conversation once again drifts to the issue of the FDA regulation of tobacco. If the member is talking more favorably, a contribution is offered, with no strings attached of course. If the member is still undecided, his objections are overcome. Once the objections are overcome, a contribution is again offered. It is important to note, that the contribution offer is woven into the conversation in a way that is seems unattached to a commitment to vote against the FDA bill. This is how outright bribery is avoided, leaving no evidence of a quid pro quo. Nothing is in writing, no firm agreements were made about how the member will vote – it is all done with a handshake.

The final part of the picture is what the member does with the contribution. He does not use it to buy a new boat. He deposits it into his fund account, and later dips into it to lease a new boat. The bottom line is, with lots of money for "contributions," enough support in Congress can be bought to kill the FDA regulation of tobacco. The little guy has no voice—that is 135 million little guys.

What will America be like as we enter the new millennium?

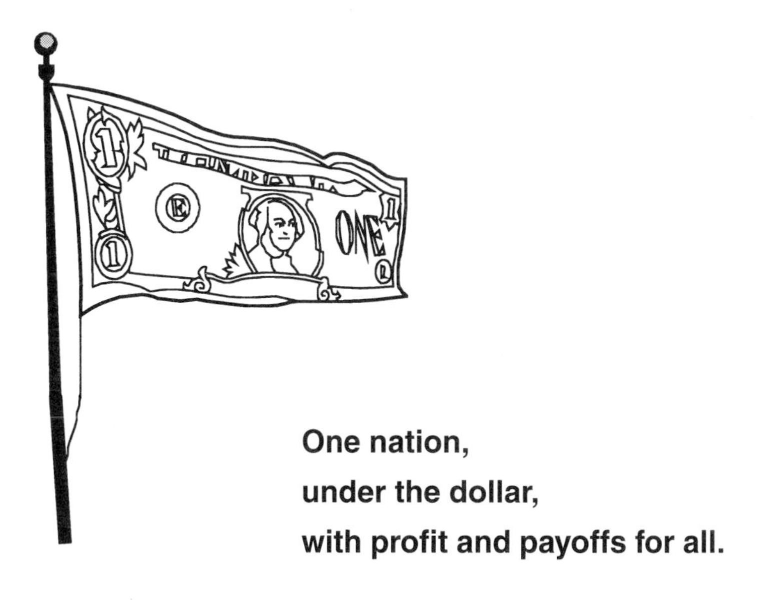

▪▪▪▪▪▪▪▪▪▪▪▪▪

You don't smoke – but smoking kills you. You don't smoke – but you pay extra taxes because others do. Rampant death and disease caused by smoking adds up to higher health care costs for everyone. Who pays for it? Do smokers pay their fair share?

"Until we reform the campaign finance system, tobacco money will continue to block such attempts to enact sound health system reform, promote the public health, and protect our children and teens from the tobacco industry."

Joseph A. Califano, Jr.

Chapter Fifteen

A Tax Burden

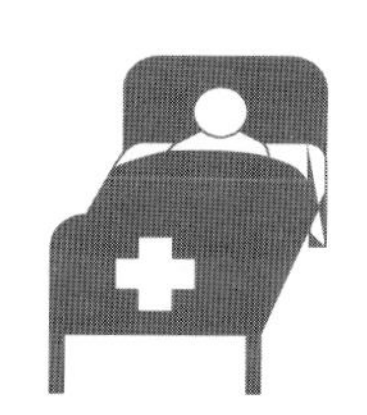

It is no wonder smokers are sick more often that nonsmokers. After all, they dump 2,000 toxic chemicals and 60 carcinogens into their blood stream on the average of every 30 minutes, 16 hours a day, every day of the year – like a continuous intravenous injection of an elixir of death. A continuous stream of poisons circulating throughout their whole body causes a continuous pathology. That means a regular smoker is never healthy; they are chronically ill. Compared to nonsmokers, smokers have more flu, pneumonia, emphysema, cancer, premature births, arteriosclerosis and heart attacks. Smokers die of cancer and heart attacks at twice the rate than nonsmokers. Smokers therefore require more heath care, doctor visits, prescription medications, longer hospitalizations, heart and lung surgery, and chemotherapy. Who pays for this monstrous health care burden?

With all the excess disease smokers have, as you would expect, their lifetime medical costs are higher that nonsmokers. Estimates of direct and indirect health care costs attributed to smoking burdens the American economy from $50 billion to over $100 billion annually.

Direct medical costs include expenses for hospitals, doctors, nursing homes, prescription drugs, home health care, burns, perinatal care for mothers who smoke, and low birth weight babies. Also, the most overlooked direct cost – the cost of health care attributed to secondhand smoke. Direct medical costs attributed to smoking is estimated by some to be 6.8% of the United States annual health care expenditures. And if that was not enough, there are indirect costs such as sick leave, life insurance, health insurance, property losses due to fires, lost Medicare taxes, and decreased productivity.

$730 Billion U.S. Annual Health Care Budget

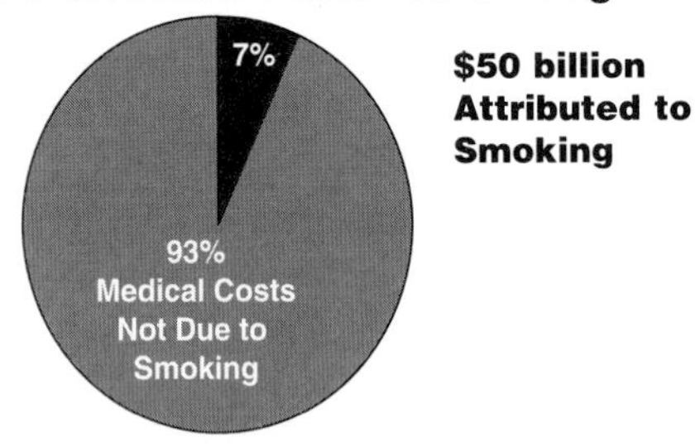

Smoker's Direct Health Care Costs

Numerous studies have been published that estimate the direct costs of smoking to society. One of the best and most widely quoted study was done by the CDC and UCB in 1993 (CDC-UCB). J.C. Bartlett, the lead author of the study, estimated the direct medical costs attributed to smoking. Medical costs were determined from actual hospital bills for diseases attributable to smoking only—heart attack, emphysema, arteriosclerosis, stroke, and cancer. Diseases or injuries not caused directly by smoking were omitted, such as doctor visits for colds or broken bones.

Health Care Costs for Smoking Related Diseases

- In 1985, the Department of Health and Human Services estimated that smoking cost the American economy $52.3 billion annually, the equivalent of $71.8 billion today adjusted for inflation.
- In 1986, a University of California -San Francisco study estimated health care costs and lost income from illness due to smoking, costs the nation $53.7 billion each year.
- The CDC estimated direct medical care attributed to smoking was $21.9 billion in 1987, and over $50 billion in 1993.
- A study published 1994, estimated that $65 billion in direct health care costs and lost productivity was attributed to smoking.
- The American Lung Association estimates that the direct and indirect costs of lung diseases attributed to smoking was $53.1 billion in 1989.
- Duke University estimated that the direct and indirect costs to society was $1.37 per pack smoked in 1994. The direct medical costs attributed to secondhand smoke was $6 billion annually.
- The Office of Technology Assessment estimated the cost of smoking to society was $2.06 per pack smoked in 1993.
- The Office of Technology Assessment estimated the indirect costs of smoking to businesses was $43 billion in lost earnings in 1985. Others estimated addition earnings loss of $8.6 billion attributed to secondhand smoke.
- Medicare costs for tobacco diseases was $16 billion in 1994.
- Medicare inpatient hospital care was $3 billion in 1994.
- 80% of the Medicare's substance abuse budget is spent on tobacco abuse.
- Smoking will drain Medicare of $800 billion in the next 20 years.

This table shows a summary of the CDC-UCB study's findings:

Direct Health Care Costs for Smokers — CDC-UCB, 1993:

$26.9 billion	Hospital Expenditures
$15.5 billion	Physician Expenditures
$4.9 billion	Nursing Homes
$1.8 billion	Prescriptions
$900 million	Home-Health Care

Dr. Bartlett found that in 1993 the cost for smokers health care was $50 billion. Since 24 billion packs of cigarettes were sold in 1993, the per pack cost was $2.06. This $2.06 per pack costs has been the target for a tobacco excise tax increase to be used to offset smokers health care costs. However, as you will see, $50 billion is too low.

$50 Billion is an Underestimation

Many authorities say the CDC-UCB figure of $50 billion is an underestimate of the total costs to our economy from smoking. One is Dr. Thomas E. Novotny, an epidemiologist and coauthor of the CDC-UCB study. Dr. Novotny said $50 billion is a "very minimum estimate," and the actual costs are "at least twice as high." There are many high dollar items not in the estimate. The CDC-UCB study does not include any of the following direct medical costs:

- Burn care from cigarette fires.
- Perinatal care for mothers who smoke.
- Low birth weight babies born to maternal smokers.
- All diseases in nonsmokers caused by second-hand smoke.

Indirect Costs Attributed to Smoking

Indirect costs associated with smoking include sick leave, life insurance, health insurance, property losses from fires, lost Medicare taxes, decreased worker productivity, premature death of valuable employees. They all have an economic impact on society and businesses. One study found that premature deaths caused by smoking, accounted for a loss of 1,198,887 years of productive work life in 1988. Productivity loss from these premature deaths cost society $40.3 billion annually.

Businesses experience losses because smokers take more frequent sick days. Work loss and disability claims cost business $6.9 billion annually. Reduced productivity, says the National Bureau of Economic Research, is one reason smokers wages are four to eight percent lower than nonsmokers. Fires caused by cigarettes also costs businesses and insurance companies $480 million annually in property losses.

Considering these direct and indirect costs, authorities say the actual costs due to smoking in 1993 were two fold higher, closer to about $100 billion. $100 billion annually puts a heavy financial burden on Medicare and Medicaid, as well as the taxpayer. From a practical point of view, when considering the costs of smoking to society, the direct medical costs are the most important. The indirect costs can be thrown out as the cost of doing business with a smoker. If they want to avoid the indirect costs, they can simply not hire or insure a smoker. The issue is: smoking puts nonsmokers in an unfair position of being forced to supplement the excessive health care needs of smokers. In addition, smokers do not pay more Medicare taxes like they usually do for life and health insurance.

Nonsmokers Health Care from ETS Exposure: The Missing Factor—The White Serpent

The CDC-UCB figure of $50 billion does not include direct medical costs such as burn care, perinatal care for smokers, and care for low birth weigh babies. Furthermore, the single largest expense not included, is the direct health care costs for 126 million nonsmokers attributed to the cumulative effects of environmental tobacco smoke. This could add another $10 billion!

Nonsmokers suffer from diseases caused by secondhand smoke which require additional health care. Medical costs for passive smoking are rarely considered when calculating heath care costs attributed to smoking. In the same manner, when the health care costs of smokers are compared to nonsmokers exposed to secondhand smoke it is ignored, which makes the difference smaller than it actually is. The only accurate way to determine the hidden costs of smokers' health care, is to compare their medical costs to nonsmokers who are not exposed to any secondhand smoke. Nonsmokers totally free from exposure to ETS should be the only group used to compare with smokers. Unfortunately only eight of every 100 nonsmokers are 100% free of any ETS chemicals in their blood.

To compound the problem, there are no good estimates available on nonsmokers health care costs attributed to the cumulative effects of environmental tobacco smoke. At the heart of the problem is a tobacco company cover-up — and the reason why there is no data on passive smoking diseases.

THE COVER-UP:

Philip Morris Suppresses Medical Information on Secondhand Smoke Related Diseases

The medical care costs for nonsmokers exposed to secondhand smoke is rarely cited because the data is difficult to obtain. On the contrary, data for all other diseases are easy to obtain from medical records. One thing that makes it is easy, is the standard code number doctors use for each disease. Doctors and hospitals use these codes when filing medical claims with private insurance, and Medicare or Medicaid. Data bases can then be searched to determine the incidence of particular diseases, like lung cancer.

There should also be a code for all diseases caused by secondhand smoke. At one time, diseases caused by secondhand smoke were assigned an E-Code number, E for disease of external cause. If this is so, then why is data on secondhand smoke illnesses difficult to obtain? The reason is because Philip Morris hired lobbyists to convince the government to stop collecting the data.

"As a practicing physician, I am frustrated when I care for a patient with chronic bronchitis, emphysema, or coronary artery disease and them am unable to use [a code] to indicate that the illness was caused, by tobacco."

-John Simmons, M.D., Putnam Hospital Center, Carmel, NY.

The Federal Government's Office of Management and Budget (OMB), made the decision to go along with Philip Morris' plan. Philip Morris accomplished this with the help of Washington lobbyist Multinational Business Services Inc. (MBI). MBI touted itself as a pro-science, but not pro-tobacco. It is interesting to note that MBI would not disclose to the *Los Angeles Times* who they worked for. Six lobbyists, including a former OSHA director, convinced OMB that assigning an E-code to diseases caused by secondhand smoke would cost the government too much money. In addition, the standard tobacco zealot defense was used claiming that secondhand smoke was not a proven cause of disease, so why collect useless data. MBI may have used "junk science" data from Health Buildings International to show ETS risks are low in offices. Whether they did or not, OMB was persuaded to go along with Philip Morris' plan. In 1995 OMB ordered the Department of Health and Human Services (DHHS), to stop using E-codes. Therefore, diseases caused by secondhand smoke do not officially exist according to the federal government. Most medical diagnosis forms that doctors, hospitals and insurance companies use are standardized with DHHS codes. So no data on secondhand smoke related diseases is available through these sources either.

How Many Nonsmokers are Poisoned by ETS?

The annual health care costs in America is some $730 billion, and rising. In the U.S., there are about 46 million smokers and 126 million nonsmokers, plus 76 million children. What may surprise you is the tremendous affect the smaller group of smokers has on nonsmokers' health and pocketbook.

The effects of secondhand smoke takes its toll on the health of 104.5 million adult nonsmokers. Nonsmokers exposed to ETS have more arteriosclerosis and heart attacks, asthma and allergy symptoms, flu and pneumonia, emphysema, cancer, and babies that are born premature or die of SIDS. The health hazards of ETS are so severe that it kills about 83,000 nonsmokers annually.

In the same manner, one in eight, some ten million children are exposed to significant amounts of ETS in and outside of the home. Medicaid as well as private insurance carriers are burdened with secondhand smoke diseases in children, costing millions in health care expenses.

Approximately 104.5 Million Nonsmokers are at Risk of Diseases Caused by Passive Smoking

Estimating the Direct Medical Costs from Passive Smoking: The 20% Rule

White and Froeb reported in the *New England Journal of Medicine* in 1980, that nonsmokers exposed to the cumulative effects of secondhand smoke suffer with 20% as much lung disease and cancer as moderate smokers do. What this means is that each nonsmoker's medical expenses are higher by the amount equal to 20% of the medical expenses of a moderate, one pack a day smoker. The 20% rule assumes that the average nonsmoker's risk is equivalent to the risk of smoking six of seven packs of cigarettes a month. If the 20% rule is applied to the CDC-UCB $50 billion ascribed to smokers direct medical costs, the direct costs from passive smoking would be $10 billion annually.

Ideally, we should be able to calculate medical expenses for nonsmokers ascribed to secondhand smoke as accurately as we can for smokers. As mentioned above, data on nonsmokers is not available because nonsmokers diseases caused by exposure to secondhand smoke do not officially exist with the Federal Government. Therefore, an alternative to applying the 20% rule directly to $50 billion, is to apply it to the direct medical costs attributed to smoking for the major disease categories: lung, heart and cancer.

A Global Estimate of the Direct Health Care Costs Attributed to Secondhand Smoke

A global estimate of the direct medical costs, of the major disease categories, lung, heart and cancer, attributed to passive smoking is found by applying the 20% rule to the direct medical costs attributed to smoking. Take the American Lung Association's (ALA) estimate that the direct and indirect costs of lung diseases attributed to smoking were $53.1 billion in 1989. To find the direct costs, we use the NCI estimate that the direct costs are 33.7% of the total costs to society. By taking 33.7% of the ALA estimate of $53.1 billion, an estimate of the direct cost attributed to smoking is $17.9 billion. Next, applying the 20% rule, yields $3.6 billion as the direct costs of health care for respiratory diseases attributed to passive smoking

The American Heart Association estimates that the total direct and indirect costs of health care for heart disease is $151.3 billion. It is generally recognized that 30% to 40% of heart diseases are caused by smoking, which is about $45.4 to $60.5 billion annually (mean $53 billion). To find the direct costs, we use the NCI 33.7% rule, which is $17.9 billion.

Rather than using the 20% rule for heart diseases, the 33% Wells rule can be used. A. J. Wells, of Kennett Square, Pennsylvania, reported in the *Journal of American College of Cardiology* in August 1994, that passive smoking is estimated to cause 33% as many deaths from heart disease as caused by active smoking. Applying Well's 33% rule, the costs of heart diseases caused by secondhand smoke is $5.9 billion.

The final major contribution to health care expenses from smoking is the largest, cancer. The National Cancer Institute estimates that the direct medical cost of health care for cancer is $35 billion. The direct costs of lung cancer to society is $5 billion, 90% of which are attributed to smoking. We know there are 3,000 cases attributed to secondhand smoke. For breast cancer, Morabia reported that 20% are caused by secondhand smoke. For the remaining cancers that cost society $19 million, 60% to 90% is attributed to smoking.

A global estimate of $12.7 billion is the total direct costs using the 20% rule estimates for all disease classes, with the exception of heart disease which is 33%. Applying the 20% rule to all the disease classes, the direct medical costs for secondhand smoke is $10.4 billion, which is about $2.3 billion low. Using the better global estimate, it is concluded that the direct health care costs caused by secondhand smoke exposure to 104.5 million nonsmokers, is about $12.7 billion annually.

Summary of the Direct Costs of Secondhand Smoke Medical Care

Diseases	Total Costs To Society	Cost Attributed to Smoking	Total Costs Attributed to Smoking	Direct Medical Costs Attributed to Smoking	Direct Medical Costs Attributed to Passive Smoking	Formula
Respiratory Diseases	NA		$53.1	$17.89	$3.6	A
Heart Diseases	$151.3	30% to 40%	$53	$17.9	$5.9	C
Lung Cancer	$5	90%	$4.5	$4.5	$0.0095	100%
Breast Cancer	$6	30%	$1.8	$1.8	$0.4	B
Other Cancers	$19	60% to 90%	$14.3	$14.3	$2.9	A
				Total	$12.7	

A = White and Froeb 20% rule - 20% of direct medical costs attributed to smoking.

B= Morabia, 20% breast cancers caused by secondhand smoke

C= Wells, passive smoking is estimated to cause 33% as many deaths from heart disease as caused by active smoking.

Considering only the direct medical costs, including $12.7 billion for the direct health care costs caused by secondhand smoke exposure to 104.5 million nonsmokers (see box), would raise the CDC-UCB per pack cost from $2.06 to $2.59.

The Real Cost of Smoking to Society

Combining the CDC-UCB direct health care cost estimate of $50 billion, with an additional $50 billion in additional and indirect costs, including the $12.7 billion for secondhand smoke, the total burden of smoking to society is $100 billion, or $4.12 per pack smoked. However, considering only the direct costs, the total is $62.7 billion.

Therefore, $2.59 is a very conservative and reasonable recommendation for a tobacco excise tax, moving the burden of health care costs attributed to smoking away from non-smokers to smokers.

Today's Tobacco Excise Tax is Insufficient

As the plague of preventable diseases attributed to smoking sweeps through America, it takes with it nonsmokers lives and their wallets. Today, smokers do not pay their fair share of the excessive health care costs they generate. The Federal Government only receives about $0.53 per pack, or about $12 billion from tobacco excise taxes annually. That leaves an estimated $50 billion, or a $2.06 per pack deficit. In all fairness, smokers should pay a $2.06 per pack increase. A per pack tax is fair, because the smoker is taxed in proportion to the number of cigarettes they smoke. The more cigarettes they smoke, the more taxes they pay to compensate for their increased health care expenses.

Current Tobacco Excise Tax Pay's only 19% of the Bill

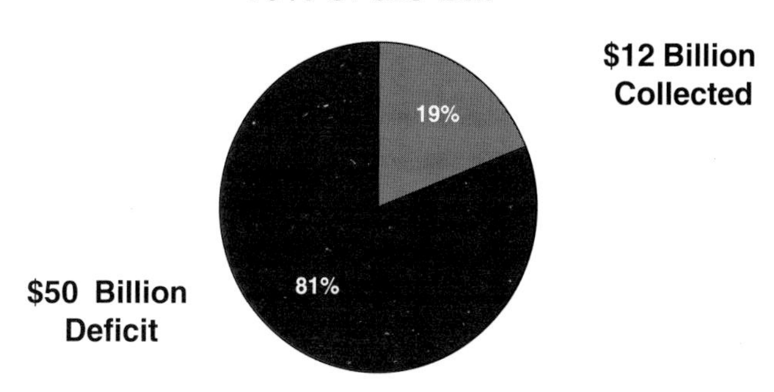

The Tobacco Industries Position on the Excise Tax

Peoples lives are cut short 15 to 20 years if they smoke. This fact is often used as a tobacco company defense. They coldly say that smokers die younger which saves our government money. This is the so called death benefit argument. In 1994 Robert Tolison, economics professor from G. Mason University and Tobacco Institute consultant, testified to Congress about the proposed increase in the cigarette excise tax. He used the death benefit argument. Mr. Tolison argued that an increase in the excise tax would decrease the number of people who would smoke. As a result, Tolison says that would cost the government money because people would live longer, "If you assume smokers expire earlier, then a tax will make them expire later." In other words, a higher cigarette excise tax is bad for the Government because it will cost more for elderly health care.

Indirect Costs Cloud the Truth

Duke University estimated the direct and indirect costs of smoking to society was $33 billion annually, of which $26.9 billion was indirect medical costs. The study was done by Kip Viscusi, an economist at Duke University. Mr. Viscusi based his estimate on data collected by W. Manning of the University of Minnesota, which was funded by the Rand Corp. Viscusi estimated direct health care expenses were $13.2 billion, which is not in the same ball park as the $50 billion to $72 billion reported in other studies. One aspect of the study is worth mentioning, Viscusi included $6 billion for secondhand smoke. $6 billion is a whopping $3.36 billion more if the 20% rule was applied. However, he admitted that his estimate was based on highly uncertain data.

Viscusi's argument included a death benefit of $46.8 billion. Interestingly, the death benefit to society was more that the expenses by $13.9 billion, which makes smoking appear to be a big cash bonus to society.

Human Deaths Justified by a Generous Profit

Premature death is cost effective? "It has to be part of the policy process," says Walter Merryman, VP of the Tobacco Institute. In a similar manner, should we put poison in our dog's food when he gets old to save on veterinary bills? Should we put all the old people outside in the rain to die so we will save on doctor bills, and decrease the surplus population? Will the Tobacco Institute ask us to stop treating AIDS patients next?

There is No Benefit when Death is the Solution

No decent human being would consider one half million deaths a year an economic bonus to society. It is important to note, that the death benefit becomes an issue only when the indirect costs to society are considered. No matter how preposterous, for the sake of the tobacco zealots, Viscusi's death benefit of $1.95 per pack smoked is less than the real cost of $4.12 per pack. This leaves a deficit to taxpayers of $2.17 per pack smoked.

In the public health arena, only the direct medical costs to society are meaningful. Morally, there is no benefit to death. Therefore, only the direct costs of $2.59 per pack smoked will be discussed further.

Since 1964, ten million people have died prematurely because of smoking. On one hand, this is denied by the tobacco cartel, on the other hand, they use it as a selling point to block efforts to raise the tobacco excise tax. Once again, they are sidestepping the issue — smoking costs society $2.59 per pack smoked. The premature death of one smoker every 73 seconds is not a benefit, and it must end.

In all fairness to nonsmoking taxpayers, new sources of funds for the health care expenses caused by smoking must be found. To solve this dilemma, there are two sources to tap. One is the tobacco excise tax, which passes the costs along to nicotine addicted smokers. The other source, is from law suits against the tobacco companies — the promoters of nicotine addition — the source of tobacco diseases and deaths.

Other Ideas for the $2.59 Tobacco Excise Tax:

- Replace tobacco industry funding of community activities, sporting events, and minority programs.
- Fund smoking cessation programs.
- Subsidize cancer Insurance for smokers.
- Subsidize hospice care for terminally ill smokers.
- Buy TV spots for public service announcements on the hazards of smoking and environmental tobacco smoke.
- Fund tobacco prevention education programs for teens and children.

The Lost Jobs Defense

When Hitler's gas chambers were finally shut down ending the Holocaust, should we have listened to pleas from the gas companies that it would put people out of work?

There are 303,000 tobacco jobs in the U.S. Interestingly, the tobacco industry claims that all of these jobs would be lost if the excise tax is increased. More realistically, we can expect a gradual decline. Furthermore, as consumers stop spending money on cigarettes, the income is redistributed to purchase other goods and services. The U.S. Bureau of Labor Statistics estimates that there will be a 2.06% annual decline in tobacco consumption until the year 2000. Economists at the University of Michigan, estimate that if tobacco consumption declined at twice the predicted rate, by the year 2000, the country would gain 19,700 jobs.

North Carolina produces 52% of all tobacco grown in the U.S. Despite this, tobacco accounts for only about four percent of the gross state product. An excise tax increase would drop domestic demand for tobacco an estimated six to 12%. The impact of a $2.59 tax seems minuscule, especially since the world demand for American grown tobacco has swollen 275% since 1985.

Jimmy Carter Says an Increased Tax Would Be Good For Farmers

Former President Jimmy Carter says that a tobacco tax would help farmers. He says that the tobacco industry has distorted the number of jobs that would be in jeopardy if the tax was passed. It is interesting to note that domestic tobacco jobs have dropped 29% over the last decade. This is largely because of actions taken by the tobacco companies themselves. They have established automated cigarette manufacturing plants in foreign countries. Many of those foreign made cigarettes are sold in the U.S. Similarly, they are training farmers in foreign countries to grow tobacco. "These actions," Mr. Carter says, "have resulted in more job loss that the tobacco excise tax ever could."

Tobacco Farmers Rebounded in 1994

The tobacco cartel is enjoying an upswing that started in 1994. Tobacco sales in America were so improved, that the U.S. Department of Agriculture increased the 1995 growing quota from 16% to 19%.

Tobacco imports have also declined. The world demand for American tobacco surged. U.S. cigarette exports to foreign markets has increased 275% since 1985. Presently things are looking good even for the small tobacco farmer, who could bring in as much as $140,000 for his crops.

A New Use for Tobacco: Transgenic Plants

The biotechnology industry may hold a new use for tobacco plants, by converting them into "biotech factories," called transgenic plants. Tobacco, like bacteria, can be genetically manipulated to produce human proteins. Acres and acres of tobacco plants could be producing insulin for diabetics, or other products like vaccines, enzymes, food additives, anticancer drugs, and antibodies. Someone will have to grow the tobacco to make these products. This technology brings a new exciting opportunity to tobacco farming. An interesting suggestion came from former President Jimmy Carter, who said that a portion of the tobacco excise tax could be used to retrain farmers to grow other crops. The tax could also be used to train tobacco farmers to grow transgenic plants.

The Tobacco Excise Tax is a Public Health Issue

A tobacco excise tax should be a health care issue and not a new tax issue, or a political issue. No one wants increased taxes. It is important to note that nonsmokers don't pay tobacco excise taxes — smokers do. Despite this, some politicians try to confuse the issue, by calling a tobacco excise tax a wholesale tax increase for everyone. "I strongly oppose any new (sin tax, tobacco excise) taxes." explained Kay Bailey Hutchison, (R-TX). Rep. Tom DeLay (R-TX), says: "You can count on my outspoken and persistent opposition to increases in any type of excise taxes." As of July 1995, Senator Hutchison has taken $49,923, and Rep. DeLay $49,450 from the tobacco industry.

States Sue Tobacco Companies to Recover Medicaid Costs

The second source of funding for the smokers' health care deficit is for the courts to mandate restitution. Mississippi was the first state to file suit against the tobacco industry to recover Medicaid health care costs to treat diseases caused by smoking. The 1994 suit seeks damages for the tobacco industries alleged 40 year strategy to "mislead and confuse the public about the true dangers associated with smoking cigarettes."

Mississippi has paid $60 to $80 million a year in Medicaid payments for 40 years. That brings the suit total to $2.4 to $3.2 billion in Medicaid costs for smoking related illnesses. Mike Moore, the state attorney general said, "It's time they quit hooking our young people on nicotine delivered through the dirty needle of cigarettes and other tobacco products."

Following Mississippi's lead, nine other states have filed suit which could pose an even greater liability for the tobacco firms. In 1994 Florida lawmakers passed a bill that would make it easier for the state to sue and recover health care costs incurred to treat diseases caused by smoking. Suits would be filed on behalf of smokers on Medicaid, where costs to treat these aliments is estimated to be $1.2 billion.

Preventative Medicine

One way to reduce health care costs is to reduce preventable deaths and disease. Scientists have spent decades of time and billions of dollars to find a cure for cancer. Eliminating the preventable diseases caused by smoking is easier, cheaper, and faster than finding a cure for them. Cessation of smoking and preventing the uptake are the keys to success of preventative medicine, and to slowing our growing health care costs. A tobacco excise tax of at least $2.00 a pack is expected to cause about 12% of smokers to quit. This will save some 50,000 lives a year.

"Congress has failed to take health promotion

and disease prevention in its sights."

-Joseph A. Califano, Jr., Columbia University,
Center on Addiction and Substance Abuse

Who are the Smokers Today?

In 1993, 46 million Americans were still smoking. Today, three million smokers are children, and another one million boys use smokeless tobacco. Today, about 25% of the population is still nicotine dependent, 27.7% of men, and 22.5% of women.

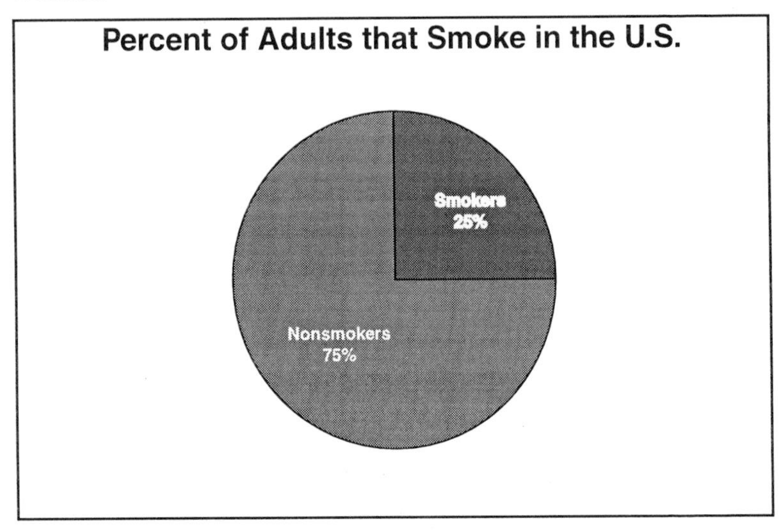

Percent of Adults that Smoke in the U.S.

The Tobacco Belt —
States with the Highest Percentage of Smokers
(25 to 30.3%, over age 18):

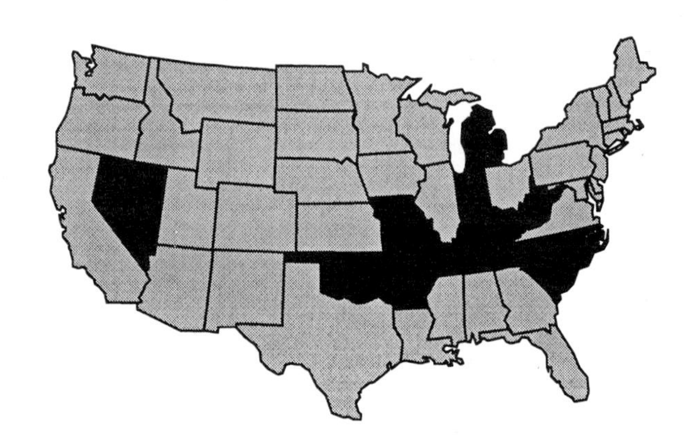

Percentage of Adults that Smoke, 1965 to 1995

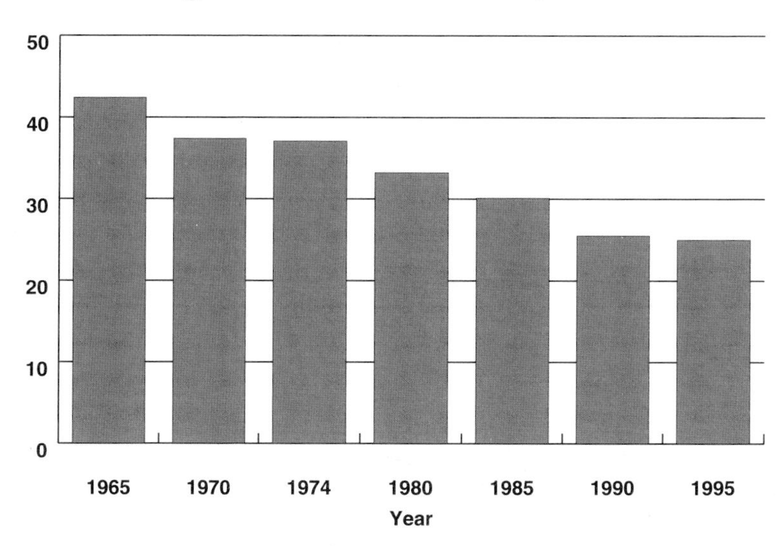

Over the last five years, cigarette smoking among adults has not changed, breaking a trend of decline since 1965.

In 1992, 26.4% of the 18 to 24 age group smoked, up from 22.9% the year before. Not only did it increase, this is the first time smoking in this age group has not decreased since 1983. There is a correlation in the increase in young smokers from 1991 to 1992, and a 16% increase in tobacco advertising and promotion budgets in 1991. The fight between the tobacco zealots and the pro-health, tobacco control forces has apparently reached a stand off.

Smokers Age 18 to 24 Smoking More

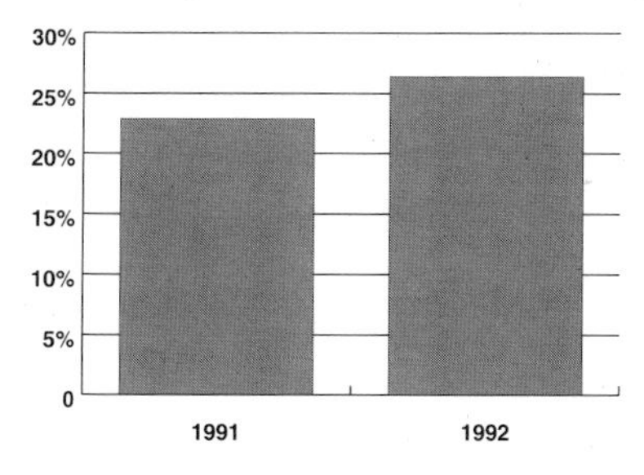

Cigarettes are the predominant type of tobacco used by women (97%). The types of tobacco used by men varies:

Types of Tobacco Used by Males

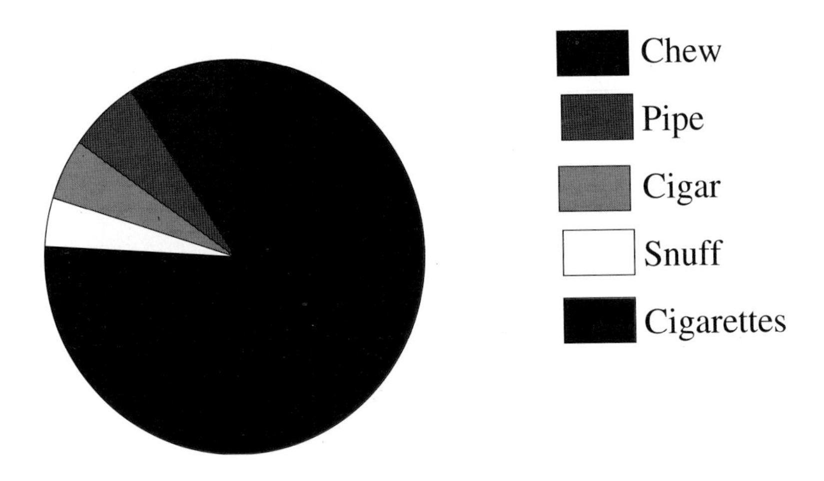

In a survey of smokers between 1987 and 1990, by the Office on Smoking and Health, CDC, smoking prevalence was 39.2% among blue collar workers, 24.2% among white-collar workers, and 34.5% among service workers.

By category of occupation, those that smoked the least, (5.5%–11.5%), were physicians, clergy, dentists, physical therapists, pharmacists, and elementary school teachers. Those that smoked the most, (51.8%–57.8%), were: roofers, crane operators, machine feeders, drywall installers, bartenders, and brick masons.

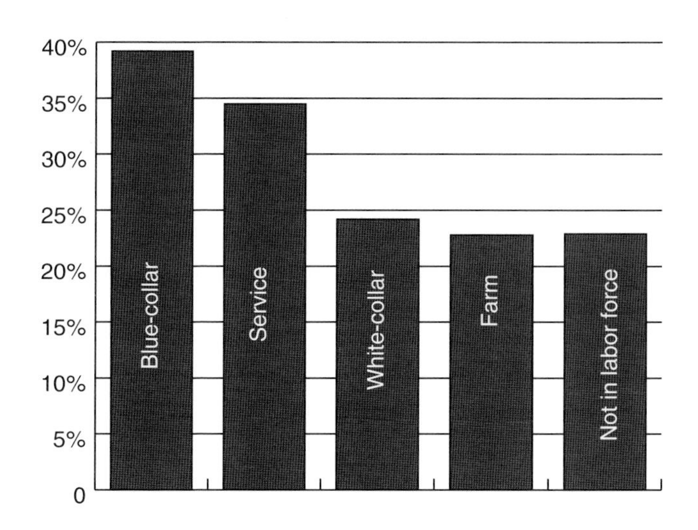

Smoking rates within ethnic groups has changed very little over the past decade. One point worthy of mention regarding smoking by race, education and sex is that Caucasian and African-American females with less than a high school education are taking up smoking at a faster rate than any other group. Smoking shows considerable variation among different races according to a 1992 survey:

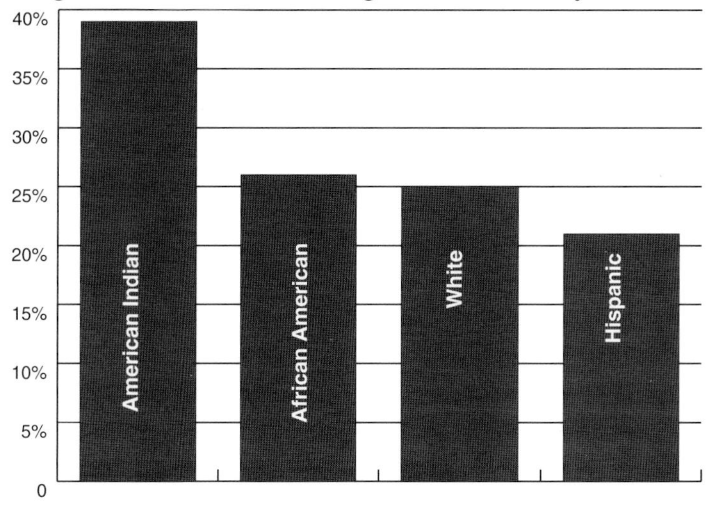

■■■■■■■■■■■■

The initiation of tobacco use starts in childhood. Congress has not stopped it. The tobacco companies can not be trusted to stop it. There is a solution to the problem that lies within the Federal Government–the FDA.

Approximately 104.5 million nonsmokers
are at risk of diseases caused by
passive smoking.

Chapter Sixteen

A Solution

The Food and Drug Administration was given power by the Federal Food, Drug and Cosmetic Act to regulate drugs. The FDA's definition of a drug is, "An article intended to affect the structure or function of the body, and it achieves this intended effects through chemical action within the human body."

Nicotine fits this definition of a drug. On August 2, 1994, an advisory panel to the FDA declared that nicotine is addictive. Testimony was heard that as few as five cigarettes a day could cause addiction in some people, and it was concluded that nicotine addiction is the major reason most people smoke.

> The FDA was given the power by the Federal Food, Drug and Cosmetic Act to regulate medical devices, such as instruments, machines, implants, pre-filled syringes, transdermal patches, and inhalers, whose primary purpose is the delivery of a drug. A drug delivery system delivers a drug into the body's circulatory system or to specific target sites in the body at predetermined, controlled rates.

Cigarettes and smokeless tobacco products fit this description of a drug delivery device. Prior to 1996, tobacco was classified as an agricultural product, not a drug. This allowed the tobacco industry to enjoy more liberties and fewer restrictions than the pharmaceutical industry. It also allowed them to sell a product that kills people when used as directed. The heart of the problem is cigarette safety is debated in Congress, which is controlled by tobacco lobbyists, and the representatives that take their money.

The FDA is the only government agency fully qualified to regulate tobacco. They don't take PAC money, and they can't accept meals or favors from the tobacco industry. Tobacco should be regulated fairly just like every other drug is today.

FDA Assures Drugs are Safe Before Approval

By law, all drugs must be proven safe before the FDA will approve it for use. Pharmaceutical companies prove their drugs are safe to doctors and drug scientists at the FDA. Drugs are put through rigorous testing for safety by clinical investigators. For the most part, with efficacy aside, the FDA assures that the cure will not be worse than the disease.

Rigorous drug testing is necessary, because often a drug will appear to be safe at first, but side-effects later develop, some lethal. We learned this through the tragic lessons of drugs like DES and thalidomide. In 1992, the FDA removed another drug from the market for safety reasons. A new antibiotic, temafloxacin, was approved because it looked safe in clinical trials. However, after it was approved, delayed adverse reactions appeared, killing six of the 174,000 patients that took it. The antibiotic was dangerous, and therefore was removed from the market. In contrast, tobacco kills 62,600 of every 174,000 smokers. Tobacco is 10,000 times more lethal. Notwithstanding, the killer antibiotic is banned, but tobacco is sold freely.

Tobacco is 10,000 times more lethal that the killer antibiotic that was banned.

The FDA's Legal Authority to Regulate Tobacco Products

The FDA has the legal authority and discretion to regulate cigarettes and tobacco as a drug, a drug delivery device, or as a combination drug/device. Under its 'drug' authority, cigarettes would have to be shown to be safe. In that case, tobacco products would be removed from the market. A ban on all tobacco products, however, is not the intention of the FDA. Therefore, cigarettes will not be regulated as a drug, but under its drug/device authority.

The FDA announced on July 12, 1995, that it was seeking approval from the White House to begin tobacco regulation. President Clinton signed the approval August 23, 1996. The director of the FDA, Dr. David Kessler M.D., approaches the regulation of tobacco sensibly—he does not want to ban tobacco.

FDA Tobacco Regulation Guidelines

The FDA's purpose is to reduce tobacco use by children and adolescents under the age of 18. The thrust of the proposal follows a two year investigation into children smoking, and will address this tragedy. A summary of the guidelines:

- The Federal minimum age for sale of tobacco is 18 years.
- Retailers are required to check the identification of the purchaser.
- Vending machines are prohibited only in areas accessible to minors, which excludes bars and nightclubs.
- Free samples, and self-service displays are prohibited.
- The sale of single cigarettes, or "kiddy packs" of less than 20 are prohibited.
- Outdoor advertising of tobacco products prohibited within 1000 feet of a school or playground.
- Advertising, outdoor billboards, transit, point of sale ads, must be in black and white only.
- Ads in teen publications must be text only, and contain a warning such as "About one in three kids who become smokers will die from their smoking."
- Promotional items, such as caps, shirts, bags, must not contain logos, brand names, or imagery.
- Advertising at events, such as entertainment or sport events, must be restricted to corporate name only.
- Manufacturers must fund a national public education campaign to prevent teenage tobacco use.

There are no provisions for a tobacco excise tax increase, new warning labels, or restrictions on environmental tobacco smoke. These issues will remain under control of Congress.

Finally, the FDA will review how effective these measures are at the end of seven years. If teen smoking and teen access to tobacco has not dropped 50% from the 1994 level, additional measures will be taken.

Kessler states that "The agency does not believe that the sudden and total withdrawal from the market would provide the best means of protecting the public health. A more reasonable approach is to focus on the problem of smoking where it begins—in young people."

The FDA's investigations found that nicotine in cigarettes and smokeless tobacco is a drug intended to affect the structure of the body, and achieves its intended effects through chemical action within the human body. In addition, cigarettes are drug delivery systems whose sole purpose is to deliver nicotine into the body in a manner in which it can be most readily absorbed by the consumer. Cigarettes are analogous to metered dose inhalers, says the FDA.

Thugs and Bullies Not Welcome

"Dr. Kessler is a thug and a bully."

- Newt Gingrich, House Speaker

Dr. Kessler needs the full backing of Congress to retain FDA jurisdiction of nicotine containing products. With the new Congress of 1995 that does not look likely. "Until Congress decides to change it's status," said Rep. Richard M. Burr, R-NC, "tobacco is a legal commodity." Rep. Howard Coble, R-NC said "I am getting annoyed by these efforts." Coble has taken $61,642 from the tobacco industry since 1985.

Another reason given for the criticism by the new GOP political powers is the length of time taken by the FDA to approve medical products. House Speaker Gingrich was prompt and outspoken in his criticism of the FDA for being too slow in approving "medical devices." Like most Congressional officials, Gingrich does not have the medical credentials to evaluate the safety of medical devices or drugs. It is no coincidence that some Congressmen considered taking away the FDA's authority to regulate medical devices. Technically speaking, cigarettes are medical devices.

When Dr. Kessler submitted his proposal to President Clinton on July 12, 1995, it bristled House Speaker Gingrich. He said the FDA has "Lost its Mind." What does Gingrich mean by that? Does he infer that the agency has gone amok, as he has said before? Or is it a threat, that if Kessler proceeds, he will be out of a job? Has Gingrich lost his concern for the health and welfare of the public in favor of some other incentive? Gingrich has taken a total of $53,750 from the tobacco industry as of December 31, 1995.

Will Congress Dismantle the Food and Drug Administration?

In 1980, U.S. Congressman Wendell Ford weakened the FTC to benefit the tobacco industry. How far will Congress go next? Will the tobacco states' representatives in Congress try to weaken the powers of the FDA? If the FDA is stripped of it's authority, tobacco products will continue to be sold as they always have been—with a few, weak regulations. This is the objective of the tobacco lobby.

Tobacco companies have the resources, money, and the support of many members of Congress, including Bob Dole. 124 House Members and 31 U.S. Senators have signed a letter to the FDA protesting the proposed tobacco regulations. Regardless of the reasons stated for dismantling, or weakening the powers of the FDA, representatives of Congress are motivated by the financial support of the tobacco industry. The average contribution from the tobacco industry to the representatives that oppose the FDA is $4,350, which is 69 times higher than contributions to those than support the FDA.

In June of 1996, Bob Dole said that cigarettes should not

be regulated by the Federal Government, rather it should be the states' responsibility. Dole has made it no secret that if he is elected president he will fire David Kessler from his FDA post. Mr. Dole says giving the FDA power to regulate tobacco is an "election gimmick," designed to divert the public's attention from the drug problem. Bob Dole has taken over $330,000 from tobacco companies during his political career.

At the end of 1995, there was a flood of bills introduced in Congress to stop the FDA. Three sponsors of bills that would prohibit the FDA from regulating tobacco, and the amount of tobacco money they have taken since 1986:

Wendell Ford (D-KY)	$76,057
Lewis Payne, (D-VA)	$92,899
Scotty Baesler, (D-KY)	$8,000

Greed Breeds Grief and Human Suffering

"Ethics, too, are nothing but reverence for life. That is what gives me the fundamental principle of morality, namely, that good consists in maintaining, promoting, and enhancing life, and that destroying, injuring, and limiting life are evil."

-Albert Schweitzer

If the Congress dismantles the FDA, drug safety, medical device safety, as well as tobacco will be in their hands. When it comes to evaluating these health issues, Congress is not qualified. Furthermore, their track record shows they are not responsible enough to regulate tobacco, much less medical products or drugs. When PAC money goes to Congress, they weave a web of protection around their interests. The health of the public goes down the drain, and they open the slippery slope to corruption. If Congress allows the pharmaceutical industry the same freedom they gave the tobacco industry, we can expect to see unregulated drugs like radioactive dog urine sold as a cure for the common cold. Congress will open up the public to risks when choosing a drug is equal to walking through the forest, randomly eating leaves from every plant.

From a practical point of view, should we trust a politician, lawyer, lobbyist, pharmaceutical representative, or a tobacco zealot, to tell us what medicines and medical devices are safe to use? Can you rely on yourself to personally evaluate the safety of an artificial heart? Do you trust your own judgment to determine if a new antibiotic is safe, and will not cause side effects such as interstitial nephritis, or disseminated intravascular coagulation? Do you feel safe taking untested herbs or food supplements? Will they interact with a prescription medication you are taking, or kill you because you have diabetes?

Tobacco Industry Files Suit to Stop FDA

In August 1995, five leading tobacco companies and an advertising agency filed an injunction to stop the FDA from regulating tobacco. This legal action is expected to drag out for years. The suit was filed in a United States District Court in North Carolina. The judge hearing the case is William L. Osteen Sr. Judge Osteen served as a tobacco lobbyist in 1974.

■ ■ ■ ■ ■ ■ ■ ■ ■ ■ ■ ■ ■

Seventy-five percent of Americans do not smoke. Yet nonsmokers' health is being harmed by tobacco smoke. Nonsmokers pocketbooks are picked to pay for smokers health care. How can you protect yourself from the White Serpent?

Our country is a democratic society. The consensus can break the grip the tobacco industry has on our country. When will the American people force the government to stop the needless deaths from tobacco? There are numerous proposals for tobacco reform in America.

Chapter Seventeen

Taking Control

There is no effective tobacco control to protect the public's health and safety in our country. It has been over 30 years since the first Surgeon General's report on tobacco and health. At that time, the Congress and the American people were made aware of a significant problem. Yet, the problem still exists today. A solution to the problem is long overdue. Several pro-health organizations have made recommendations to resolve this public health calamity.

The Coalition on Smoking OR Health, Washington, D.C.

The Coalition on Smoking OR Health is made up of three health agencies: The American Cancer Society, American Heart Association, and American Lung Association. Their recommendations:

THE PRESIDENT:

- Make all federal buildings smoke free.

FOOD AND DRUG ADMINISTRATION:

- Prohibit advertising and promotion of low-tar and low-nicotine products.
- Seek full regulatory authority over all tobacco products.

FEDERAL TRADE COMMISSION:

- Prohibit the Joe Camel advertising campaign.
- Prohibit advertisements that suggest certain tobacco products are safe, non-addictive, or as a way to lose weight.

JUSTICE DEPARTMENT:

- Prohibit brand-name sponsorship of televised sporting events by tobacco companies.
- Prohibit tobacco advertising at televised sporting events.

CONGRESS:

- Increase federal excise tax to $2.00 a pack.
- Use part of taxes collected to assist tobacco farmers to switch crops, pay for buy outs, or to retrain for other jobs.
- Prohibit smoking in public places, especially where there are children.

- Give the FDA full authority to regulate the manufacture, sale, distribution, advertising, and promotion of tobacco products.
- Enact educational reforms that include smoke-free schools, and education on the hazards of smoking and ETS.
- Authorize and appropriate money to the Department of Health and Human Services for paid advertising campaigns to counter tobacco advertising.

The American Medical Association

"The U.S. public has been duped by the tobacco industry."

-American Medical Association, July 19, 1995

The AMA, in July 1995, pledged steps to help eradicate tobacco related diseases. Highlights of the AMA's recommendations are listed below:

- Tobacco should be regulated by the FDA as a drug.
- All tobacco advertising should be eliminated, including advertising at televised sports events.
- Tobacco purchases should be strictly limited to adults.
- Tobacco excise taxes should be increased.
- OSHA should act to ban smoking in the workplace.
- Politicians should not accept money from the tobacco industry, and those that do should be publicly identified.
- Increase efforts to educate all on the health hazards of tobacco and addictive nature of nicotine.
- Researchers should not accept grants from the tobacco industry.
- Ban the export of tobacco to foreign countries.

Henry Waxman's Plan

Representative Henry Waxman, D-Cal, recommends a four step that will protect the public's health. The chief beneficiary of Mr. Waxman's plan are children.

- Pass a smoke-free environment law, prohibiting smoking in public.
- Raise the tax on tobacco to $2 a pack.
- Restrict cigarette advertising.
- Remove nicotine from cigarettes.

The Critical Issues

These four critical issues need your attention and support:

I. FDA regulation of tobacco products.

II. A 50 year ban all advertising, and promotion of tobacco products.

III. Increase the Tobacco Excise Tax $2.06 per pack.

IV. Prohibit smoking in all public places.

I. Support the FDA Regulation of Tobacco

Congress has failed for thirty years to protect the public. Ten million people have perished during that time. It is appropriate for the FDA to fully regulate tobacco products. Here again is a summary of what the FDA will do:

Reduce Teen Access to Tobacco by:

- Establishing a minimum age requirement of 18 years of age.
- Requiring retailers to check IDs (photo IDs only).
- Prohibiting vending machines where accessible to minors, and free tobacco samples.

- Prohibiting self-service displays to discourage shoplifting of cigarettes and smokeless tobacco.
- Prohibiting the sale of single cigarettes or "kiddy packs" of less than 20 cigarettes.

Curtail advertising directed at children, the number one reason kids smoke, by:

- Prohibiting outdoor advertising of tobacco products within 1000 feet of a school or playground.
- Requiring that advertising, outdoor billboards, bus, taxi, trains, point of sale ads, must be in black and white only.
- Requiring the warning "About one in three kids who become smokers will die from their smoking" in teen publications. They must be text only, no color cartoons or positive imagery.
- Requiring that promotional items, such as caps, shirts, bags, must not contain logos, brand names, or imagery.
- Restricting advertising at entertainment or sport events, to corporate name only.
- Require an education program to prevent children from smoking.
- Manufactures must fund national public education campaign to prevent teenage tobacco use.

There are no provisions for a tobacco excise tax, new warning labels, restrictions on environmental tobacco smoke, or a ban on tobacco.

Write your representatives in Congress at ask them to support the FDA's authority to regulate tobacco products.

II. A 50 Year Moratorium on Tobacco Advertising and a Plan Cigarette Pack Law.

The tobacco industry should lose the right to advertise forever, simply because they have exceeded all reason and decency—they promote cigarettes to children. Advertising encourages teens to use a product harmful to their health. For the sake of our future generation's health, steps must be taken. Rather than a permanent ban, a 50 year moratorium on all tobacco advertising and promotion is more appropriate and reasonable.

A 50 year ban will start the de-normalizing process of tobacco. Without the positive imagery of advertising, society's image of smoking will erode away. After all their tobacco advertisements are long forgotten, they could be allowed to resume advertising with these restrictions:

- Black and white print ads with no imagery, in publications read only by adults.
- No point of sale advertising.
- No cartoon advertising.
- No free sampling.
- No sponsorship of sports, cultural, or community events.
- No tobacco paraphernalia or promotional item giveaways.
- A plain-pack restriction.

PLAIN-PACK Restriction

Drug prescriptions come from the pharmacy in plane brown bottles with typed labels. Since nicotine is a drug, it should look like a drug. Glamorous, Madison Avenue cigarette packaging helps attract children. Lorillard Tobacco hired a promotion firm to design a new cigarette package, and in 1970 directed them to "design a package that is attractive to kids."

Enticing tobacco packages should be replaced with a plain white wrapper. Below is an example of what a plain cigarette pack would look like.

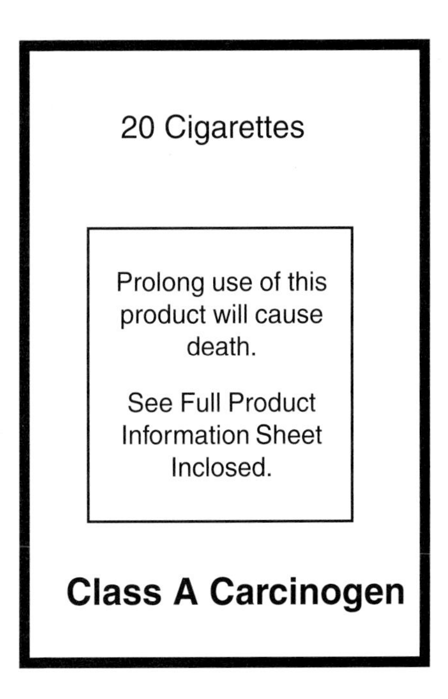

III. INCREASE the TOBACCO EXCISE TAX $2.06 per pack

The Tobacco Excise Tax is a Health Care Issue

A tobacco excise tax is a health care issue and not a new tax issue. In all fairness, smokers should pay a tobacco excise tax of $2.59 per pack. A per pack tax is fair because it is proportional to the amount of tobacco used, and to the health damage done to themselves and to those that breathe their secondhand smoke. And best of all, an increased excise tax will reduce smoking six percent, and save about 25,000 lives a year.

Other Ideas for the Increased Revenue from a $2.59 Tobacco Excise Tax.

- Pay for the $16 million annual tobacco subsidy.
- Replace tobacco industry funding of community activities, sporting events, and minority programs.
- Fund smoking cessation programs.
- Subsidize cancer insurance for smokers.
- Subsidize hospice care for terminally ill smokers.
- Buy pro-health television advertising that encourages smokers to quit, and to prevent teens from starting.

IV. Pass a Smoke-Free Environment Act to Accommodate 214 Million Nonsmoking Americans

Nonsmokers should be accommodated with a smoke-free environment in all public buildings. Today, nonsmokers do not have the freedom to move from public place to public place, in all 50 states, without being forced to breathe tobacco smoke. For all Americans to have equal protection from ETS in any city, and in any state, federal regulations are in order to protect individual rights.

A smoke-free environment act would also motivate about three to six percent of smokers to quit. A survey done by the National Bureau of Economic Research found that smoking among office workers dropped from 31% in 1985, to 26% in 1993. The decline in smoking was attributed to enforcement of no smoking policies in the workplace. Furthermore, workers who did not quit, cut back smoking ten percent. In those worksites that allow smoking, smokers there said they smoked an average 20.6 cigarettes a day. This means the workplace is still hazardous area for millions of workers. Without a uniform, national ban on smoking in public, the annual tobacco death toll will rise from 434,000 to 700,000 a year by the year 2000.

Where There's Smoke, There's Cancer!

You should not have to breathe any amount of ETS. If you want you and your family to stay healthy, your goal should be zero tolerance to ETS. Today's ways of separating smokers from nonsmokers to prevent drift is not a protective measure. As the white serpent coils it's way up, it becomes invisible. Sitting in a "no smoking" section is like opening an umbrella to protect yourself from a speeding bullet. Demand a smoke-free environment at the eating establishments that you frequent. Let restaurant managers know that you will not come back until smoking is not allowed.

Freedom and Rights for Nonsmoking Americans, for all Intents and Purposes, is the Freedom to Enter any Public Building in America and be Accommodated with a Smoke-Free Environment.

A Model Smoke-free Environment Act

An overriding concern for public health motivated six former Surgeon Generals of the U.S., as well as the EPA to speak in favor of a national smoke-free environment law. Representative Henry Waxman and Senator Frank Lautenberg introduced a Smoke Free-Environment Act (SFEA) in 1994.

The proposed bill was watered down and finally killed by the tobacco zealots when Rep. Thomas Bliley replaced Henry Waxman as chairman of the Subcommittee on Health and the Environment. Although it is not law today, it has the elements essential to protect the health of the public.

- A ban on smoking in all public buildings where over 12 persons visit in a week's time. (Including nicotine delivery devices of any kind, such as Eclipse.)
- Where smoking is permitted, smokers will be consolidated into smoking rooms, that have separate ventilation systems, vented to the outdoors.
- Enforcement will be administrated through federal district courts, with fines up to $5,000 a day for violations.

Experience has shown that in cities that have smoke free environment laws passed, there have been no arrests for violations. The public cooperates with widespread no smoking laws, as they do in elevators and in no smoking areas today. From a practical point of view, it will enforce itself. Requiring federal smoking police is a fantasy the tobacco industry used to cause fear among antigovernment concerns.

Restaurant owners will have the choice to prohibit smoking, or to build a smoking room. "A total smoking ban would be the cheapest way to go," says a spokesman for the Building Owners and Managers Association. A "no smoking sign" only costs a few dollars. This is a very inexpensive alternative to building a smoking room. Restaurant associations always resist this idea, arguing that restaurants will lose business. Research in cities with nonsmoking ordinances prove that these fears are unfounded. Smoke-free ordinances do not decrease restaurant sales. On the contrary, in some areas sales have increased.

An EPA report, written in 1994 by Dr. David H. Mudarri, an economist, outlined the cost saving of a national smoke-free law:

- Savings will range $39 to $72 billion annually.
- Cost $2.5 to $3.5 billion for enforcement, and smoking room construction.

The savings SFEA would bring will outweigh the costs, by a least $36 billion. SFEA would save businesses expenses in other ways. The major cause of building fires are cigarettes. This would improve safety and lower fire insurance costs. Building maintenance would be reduced $4 to $8 billion, because air filters, carpets and windows stay cleaner, and there would be no maintenance of ashtrays.

No Ban on the Sale of Tobacco!

It is important to note that none of the proposals in this chapter recommend a ban on tobacco. The proposed smoke-free environment law, and the FDA regulation guidelines are not attempts to ban the sale of tobacco. Banning tobacco is unreasonable and it would cause chaos. The "prohibition scare" is a tactic created by the tobacco industry, in an effort to enrage smokers and rally them together. Furthermore, the individual's right to smoke is respected. However limits must be placed on where they can smoke, and who pays for their health care. The right to smoke ends when smoke enters another persons lungs.

The Critical Issues: What Can You Do?

The Dilemma

You have made the decision not to smoke, like the majority of Americans. Yet, one nonsmoker dies from exposure to secondhand tobacco smoke every 6 ½ minutes. You don't smoke, but you pay taxes for smokers' health care. You don't buy tobacco, yet you pay taxes to subsidize tobacco. You don't want your children to smoke, but one teen starts smoking every 30 seconds. What is wrong with this ugly picture?

Most nonsmokers have no objection to adults that want to smoke. However, they do not want smoking to affect their own lives in such a dramatic way. People who have chosen not to smoke don't want to be killed or pay more taxes because someone else has chosen to smoke. Nonsmokers will not have peace, good health, freedom or rights they deserve until secondhand tobacco smoke and tobacco is under control.

The Government's Duty

The Federal Government protects you from ground glass and metal shavings in your food, and from *Salmonella* bacteria in your eggs or poultry. The government protects you from benzene and other harmful chemicals in the water supply. They protect you from asbestos and lead. They make efforts to protect you from being killed by a drunk driver, or by a terrorist attack. Yet they do little while secondhand smoke kills one person every six and one half minutes.

While the public slept, Congress failed to pass most of the 1,000 tobacco control bills proposed since 1964. They have given the tobacco industry the equivalent of hand slaps, and they have fed us pieces of candy as pacifiers. Our legislators were elected to represent the people of their districts. Above all, they should:

- **Represent the concerns of the people that elected them.**
- **Protect the public's health and safety.**

Congress has turned their backs on America for millions of dollars from the tobacco industry. For us to regain our right to be protected, and in the interest of public heath, we must circumvent the political and economic power blocs. Tobacco control must be removed from the hands of politicians.

Tell Your Representatives What You Want

Voters can break the economic and political power bloc the tobacco industry has had on Congress for over 30 years. Let your representatives know you will vote for the candidate that supports your position. Let them know your opinion and tell them how you want them to vote on tobacco issues. Write, call or fax your representatives in Congress, as well as the President, and tell them what you want.

Referendum

There is another path voters can take around the political stranglehold. The "one person one vote: the I'm mad as hell and I'm not going to take it any longer," attitude. Nonsmokers can take the movement directly over the heads of their politicians, and directly to the people.

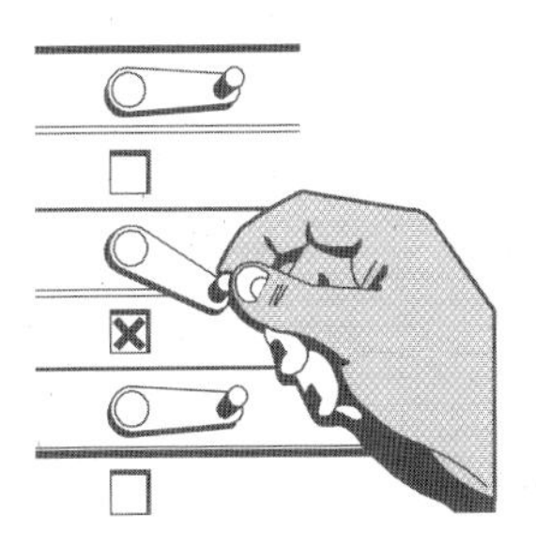

A citizen's ballot, a referendum, is as a form of direct democracy that circumvents the traditional political and economic power blocs. The voters enact legislation by voting yes to a proposition placed on the ballot at election time.

In a 1977 Gallup Poll, adults were asked if they favored a referendum:

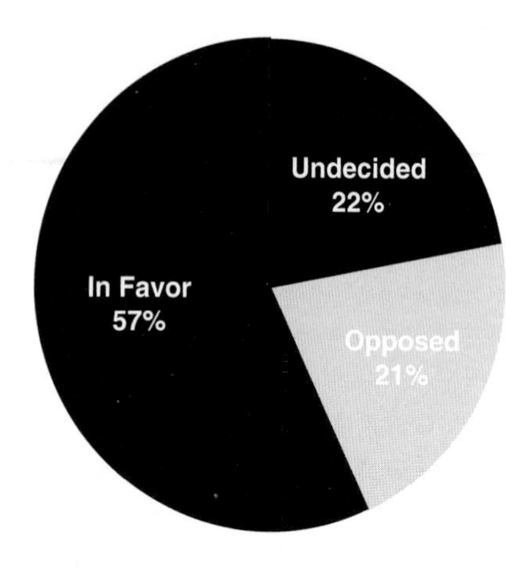

A referendum to pass antismoking laws may be an alternate approach for some states. Some types of referendum, or direct legislation are:

Referendum by popular petition: Voters file a petition demanding certain measures be adopted by the government; with a minimum number of signatures, the referendum must be held; majority wins.

Popular initiatives: Voters file a petition demanding certain measures which the government has not adopted, be referred to the voters. The petition contains the required number of valid signatures; if majority of voters are in favor, it becomes law.

From 1898 to 1977, about twenty-three states have had some kind of referendum.

State	Number	Percent Approved
California	159	27%
Colorado	119	35%
North Dakota	137	47%
Oregon	207	32%
Constitutional Amendments	539	35%
Statute Initiatives	685	38%

Proposition 99

A major antismoking referendum in California, Proposition 99, was approved by voters in November 1988. It increased tobacco taxes by 35 cents a package. Twenty percent of the tax was to be spent on smoking prevention and cessation advertising, smoking prevention programs, and education on the health hazards of smoking.

Proposition 99 has been successful in reducing the number of smokers by one million (smoking prevalence now 19.1%). The California Department of Health Services says they have saved $386 million in health care costs for treating tobacco related disease in 1993.

The year before the vote on Proposition 99, the tobacco industry spent $3.1 million on lobbying in California. Willie Brown, the current mayor of San Francisco, and former speaker of California's State Assembly, has collected over $646,000 from tobacco interests since 1980. Tobacco companies gave other political candidates and members of the state legislature $572,000. Other estimates were as high as $22 million spent in an effort to get Proposition 99 to fail. A referendum win, such as Proposition 99, is devastating to the tobacco cartel.

A National Referendum?

There has never been a referendum at the national level. A national referendum would be highly unlikely today. However, the issue has been considered in Congress. In 1977, Senator James Abourezk (South Dakota), introduced a bill in the Senate, proposing an amendment to the U.S. constitution under which most subjects could be set before the voters by popular petition.

The proposed amendment would require a minimum number of signatures: three percent of ballots cast in the most recent presidential election, and signed by three percent of voters in at least ten states. It, of course, excluded declaration of war or military action. If passed by popular vote, it would become law in thirty days. The law could be repealed by two thirds of Congress during first two years; and thereafter only by a majority of congress. Unfortunately, Abourezk's bill was defeated.

Join a Pro-Health Tobacco Control Advocacy Group

Support a pro-health tobacco control advocacy group. Join hands with others to form a wall between the tobacco pusher and your children. See the list of pro-health tobacco control advocate groups listed in Appendix H. They will provide you with information on the issues, what they are doing about it, and how you can help.

Local Tobacco Control Coalitions

Coalitions are groups of individuals and organizations

with similar pro-health interests that come together with a common goal. A group is more likely to achieve results that are difficult to achieve alone. Some of the major strategies of tobacco control advocacy coalitions today are:

- Raise the publics awareness about issues such as teen access to tobacco.
- Promote public policy to protect the health of the public — pass a local smoke-free ordinance.
- Prevent teen tobacco use.
- Promote tobacco cessation.

Coalitions have successfully accomplished all of these with the help of the American Cancer Society, American Heart Association, and American Lung Association. These organizations have established coalition guidelines and are happy to get involved. They generally can offer coalitions staff support, meeting facilities, secretarial support, and volunteer resources. Having the big three as coalition members makes it easier to get local hospitals, medical associations, school districts, health departments, health care professionals, and interested individuals to join.

If you are interested in joining a coalition, or want to help start one in your city, call your local American Cancer Society, and ask for the prevention director. See Appendix I, for an example of coalition bylaws.

Make a pledge now, in the memory of the ten million tobacco victims. Pledge in the name of your loved ones, your friends, or family members that have died prematurely from smoking. Help stop the pain and suffering. Speak out for those that can't speak, because they have lost their voice box to cancer. Protect your children from being seduced into nicotine addiction.

Make This Pledge in Honor of
the Ten Million Dead from Smoking.

I Pledge to Take this Action Today:

1. I will support the FDA regulation of tobacco.
2. I will support a federal smoke-free environment law, to make all public buildings and all workplaces smoke-free.
3. I will not allow my spouse, family member, or friend to smoke in my home.
4. I will protect my children from exposure to ETS, in public, in private, and in cars.
5. I will eat only at 100% smoke-free restaurants.
6. I will demand a $2.06 per pack increase in tobacco excise tax.
7. I will demand a 50 year moratorium on all tobacco advertising and promotion.
8. I will write my public officials about my demands. I will make my opinion heard in Congress.
9. I will join and support at least one pro-health tobacco control advocacy group.
10. I will encourage at least one person to stop smoking.

Signed______________________________

Date_______________________________

■ ■ ■ ■ ■ ■ ■ ■ ■ ■ ■ ■ ■ ■

Ten million Americans have needlessly died — poisoned. How many million more will suffer in pain and die before the tobacco epidemic is stopped? Stop the chemical warfare that is killing 83,000 innocent nonsmokers, including 3,700 infants every year. Put all your efforts into your pledge now, and help stop this crime in progress. Write a letter now.

Help get back America to who it belongs — the people. Stop the tobacco bullies that have bled away the power of the majority with dirty tobacco money. Let public officials know that profits do not justify the loss of one single human life.

Turn your back no longer!

Join the public outrage at those responsible for the seduction of children into a life of nicotine addiction at the rate of 3,000 a day. The volcanic pressure of public opinion is building.

Call your representatives in congress now.

If the FDA does not retain authorization to regulate tobacco, future generations of Americans will not be safe from the tobacco zealots. The death rate from tobacco will continue to rise. But you can help save millions of lives.

Let your voice be heard!

The public is outraged and is about to erupt! When the pressure can be held back no longer, you will hear the call to march in Washington— pack your bags!

It's time to fight back!

The street is my ashtray.

Epilogue

What if Cocaine Was Legal Today?

A suitable climate and proper soil conditions made tobacco a successful cash crop in American. In another part of the world, Peru's unique climate, altitude, and soil conditions made coca a successful cash crop there. In America, coca does not have the legal status, or the social acceptability of tobacco.

Consider what it would be like if the growing areas of these two plants were reversed—coca was grown in the U.S., and tobacco was grown in Peru. Would the legal status of each be reversed today? If history could be rewritten, would cocaine be a legally sold product, and tobacco an illicit, dangerous drug? Would cocaine be "normalized" in society like tobacco is today? If history was rewritten, the cocaine and tobacco issues could look this way today.

Since the early 1900's, coca leaves became an important cash crop in the U.S.. The only coca farms in the world were in America. 250,000 coca growers were dependent upon the coca leaf for their livelihood. Coca brings in four times more profit per acre than corn or wheat.

Coca was first introduced to the public in Coca-Cola, a popular, refreshing beverage. In 1906, the makers of Coke began using de-cocainized coca leaves in its production. However, the public continued to chew, smoke, and inhale cocaine.

Tobacco use, although less popular than cocaine, was on the increase. Since tobacco was grown only in Peru, it was expensive and in short supply. Tobacco was chewed and smoked by a small percentage of the American population. Tobacco users were called nicotine fiends. The smoke from tobacco was intolerable to other people. Tobacco was a health hazard, the cause of cancer, heart disease and death.

In 1914, the *Harrison Narcotic Act* classified tobacco as a drug. Possession or sale of tobacco was subject to fines and jail terms. Tobacco continued to be smuggled and illegally sold in America. On the other hand, coca slipped by the Harrison Act because little was known about it. Coca was classified as an agricultural product, not a drug. No one had any concern about cocaine's harmful effects or its habit forming properties.

The cocaine cartel launched a major advertising campaign that made cocaine use normal. By 1950, almost half of all adults in America used it. Advertising was responsible for creating a respectable image for cocaine. Imaging was used to associated it with good health, vigor, beauty, popularity, and independence. Cocaine quickly became as American as apple pie. Children were targeted with cartoon advertising. Cocaine became the most successfully marketed product in U.S. history.

In 1964, the Surgeon General's report revealed to the public for the first time the hazards of cocaine. Cocaine, inhaled over long periods of time erodes nasal passages, causes heart attacks, strokes, induces psychosis, and causes physiological dependence. Chewing the leaves erodes the gums. Cocaine killed about 20,000 people each year. The burden on the health care system from cocaine abuse was $5 billion a year.

Cocaine was addictive—46 million people used it. Most used it once or twice a day, and some as often as five to ten times a day. Users were spending from $2.50 to $12.00 a day on the cocaine habit. Teens were taking up the coca chew at the rate of 3,000 a day. Cocaine was readily available in vending machines everywhere.

The cocaine zealots—the coca growers, and cocaine manufactures, overlooked the deaths from cocaine. Political campaign financing relied heavily on cocaine PAC money, which made the cocaine industry a very powerful influence in Congress.

Publicly, the cocaine industry denied the health hazards, and the addictive power of cocaine—while in private, they openly discussed cocaine's hazards, addictiveness, and how to overcome those objections.

The Cocaine Institute became the propaganda arm of the cocaine industry. They denied that cocaine was addictive or that it had any health consequences. Massive promotional and advertising campaigns were used to sweeten the public's eroding image of them. To create an image associated with decency and good health, they sponsored the arts, sporting events, and other cultural activities. The Cocaine Institute was a den of misinformation and false statements.

Anti-cocaine forces started applying pressure to halt the advertising and promotion of cocaine, and its sale to children. Cocaine was often compared to smoking tobacco, which is as addictive as cocaine, but very toxic, and causes a high rate of cancer, heart disease and death.

There was an imbalance of coca interests in Congress. Only ten percent of the 531 Congressional districts grew coca. However, coca zealots controlled Congress. Congressional representatives, from the major coca growing states, and cocaine zealot lobbing efforts were able to fend off all attempts at cocaine regulation. Cocaine was classified as an agricultural product, not a drug. Therefore, cocaine was not regulated. From 1964 to 1994, over 1,000 major bills attempting to regulate cocaine were defeated. Bills to regulate advertising, promotion, to require adequate health warnings, and to curtail sales of cocaine to children were defeated. The government even subsidized the coca farmers crops.

When the FTC tried to regulate cocaine, the Congress crippled its powers. The FDA now wanted to regulate cocaine, but was met with great political resistance. The cocaine zealots were prepared to dismantle the FDA. They maintained that coca was a natural product, and everyone's individual right to use it. The cocaine zealots had the support of 250,000 motivated coca growers, and 46 million addicted coca users.

A reporter, Al Taylor, interviewed the Cocaine Institute's spokesman, Barry Sharp. Al had been an acquaintance of Barry for ten years. Barry Sharp was from North Carolina. He was a middle aged gentleman with silver hair, and an amenable manor. His trademark was a lump of coca chew in his cheek. He was adorned with a gold cocaine spoon around his neck. His office was decorated with symbols of the divine coca plant. He had lobbied Congress for 25 years. He was golf buddies with many senators. The Cocaine Institute donated large sums of money to their reelection campaigns, and they gave larger sums to the senators' wives favorite charities. They gave over $400,000 to a presidential candidate.

The Interview

AT: Mr. Sharp, the cocaine industry has been accused of deceptive advertising, and failing to disclose adequate health warnings. Cocaine causes heart attacks, stroke, and is addictive. The past six Surgeon Generals have called for a ban on all coca products. Many are calling for a cocaine-free society by the year 2000. What is the future of cocaine in America?

BS: Al, from the beginning of American history, cocaine has been part of it. It helped finance the American revolution, and helped build our new nation. There have been anti-cocaine zealots around since then, with their moral opposition to cocaine. The prudes unfairly called it "white death," and users were called "coca fiends." But the colonist continued to grow and chew coca as a part of their free choice—cocaine became a tradition.

The anti-cocaine zealots think their world should be the way it ought to be. They are calling for a ban by year 2000—that's a fool's paradise. They say this nonsense to get in the newspapers. It is just not going to happen. No cocaine today, what tomorrow—no sugar, no salt, no french fries, no red meat—where does it end? It's a slippery slope to prohibition. Forty-six million adults use coca today because they want to. Prohibition did not work in 1920, and it will not work in the 1990's. A utopian world without cocaine will come only with the loss of our precious freedom, the freedom of choice—to use cocaine. That is paradise lost.

AT: Consumer groups are concerned today that the cocaine industry is not properly disclosing the health hazards of cocaine. When are you going to give full disclosure?

BS: Everyone knows cocaine is bad for you. The federal government requires a statement on each package, (he holds up a pack): "Don't use it very much, it might not be good for your health. Contains sugar." You see Al, we are in compliance with all federal government regulations.

AT: That's not an adequate warning. The heart of the matter is that cocaine has been shown to be a habit forming drug, as addictive as heroin, alcohol or nicotine. It has been called as addictive as tobacco by the Surgeon General. Cocaine is used by 46 million Americans, and that is a lot of customers for something your industry claims is not addictive. What is your position? Is cocaine addictive?

BS: I deny that cocaine is addictive. Anti-cocaine zealots want to make us feel guilty, like drug addicts. There is a big difference between the executive that enjoys a snort of cocaine after lunch, or a coca chew in the morning with coffee, and the tobacco smoker. Smokers must feed their addiction as often as every 30 minutes, and they die of cancer and heart attacks. No one has ever been arrested for driving while intoxicated on coca. Unlike tobacco, coca only affects the user. Tobacco kills those that breath the smoke around them too.

AT: Surveys say that most cocaine users want to quit but can not. Only 30% are able to quit. If cocaine was not addictive, it would be easy for all to quit. Don't you think that spells addiction Barry?

BS: Thirty of every hundred cocaine customers have easily quit using cocaine. Nicotine is very addictive, and is very difficult to quit. By comparison, only two or three of 100 tobacco junkies are able to quit smoking. My goodness, there is no comparison between a hard drug like nicotine and cocaine. The cocaine habit is more like enjoying a snack, eating cookies, or drinking a cup of coffee. People use cocaine because they enjoy it. No, cocaine is no more addictive than buttermilk.

AT: Cocaine is blamed for 20,000 deaths every year. How do you explain that if cocaine is not harmful?

BS: That is a computer generated number. No one has proven cocaine is harmful, or causes heart attacks. If tobacco were used by 46 million people today, over 400,000 would die every year. No one has ever gotten cancer from the cocaine habit.

AT: What cocaine death figure would you agree on?

BS: Al, coca products have been accused of killing people, so what else is new?

AT: The additives in cocaine have never been tested for safety. Two are known carcinogens. Doctors say coca chew is the cause of oral cancer.

BS: We have tested the additives we use, and they are safe. We add them to chew for flavor. Coca is a natural product. I am not convinced that cocaine causes death. Coca has not been proven in a court of law, or by the Congress to cause oral cancer. The judges and the juries have always agreed with our position, cocaine does not cause cancer. My grandmother lived to be 95, and she chewed coca all her adult life. Besides, everyone has to die sometime.

Our industry today represents over 280,000 Americans. We are proud of our industry, our people, and our coca products. We make the best cocaine money can buy.

AT: Mr. Sharp, the cocaine cartel has been accused of targeting children in their advertising for cocaine use. Three thousand teens a day start using coca chew. They use the most heavily advertised brand—White as Snow. It looks like bubble gum. The cartoon horse, Cocaine Charlie, appeals to children. Recent studies prove that Cocaine Charlie advertisements seduce children into cocaine addiction.

BS: If I thought that Cocaine Charlie ads made children use cocaine I would pull it in a heart beat, but our research shows that it does not. Besides, I have never seen an advertisement that made someone buy something they did not want. Our advertising is effective in getting adults already using another cocaine brand to use White as Snow. Our studies show that children do not use cocaine, therefore we are not responsible for a program to stop them from using it.

AT: The FDA is calling for a ban on advertising and promotion of coca.

BS: This is another attempt of the anti-cocaine zealots to ban cocaine. Cocaine is a legally sold product. Banning advertising of a legally sold product would be a violation of the freedom of speech that the Constitution guarantees. The FTC has tried this before and failed.

AT: Thanks to your cocaine cartel, the FTC has weaker powers now to protect the public. But the FDA does have the power to regulate cocaine now that it has been reclassified as a drug. Some say you are out of luck.

BS: Out of luck—it's not over until the fat lady sings Al. Cocaine is not a drug—it's more like caffeine. Coca is fully regulated now, from seed bed to chew and snort powder. The FDA has blown this out of proportion—as another political move toward backdoor prohibition. The FDA, like the FTC gets its power from Congress too, and as you know, Congress is not a problem.

Off the record Al, we have had the Congress in our pocket for 30 years. We own the Republican party, and we are going to own the next Republican president. Election campaigns costs lots of money, and we have deep, deep pockets. You have to spend the dollars to get elected, and politicians know they can count on us for a large contribution. Banning cocaine advertising is just not going to happen. The FDA is on a witch hunt, and we are going to have Congress dismantle the agency. We have 40 bills in Congress to kill the FDA right now. And we have all gotten together and we are suing the tar out of the government. Those damned FDA thugs, I'm going to get the director put on the gonorrhea detail in Detroit.

AT: Mr. Sharp, are you confident that you will continue to operate as usual, despite a new barrage of accusations, cover-ups, and a Justice Department investigation. Is there anything that poses a threat to your industry's viability?

BS: What the anti-cocaine people do not understand, and it's good for us they don't, is that the biggest threat is how people vote. If they vote for the candidate who takes the position to ban cocaine advertising, and to give the FDA the power to regulate cocaine as a drug, we are dead in the water.

When these anti-cocaine zealots' activities go through normal channels, lobbing, grass roots organizations, rallying, they are of no threat. They have been doing that for 30 years, and we are still in business. These radical social engineers are more like a pesky gnat flying around your face on a summer day.

But if they ever take the matter over the heads of the politicians, we are in deep doodoo. An initiative, a referendum to ban advertising, or anything that would take the control of cocaine out of the hands of politicians and into the hands of the voters, would surely bring our house down.

AT: Cocaine users are outnumbered by three to one, they are in the minority. Non-cocaine users could make some changes. There will come a time when they are going to get mad as hell and not take it any more.

BS: We have controlled the public in numerous ways in the past. Every time the public's blood boils, we give in an inch—we agree to add this little warning, we agree not to advertise at ball games on television, or we send out messages that cocaine is not for kids—it's an adult pleasure. That cools them down. We find other ways to advertise, and it's business as usual. Our latest scheme is workin' better that we ever expected. This Government intervention thing we dug up from the 1960's Roper report is working miracles for us Al, and Congressmen are helping.

Human nature is on our side because most people don't have the motivation to vote. Some people don't care, they have other problems in their lives. Some just don't care enough to do a damn thing about it. Most don't really know what is going on.

Forty-six million happy cocaine customers make a highly motivated group of individuals. When we hold a rally in DC, all we have to do is announce "no more cocaine," and the growers, users, the whole industry marches. They know we will help protect their basic American rights.

AT: Yes, but you are getting richer, at the cost of people dying.

BS: Profits at the sacrifice of human lives? You break my heart. Using cocaine is a risk—skydiving is a risk; bungee jumpin' is a risk. Adults have the right to pursue risky activities. People take chances everyday from being killed by some fool driving down the middle of the highway. Why don't you go after the automobile industry?

AT: They don't sell defective cars that cause 20,000 preventable deaths a year. They don't target children with reckless driving cartoons that say "Driving reckless is sexy—floor it!" They practice responsible marketing, something you do not do.

BS: Watch your mouth son. I can appreciate your concern. Relax. Live and let live. Enjoy life, take some risks. Here, have a little bump. Got time for a round of golf?

End of interview.

You may deceive all the people part of the

time, and part of the people all the time,

but not all the people all the time.

Abraham Lincoln

Bibliography

Chapter one:

Brecher, E.M., and Editors of Consumer Union, Licit and illicit drugs, Consumers Union, New York, 1972.

Collier's Encyclopedia, P.F. Collier, Inc., 1993.

Fredman, Alix M., and L.P. Cohen, "How cigarette maker keep health question 'open' year after year," The Wall Street Journal, February 11, 1993.

Goodman and Gilman's, The pharmacological basis of therapeutics, Macmillian Publishing Co., Inc., New York, 1980, A.G. Gilman, et al, editors.

Hwang, S.L., "Filter bits may lodge in smokers' lungs," The Wall Street Journal, Jan.13, 1995.

Jacobson, B., The ladykillers-why smoking is a feminist issue, Continuum, New York, 1981.

Robert, Joseph C., The story of tobacco in America, The University of North Carolina Press, Chapel Hill, 1967.

Russell, M.A.H,. "The nicotine addiction trap: a 40-year sentence for four cigarettes," British J. Addiction, Vol. 85, 1990, pg. 293-300.

Slade, John, "The tobacco epidemic: lessons from history," J. Psychoactive Drugs, Vol. 24, no.2, Apr-Jun, 1992, pg. 99-109.

"Smoking, Tobacco and Health -A fact book," U.S. Department of Health and Human Services, 1989, DHHS Publication No. (CDC) 87-8397.

Taylor, P., The Smoke Ring, Pantheon Books, New York, 1984.

The Wall Street Journal, March 8, 1994.

Wagner, Susan, Cigarette Country-Tobacco in American History and Politics, Praeger Publishers, New York, 1971.

White, Larry C., Merchants of Death-The American Tobacco Industry, Beech Tree Books, W. Morrow and Co., New York, 1988.

Wynder, E.L., and E.A. Grahn, "Tobacco smoking as a possible etiologic factor in bronchiogenic carcinoma," JAMA, Vol. 143 no. 4, May 27, 1950, pg. 329-338.

Chapter two:

"Cancer facts & figures— 1995," American Cancer Society, Jan, 1995.

Carter, Jimmy, "A healthy tobacco tax could help farmers too," The Houston Chronicle, February 11, 1994.

"Executive Pay," The Wall Street Journal, April 11, 1996, R17.

Glantz, S.A., D. E. Barnes, L. Bero, P. Hanauer, and J. Slade. "Looking through a keyhole at the tobacco industry: The Brown and Williamson Documents," JAMA, Vol. 274, No. 3, July 19, 1995, pg. 219—224.

Hilts, P.J., "Tobacco firm knew of cigarette dangers in 1964,' The Houston Chronicle, May 8, 1994.

Levy, D., "Horrible price paid for not knowing," USA Today, May 19, 1994.

Levy, D., "Tobacco firms knew of dangers," The Houston Post, June 6, 1994.

Mooshil, J., "Marlboros for export that land in U.S. are spelling trouble," The Wall Street Journal, May 16, 1994.

Naj, A. K., "Tobacco has new role: medicine factory," The Wall Street Journal, May 12, 1994.

Peto, R, A.D. Lopez, J. Borehan, M. Thun, and C. Heath, Jr., "Mortality from tobacco in developed countries: indirect estimation from national vital statistics," The Lancet, Vol. 339, 1992, pg. 1268—1278.

Slade, John., L. Bero, P. Hanauer, D.E. Barnes, and Stanton. A. Glantz. "Nicotine and Addiction: The Brown and Williamson Documents," JAMA, Vol. 274, No. 3, July 19, 1995, pg.. 225—233.

Smothers, Ronald, "After year of despair, tobacco farmers enjoy prospect of better times," The New York Times, December 15, 1994.

Taylor, P., The Smoke Ring, Pantheon Books, New York, 1984.

The Tampa Tribune, April 26, 1994.

White, Larry C., Merchants of Death, Beech Tree Books, New York, 1988.

Chapter three:

Collins, Glenn, "Group seeks a reopening of hearings on tobacco," The New York Times, June 13, 1995.

Collins, Glenn, "Legal attack on tobacco intensifies," The New York Times, June 9, 1995.

Collins, Glenn, "Tobacco firm announces recall of faulty cigarettes -Chemical contaminants found in filters," The New York Times, May 26, 1995.

Davis, R., "No longer David vs. Goliath," USA Today, May 19, 1994.

Fisher, Ian, "Tobacco funds go to black officials," The New York Times, November 19, 1995 A21.

Freedman, Alix M., "Philip Morris memo likens nicotine to cocaine," The Wall Street Journal, December 8, 1995, B1.

Glantz, S.A., D.E. Barnes, L. Bero, P. Hanauer, and J. Slade. "Looking through a keyhole at the tobacco industry: The Brown and Williamson Documents," JAMA, Vol. 274, no. 3, July 19, 1995, pg. 219-224.

Hilts, P.J., "U.S. turning to grand juries to scrutinize tobacco industry," The New York Times, July 26, 1995, A1.

Neergaard, Lauran, "Tobacco company chewed over idea for nicotine candy," The Houston Chronicle, August 22, 1995, 6A.

Novak, Viveca, and A.M. Freedman, "Tobacco industry facing 2 criminal investigations," The Wall Street Journal, July 25, 1995, A3.

Robison, Clay, "Texas Democrats to refuse money from tobacco concerns," The Houston Chronicle, June 11, 1996, 19A.

Schwarts, John, "UCSF battling tobacco firm," The Washington Post, February 26, 1995.

"Seven congressmen seek federal inquiry into tobacco makers," The Houston Chronicle, May 28, 1994.

Slade, J., L. Bero, P. Hanauer, D.E. Barnes, and S.A. Glantz. "Nicotine and Addiction: The Brown and Williamson Documents," JAMA, Vol. 274, no. 3, July 19, 1995, pg. 225-233.

U.S. Public Interest Research Group, March 96, 1996.

Chapter four:

"A Study of public attitudes towards cigarette smoking and the tobacco industry in 1978," May 1978, Ed. Roper Organization, 1978, 1.

ASH Smoking and Health Review, Vol. XXIII, No. 6, Nov-Dec 1993.

ASH Smoking and Health Review, Vol. XXV, No 3, May-June 1995

Barro, R.J., "Send regulations up in smoke," The Wall Street Journal, June 3, 1994.

Barron's, May 16, 1994.

Blum, Alan, "Sounding Board, The Marlboro Grand Prix: Circumvention of the television ban on tobacco advertising," NEJM, Vol. 324, no. 13, March 28, 1991, pg.. 915-916.

Collins, Glenn, "Big advertising company bars billboard ads for tobacco," The New York Times, May 3, 1996, C19.

Department of Health and Human Services, Public Health Service. "Preventing tobacco use among young people," a report of the Surgeon General, Washington, D.C.: Government Printing Office, 1994.

Editors note, The Houston Chronicle, January 8, 1989/

Elliott, Stuart, "Advertising," The New York Times, April 10, 1996.

Elliott, Stuart, The New York Times, March 21, 1995.

Feder, Barnaby J., The New York Times, December 17, 1995, pg. 4-2.

Federal Trade Commission, "Report to Congress for 1993, pursuant to the Federal Cigarette Labeling and Advertising Act," 1995.

Federal Trade Commission. "Report to Congress pursuant to the Federal Cigarette Labeling and Advisory Act of 1992," Washington, D.C.: GPO, (1994):3.

"Former Marlboro Man Dies," The Houston Chronicle, October 21, 1995.

Fredman, Alix M., and L.P. Cohen, "How cigarette maker keep health question 'open' year after year," The Wall Street Journal, February 11, 1993.

Hazan, A. R., H.L. Lipton, and Stanton A. Glantz, "Popular films do not reflect current tobacco use," AJPH, Vol. 84, no. 6, 1994, pg. 998-1000.

Helyer, J., "Signs sprout at sports arenas as a way to get cheap TV advertising," The Wall Street Journal, March 8, 1994.

Hwang, Suein L., "Philip Morris agrees to stop placing ads in view of TV," The Wall Street Journal, June 7, 1995.

Hwang, Suein L., "RJR unit tightens rules on distribution of cigarette samples-proof of age requirement precedes a TV broadcast on easy access to minors," The Wall Street Journal, November 3, 1995.

Hwang. Suein L., "Teenage smoking on rise, particularly among the youngest, U.S. study finds," The Wall Street Journal, July 20, 1995

Jacobson, B., The ladykillers-why smoking is a feminist issue, Continuum, New York, 1981.

JAMA, October 28, 1950 , pg. 49.

Jouzaitis, Carol, "Teen smoking soars," The Houston Chronicle, July 20, 1995.

Krauthammer, Charles, "Why single out smoking as target for repression," The Houston Chronicle, June 12, 1994.

Mahaney Jr., F. X., "Old-time ads tout health benefits of smoking: Tobacco industry had doctors' help," Journal of the National Cancer Institute, Vol. 86, No. 14, 1994, pg. 1048-1049.

"Marlboro Man is dead," The Houston Chronicle, July 24, 1992.

MMWR, Vol. 43, no. 19, May 20, 1994, pg. 341-346.

MMWR, Vol. 39, no. 16, 1990

New York Times, May 5, 1996.

Noah, Timothy, "Al Gore criticizes comments by Dole concerning the health risks of tobacco," The Wall Street Journal, June 18, 1996, B11.

Ono, Yumiko, "RJR's new ad campaign: It's hip to smoke," The Wall Street Journal, April 16, 1996, B1.

Roberts, S.V., and T. Watson, "Teens on tobacco," U.S. News & World Report, April 18, 1994.

Salinger, Pierre, "After we persecute smokers, who's next?," USA Today, November, 1994.

Schelling, T.C., "Addictive Drugs: the Cigarette Experience," Science, Vol. 255, 1992, pg. 430-433.

"Showdown on Tobacco Road," a film by David Hoffman , Kirk Wolfinger, Produce by Terri Randall, written by Harvey Ardman, Varied Directions, 1987.

Sullen, J., "Just how bad is secondhand smoke?," National Review, May 16, 1994.

Taylor, P., The Smoke Ring, Pantheon Books, New York, 1984

Tee, J.B., "Cigarette ads in kid's movies," Tobacco Youth Reporter, Vol. 4, no.1, 1989, pg. 1-2.

Thurow, R., R. Thompson, and K. Goldman, "Ban on tobacco ads might stall auto racing," The Wall Street Journal, August 14, 1995, B1.

The Wall Street Journal, April 29, 1994.

The Wall Street Journal, May 19, 1994.

Warner, K.E., et al, "Cigarette advertising and magazine coverage of the hazards of smoking," NEJM, Vol. 326, no. 5, pg. 305.

White, Larry C., Merchants of Death, Beech Tree Books, New York, 1988.

Yoder, Edwin M., "'War on cigarettes' would give criminals another illegal drug to fight over," The Houston Chronicle, April 6, 1994.

Chapter five:

Aloise-Young, P.A., J.W. Graham, and W.B. Hansen, "Peer influence on smoking initiation during early adolescence: a comparison of group members and group outsiders," J. Applied Psychology, Vol. 79, no. 2, 1994, pg. 281-287.

JAMA, Oct. 14, 1950, pg. 63.

Brody, Jane. E., "Study links ads to 60's-era smoking," The New York Times, February 23, 1994.

CDC Editorial, "Minors' access to cigarette vending machines-Texas," MMWR, 1994; Vol. 43, pg. 625-627.

CDC, "Changes in the cigarette brand preferences of adolescent smokers-United States, 1989-1993," MMWR, Vol. 43,1994, pg. 577-581.

CDC, "Trends in smoking initiation among adolescents and young adults- United States, 1986-1989," MMWR, Vol. 44, No. 28, July 21, 1995, pg. 521-524.

Center for Disease Control, MMWR, Vol. 39, 1990, pg. 261-265.

"Cigarette ads lure young, study says," The New York Times, April 4, 1996, A15.

"Cigarette Smoking Among Adults, U.S., 1993," MMWR, Vol. 43, 1994, pg. 925-930.

Department of Health and Human Services, Public Health Service, "Preventing tobacco use among young people, a report of the Surgeon General, Washington, D.C.: Government Printing Office, 1994.

DiFranza, J.R, and J.B. Tye, "Who profits tobacco sales to children?," JAMA, Vol. 263, no. 2, pg. 2785-2786, 1990.

DiFranza, J.R., J.A. Savageau, and B.F. Aisquith, "Youth access to tobacco: The effects of age, gender, vending machine locks, and 'It's the Law' programs," AJPH, Vol. 86, no.2, February 1996, pg. 221-224.

DiFranza, J.R., J.W. Richards Jr, P.M. Paulman, et al, "RJR Nabisco's cartoon camel promotes camel cigarettes to children," JAMA, Vol. 266, no. 22, 1991, pg. 3149-3153.

Document no 89: Imperial Tobacco Ltd. and R.J. Reynolds-MacDonald Inc. v Le Procurer General du Canada, Quebec Superior Court, 1990.

Evans, N. et al., "Influence of tobacco marketing and exposure to smokers on adolescents susceptible to smoking," J. of the National Cancer Institute, Vol. 87, No. 20, October 18, 1995, pg. 1538-1545.

Feder, Barnaby J., "Increase in teenage smoking sharpest among black males," The New York Times, May 24, 1996.

Fischer, P. M., M. P. Schwartz, J. W. Richards, A. O .Goldwstein, and T. H. Rojas, "Brand logo recognition by children aged 3 to 6 years — Mickey Mouse and Old Joe the Camel," JAMA, Vol. 266, no. 22, December 11, 1991, pg 3134-3148.

Freedman, Alix .M., E. Jensen, and A. Stevens, "CBS legal guarantees to '60 minutes' source muddy tobacco story," The Wall Street Journal, November 16, 1995. A1.

George H. Gallup International Institute, "Teenage attitudes and behavior concerning tobacco: report of the findings," Princeton, New Jersey: George H. Gallup International Institute, 1992.

Gilpin, E.A, L. Lee, N. Evans, and J.P. Pierce, "Smoking initiation rates in adults and minors: united States, 1944-1988," Amer. J. Epidemiology, Vol. 140, no. 6, pg. 535-543.

Hilts, Philip J., "Ads linked to smoking by children-new studies dispute industry arguments," The New York Times, October 18, 1995.

Hilts, Philip J., " Study Finds Tobacco ads nearer schools-California survey say promotion are often place near candy," The New York Times, August 3, 1995, A11.

Hilts, Philip J., "Survey finds surge in smoking by young," The New York Times, July 20, 1995.

The Houston Chronicle, November 5, 1995.

The Houston Post, January 23, 1994

Hwang, Suein L., "Study links rise in teen smoking to ad spending," The Wall Street Journal, July 21, 1995.

Hwang. Suein L., "Teenage smoking on rise, particularly among the youngest, U.S. study finds," The Wall Street Journal, July 20, 1995

Kessler, David A., "Nicotine addiction in young people," NEJM, Vol. 333, no. 3, July 20, 1995, pg. 186-189.

Levin, Myron, "States not enforcing bands on tobacco sales to kids, study finds," The Houston Chronicle, April 26, 1995.

Memorandum: J. P. McMahon, Divisional Manager, RJR Sales Co., 1-10-90, in: Kessler, David A., "Nicotine addiction in young people," NEJM, Vol. 333, no. 3, July 20, 1995, pg. 186-189.

Memorandum: R.G. Warlick, Division Manager, RJR Reynolds, 4-5-90. in: Kessler, David A., "Nicotine addiction in young people," NEJM, Vol. 333, no. 3, July 20, 1995, pg. 186-189

MMWR, May 20, 1994, Vol. 43, no. 19, pg. 341-346.

Noah, Timothy, " Study says minors respond more to cigarette ads than do adults," The Wall Street Journal, April 4, 1996, B1, in the *Journal of Marketing*, April 1996.

Noah, Timothy, "Cigarettes are sold on Internet Web sites," The Wall Street Journal, January 24, 1996, B1.

Ono, Yumiko, "Ads do push kids to smoke, study suggests," The Wall Street Journal, October 18, 1995.

Patton, G. C, M. Hibbert, M.J. Rosier, J.B. Carlin, J. Caust, and G. Bowes, "Is smoking associated with depression and anxiety in teenagers?," AJPH, Vol. 86, no. 2, February 1996, pg 225-230.

Pierce, J.P, and E. Gilpin, "How long will today's new adolescent smokers be addicted to cigarettes?," American Journal of Hospital Pharmacy, Vol. 86, no. 2, February 1996, pg. 253-256.

Pierce, J.P., E. Gilpin, D.M. Burns, E. Whalen, B. Rosbrook, D. Shopland, and M. Johnson, "Does tobacco advertising target young people to start smoking?," JAMA, Vol. 266, no 22, pg. 3154-3158.

Pierce, J.P., L. Lee, and E.A. Gilpin, "Smoking initiation by adolescent girls, 1944 through 1988," JAMA, Vol. 271, no 8, pg. 608-611, February 23, 1994.

Raeburn, Paul, "Study smokes out Weekly Reader-Newsletter accused of touting views of the tobacco industry," The Houston Chronicle, November 1, 1995.

Reilly, Partick M., "A KKR vehicle finds profit and education a rich but uneasy mix," The Wall Street Journal, October 12, 1994.

Robert, Joseph C., The Story of Tobacco in America, The University of North Carolina Press, Chapel Hill, 1967.

Roberts, S.V., and T. Watson, "Teens on tobacco," U.S. News & World Report, April 18, 1994.

Russell, M.A.H., "The nicotine addictions trap: a 40-year sentence for four cigarettes," British J. Addiction, Vol. 85, 1990, pg. 293-300.

Schwartz, John, "Cigarette access on rise," The Houston Chronicle, February 16, 1996, A13, in MMWR, February 1996.

Schwartz, John, "Document could disprove claim firm didn't target teen smokers," The Houston Chronicle, April 23, 1996, 5A.

Schwartz, John, "Official made plan to draw teen smokers-company says it didn't act on memo," The Houston Chronicle, October 4, 1995.

"Showdown on Tobacco Road," a film by David Hoffman and Kirk Wolfinger, Produced by Terri Randall, written by Harvey Ardman, Varied Directions, Inc., 1987.

Stolberg, Sheryl, "Underage smokers three times as likely to be influenced by ads," The Houston Chronicle, April 4, 1996, A18.

Taylor, P., The Smoke Ring, Pantheon Books, New York, 1984. From: Brown and Williamson, Document AO11345, 1975 Viceroy Marketing Research, Done by Marketing & Research Counselors, Inc.

U.S. Department of Health and Human Services. "Preventing tobacco use among young people: a report of the Surgeon General," Atlanta: U.S. Department of Health and Human Services, Public Health Services, CDC, National Center for Chronic Disease Prevention and Health Promotion, Office on Smoking and Health, 1994.

White, L.C., Merchants of Death, Beech Tree Books, New York, 1988.

Wildey, M.B., S.I. Woodruff, S. A. Pampalone, and T. L. Conway, "Self-service sale of tobacco: how it contributes to youth access," Tobacco Control, Vol. 4, no. 4, 1995, pg 355-361.

Chapter six:

"Accessibility of Cigarettes to Youths aged 12-17," MMWR, Vol. 41, 1992, pg. 485-488.

American Psychiatric Association, Diagnostic and statistical manual of mental disorders, rev.3rd. edition, American Psychiatric Association, Washington, D.C. 1987.

Benowitz, Neal L. and P. Jacob III., "Daily intake of nicotine during cigarette smoking," Clinical Pharmacology and Therapeutics, Vol. 35, 1984, pg. 499-504.

Benowitz, Neal L., "Pharmacologic aspects of cigarette smoking and nicotine addiction," NEJM, Vol. 319, No. 20, Nov. 17, 1988, pg. 1318-1330.

Benowitz, Neal L., and Jack E. Henningfield, "Establishing a nicotine threshold for addiction," NEJM, July 14, 1994, Vol. 331, no. 2, Pg. 123-125.

Benwell, M.E.M., D.J.K. Baiforr, and J.M. Anderson," Evidence that tobacco smoking increases the density of nicotine binding sites in human brain," Journal of Neurochemistry, Vol. 50, 1988, pg. 1243-1247.

Bishop, Jerry E., "Nicotine's effect on brain cells explained in study," The Wall Street Journal, September 22, 1995.

Blumbergn H.H., S.D. Cohen, B.E. Dronfienld, E.A.. Mordecai, J.C. Roberts, and D. Hawks, "British opiate users: I, people approaching London drug treatment centers," International Journal of Addiction, Vol. 9, 1974, pg. 1-23.

Burt, A, D. Illingworth, T.R.D. Shaw, P. Thornely, P. White, and R. Turner, "Stopping smoking after a coronary infarction," Lancet, 1, 1974, pg. 304-306.

"Cigarette smoking among adults- United States, 1993," MMWR, Vol. 43, 1994, Pg. 925-939.

CNN/Gallup/USA Today survey, USA Today, March 16, 1994.

Condor, Bob, "Cigar smokers also exposed to health risks," The Houston Chronicle, February 2, 1996, 1D.

Corrigall, W.A. and K.M Coen, "Nicotine maintains robust self-administration in rats on a limited-access schedule," Psychopharmacology, Vol. 99, No. 4, 1989, pg. 473-478.

Daughety, V.S., S.M. Levy, K.L. Ferguson, P.R. Pomrehn, and S.L. Brecker, "Surveying smokeless tobacco use, oral lesions and cessation among high school boys," JADA, Vol. 125, Feb. 1994, pg. 173-180.

Dorland's Pocket Medical Dictionary, W.B. Saunders Co., 23rd Edition, 1982

Fowler, J.S,. N.D. Volkow, et al, "Inhibition of monoamine oxidase B in the brains of smokers," Nature, Vol 379, February 22, 1996, pg. 733-736.

Freedman, Alix M., "Juiced up: how a tobacco giant doctors snuff brands to boost their 'kick," The Wall Street Journal, October 26, 1994.

Freedman, Alix M., "Philip Morris memo likens nicotine to cocaine," The Wall Street Journal, December 8, 1995, B1.

Freedman, Alix M., T. K. Smith, and J. Helyar, "Liggett ordered to pay $400,000 in damages for smoker's death," The Wall Street Journal, June 14, 1988.

"From one bad habit to another," JAMA, Vol. 275, No. 16, April 24, 1996, pg. 1223.

Glantz, S.A., D.E. Barnes, L. Bero, P. Hanauer, and J. Slade, "Looking through a keyhole at the tobacco industry: The Brown and Williamson Documents," JAMA, Vol. 274, No. 3, July 19, 1995, pg. 219-224.

Glasman, Alexander H., and George F. Koop, "Psychoactive Smoke," Nature, Vol. 379, February 22, 1996, pg. 677-678..

Goodman and Gilman's, The Pharmacological Basis of Therapeutics, Macmillian Publishing Co., Inc., New York, 1980, A.G. Gilman, et al editors.

Harris, Richard, National Public Radio, May 9, 1994.

"The health consequences of smoking: Nicotine addiction. A report of the Surgeon General," U.S. Department of Health and Human Services, U.S. Government printing office, Washington, D.C., 1988.

Henningfield, J, and R. Keenan, "Nicotine delivery kinetics and abuse liability," J. Consult. Clinical Psychology, Vol. 61, 1992, pg. 743-750.

Henningfield, J.E., L.T. Kozlowski, and N.L. Benowitz, "A proposal to develop meaningful labeling for cigarettes," JAMA, Vol. 272, no. 4, July 27,1994, pg. 312-314.

Henningfield, J.E., "How tobacco produces drug dependence," In: Ockene, J.K., ed. The pharmacologic treatment of tobacco dependence: proceedings of the world congress, November 4-5, 1985. Cambridge, Mass.: Institute for the study of smoking behavior and policy, 1986; pg. 19-31.

Hilts, Philip J., "FDA panel takes step toward setting control on nicotine," The New York Times, August 2, 1994.

Hilts, Philip J., The New York Times, April 1, 1994.

Hilts, Philip J., "Tobacco firms knew of cigarette dangers in 1963," The Houston Chronicle, May 8, 1994.

Hilts, Philip J., "Scientist say Philip Morris withheld nicotine findings," The New York Times, April 29, 1994.

Hilts, Philip J., "FDA panel takes step toward setting control on nicotine," The New York Times, August 2, 1994.

Hilts, Philip J., "Tobacco maker studied risk but did little about results," The New York Times, June 17, 1994.

Hilts, Philip. J., "Survey finds surge in smoking by young," The New York Times, July 20, 1995.

Hilts, Philip J., The Wall Street Journal, April 15, 1994.

The Houston Chronicle, April 15, 1994.

Hurt, R.D, K. P. Offord, I.T. Croghan, L. Gomez-Dahl, T.E. Kottke, R. M. Morse, and L. J. Melton, "Mortality following inpatient addictions treatment," JAMA, Vol. 275, no. 14, April 10, 1996, pg. 1097-1103.

Hwang, S.L., and A.M. Freedman, "RJR is testing a 'Smokeless Cigarette' after attempt failed five years ago," The Wall Street Journal, November 28, 1994, pg. A5.

Hwang, Suein L., Alix M. Freedman, "Smokers may mistake 'clean' cigarette for safe," The Wall Street Journal, April 30, 1996. Pg. B1.

Internal Philip Morris memo, ABC *Day One*, February 28, 1994.

Jones, Ernest, The life and work of Sigmund Freud, Basic Books, New York, 1953, pg. 331.

Kessler, David A., "Nicotine addiction in young people," NEJM, Vol. 333, no. 3, July 20, 1995, pg. 186-189.

Kessler, David, "Statement on nicotine-containing cigarettes," Tobacco Control, Summer 1994.

Lee, E.W., and G. E. D'Alonzo, "Cigarette smoking, nicotine addiction, and its pharmacologic treatment," Archives of Internal. Medicine, Vol. 153, no.1, Jan. 11, 1993, pg. 34-48.

Lynch, B.S., and R.J. Bonnie, editors, Growing up tobacco free: preventing nicotine addiction in children and youths, Washington, D.C., National Academy Press, 1994:8.

Mahar, Maggie, "Tobacco's Smoking Gun," Barron's, May 16, 1994.

McGehee, D.S., M.J.S. Heath, S. Gelber, P. Devay and L.W. Role, "Nicotine enhancement of fast excitatory synaptic transmission in CNS by presynaptic receptors," Science, Vol. 269, Sept. 22, 1995, pg.1692-1696.

McGinley, Laurie, "Cigarettes now on market are addictive, FDA drug abuse advisory panel finds," The Wall Street Journal, August 3, 1994.

Miller, N.S., and J.A. Cocores, "Nicotine dependence: diagnosis, pharmacology and treatment," Journal of Addictive Diseases, Vol. 11, no. 2, 1991, pg. 51-65.

Moss, A.J. K.F. Allen, G.A. Giovino, et al. "Recent trends in adolescent smoking, smoking-uptake correlates, and expectations about the future, Advance data from vital and health statistics," No. 221, Hyattsville, MD, National Center for Health Statistics, 1992. (DHHS pub. no. (PHS) 93-1250.

Neergaard, Lauran, "Tobacco company chewed over idea for nicotine candy," The Houston Chronicle, August 22, 1995. 6A.

"The Nicotine War", FRONTLINE, Written, produced and directed by Joh Palfreman. Assoc. producers: Michelle Nicholasen, and Michaela Barnes. Editor: Bill Lattanzi. Field Producers: Michelle Nicholasen, Michaela Barnes, and Kathy Boisvert, Narrator: Will Lyman, PBS, Jan. 3, 1995.

Nowak, Rachel, Science, Vol. 263, March 18, 1994, pg. 1555-1556.

Pearl, Rebecca, National Public Radio, April 28, 1994.

Peto, R., A.D. Lopez, J. Boreham, M. Thun, and C. Health Jr., "Mortality from tobacco in developed countries: indirect estimation form national vital statistics," Lancet, 1992, Vol. 339, pg. 1268-78.

Pierce, John P., and E. Gilpin, "How long will today's new adolescent smokers be addicted to cigarettes?," AJPH, Vol. 86, no.2, February 1996, pg. 253-256.

"Researchers discover feel-good spot for nicotine," The New York Times, September 22, 1995.

"Reducing the health consequences of smoking: 25 years of progress," A report of the Surgeon General, Wash. D.C., US Dept. of Health and Human Services, CDC, 1989, DHHS pub. CDC 89-8411.

Roberts, S.V., and T. Watson, "Teens on tobacco," U.S. News & World Report, April 18, 1994.

Russell, M.A.H., "The nicotine addictions trap: a 40-year sentence for four cigarettes," British J. Addiction,. Vol. 85, 1990, pg. 293-300.

Schelling, T.C., "Addictive Drugs: The Cigarette Experience," Science, Vol. 255, (5043), 1992, pg. 430-433.

Shapiro, Eben, "Scientist say Philip Morris suppressed his research on nicotine addiction," The Wall Street Journal, April 29, 1994.

Shapiro, Eben, "Tobacco firms may face new pressure with disclosure of executive's memo," The Wall Street Journal, May 9, 1994.

Slade, J., L. Bero, P. Hanauer, D.E. Barnes, and S.A. Glantz, "Nicotine and Addiction: The Brown and Williamson Documents," JAMA, Vol. 274, no. 3, July 19, 1995, pg. 225-233.

Slade, John, "The tobacco epidemic: lessons form history," J. Psychoactive Drugs, Vol. 24, 1992, pg. 99-109.

Surgeon Generals Report 1994, in The Houston Chronicle, Feb. 25, 1994.

Taylor, P. In: Goodman and Gilman's, The Pharmacological Basis of Therapeutics, Macmillian Publishing Co., Inc., New York, 1980, A.G. Gilman, et al editors.

Taylor, Peter, The Smoke Ring, Pantheon Books, New York, 1984.

"Teenage attitudes and behavior concerning tobacco: a report of the findings," N.J.: Gallup International Institute, 1992:54.

"Teenagers and the 'madness' of drugs", US. News & World Report, November 13, 1995, pg. 25.

Tobacco-Free Youth Reporter, Vol. 6, no.1, 1994.

Tilashalski, K., B. Rodu, and C. Mayfield, "Assessing the nicotine content of smokeless tobacco products," JADA, Vol. 125, May 1994, pg. 590-594.

Vedantam, Shankar, "Tobacco industry government debate researchers' findings," The Houston Chronicle, March 30, 1996, 6A.

The Wall Street Journal, April 1, 1994.

The Wall Street Journal, March 2, 1994.

Warner, K.E., "Profits of Doom," AJPH, Vol. 83, no. 9, 1993, pg. 1211.

White, Larry C., Merchants of Death , The American Tobacco Industry , Beech Tree Books, William Morrow and Company, 105 Madison Ave., New York, NY 10016, 1988.

Chapter seven:

ABC *Day One*, February 28, 1994.

Campbell, William I., CEO Philip Morris, The New York Times, March 15, 1994. Letter to editor.

Cimons, M., "Papers tell how tobacco firms can boost nicotine levels," The Houston Chronicle, April 14, 1994.

Collins, Glenn, "Disputed documents could be used in class-action suit against tobacco companies," The New York Times, April 10, 1996, A11.

Freedman Alix M, and Suein L. Hwang, "Three ex-employees say Philip Morris deliberately controlled nicotine levels," The Wall Street Journal, March 19, 1996, B1.

Freedman, Alix M., "Former Philip Morris scientist alleges company knew nicotine acts like drug," The Wall Street Journal, March 18, 1996, A3.

Freedman. Alix M., "Tobacco firm show how ammonia spurs delivery of nicotine," The Wall Street Journal, October 18, 1995, A1.

Geyelin, Milo, A. M. Freedman, "R.J. Reynolds once linked the success of rival brands to 'nicotine kick' boost," The Wall Street Journal, May 23, 1996. A-10.

Hilts, Philip J., "Lawmaker applies pressure for regulation of nicotine," The New York Times, August 1, 1995, A9.

Hilts, Philip J., The New York Times, April 15, 1994.

Hilts, Philip J., "Scientist say Philip Morris withheld nicotine findings," The New York Times, April 29, 1994.

Hilts, Philip J. The Wall Street Journal, April 1, 1994.

Hwang, Suein L., "Young snuff users advance to brands with more nicotine, 2 studies suggest," The Wall Street Journal, April 27, 1995.

Leary, W.E., "Cigarette company developed a potent gene-altered tobacco," The New York Times, June 22, 1994.

Mahar, Maggie, "Tobacco's smoking gun," Barron's, May 16, 1994

McGinley, L., "FDA chief says firm developed altered tobacco," The Wall Street Journal, June 22, 1994.

National Public Radio, "Tobacco Additives," April 8, 1994.

Neergaard, Lauran, "Cigarette critics attack tobacco debris process used by Philip Morris", The Houston Chronicle, March 27, 1996, 14A.

"The Nicotine War", FRONTLINE, Written, produced and directed by Joh Palfreman. Assoc. producers: Michelle Nicholasen, and Michaela Barnes. Editor: Bill Lattanzi. Field Producers: Michelle Nicholasen, Michaela Barnes, and Kathy Boisvert; Narrator: Will Lyman. PBS, Jan. 3, 1995.

Noah, Timothy, "Waxman says data suggest nicotine was boosted in Philip Morris cigarettes", The Wall Street Journal, August 1, 1995

Shapiro, Eben, The Wall Street Journal, March 25, 1994.

Shaprio, E., "Philip Morris may sue ABC for TV report," The Wall Street Journal, March 24, 1994.

Shaw, Angela, The Wall Street Journal, February 28, 1994.

Slade, J., L. Bero, P. Hanauer, D.E. Barnes, and Stanton A. Glantz, "Nicotine and Addiction: The Brown and Williamson Documents," JAMA, Vol. 274, no. 3, July 19, 1995, pg. 225-233.

"Snuff makers target kids, scientists say," The Houston Chronicle, April 27, 1995.

White, Larry C., Merchants of Death, Beech Tree Books, New York, 1988.

Chapter eight:

"Annual Report on Carcinogens," U.S. Department of Commerce, 1991.

All Things Considered, National Public Radio, April 14, 1994 .

Barnes, D.E., P. Hanauer, J. Slade, L. Bero, and S.A. Glantz, "Environmental tobacco Smoke: The Brown and Williamson Documents," JAMA, Vol. 274, No. 3, July 19, 1995. pg. 248-253.

Bartecchi, C.E., T.D. MacKenzie, and R.W. Schrier, "The Human costs of tobacco use," NEJM, Vol. 330, No. 13, Pg. 907-912.

Bishop, J.E. "Snuff found to contain heavy doses of cancer-causing chemical in study," The Wall Street Journal, December 20, 1995, B6, from *J. of Nat. Cancer Institute*, Hoffmann, D, M.V. Djordjevic, T. Glynn, N. Connolly, December 1995.

Brecker, C., and T. Dubin, "Activation of factor XII by tobacco glycoprotein," J. Experimental Medicine, Vol. 146, 1977, pg. 457-467.

Brecker, C., T. Dubin, and H. Wiedemann, "Hypersensitivity to tobacco antigens," Proc. Natl. Acad. Sci., Vol. 73, 1976, pg. 1712-1216.

Brownson, R.C., T.E. Novotny, and M.C. Perry, "Cigarette smoking and adult leukemia: a meta-analysis," Arch. Intern Med., Vol 153, 1993; pg. 469-75.

CDC Editors note, JAMA, Vol. 271, No 6, pg. 419.

Center for Disease Control, DHHS Publication No (CDC) 89-8411, 1989.

"Chemical Substance Inventory," Toxic Substance Control Act, EPA, July 1990, TS-799.

Eisler, H., "Polonium-210 and bladder cancer," Science, Vol. 144, pg. 952-53.

Environmental Protection Agency, "Respiratory health effects of passive smoking: lung cancer and other disorders," Washington, D.C. : Office of Health and Environmental Assessment , 1993.

"Environmental tobacco smoke in Workplace; Lung Cancer and other health effects," [DHHA publication no.(NIOSH)91-108], in JAMA, July24/31, 1991, Vol. 266, no 4, pg. 471.

Glantz, Stanton A, and W. W. Parmley, "Passive smoking and heart disease: Mechanism and risk," JAMA, Vol. 273, No. 13, April 5, 1995.

Goodman and Gilman's, The Pharmacological Basis of Therapeutics, Macmillan Publishing Co., Inc., New York, 1980, A.G. Gilman, et al editors.

Grolier's Encyclopedia

"Health effects of passive smoking: Assessment of lung cancer in adults and respiratory disorders in children," Washington, DC; US environmental Protection Agency, Office of Health and Environmental Assessment, Office of Atmospheric and Indoor Air Programs, 1990, report no. EPA 600-6-90-006A.

Hecht, S., and D. Hoffmann, "Tobacco-specific nitrosamines, an important group of carcinogens in tobacco and tobacco smoke," Carcinogenesis, Vol. 9, 1988, pg. 875-84.

Hecht, S. S., et al., "Tobacco-specific lung carcinogen in the urine of men exposed to cigarette smoke," The New England Journal of Medicine, Vol. 329, No. 21, pg. 1543.

Hennekens, C.H., J.E. Buring, R. Peto, et al, "The effects of vitamin E and beta carotene on the incidence of lung cancer and other cancers in male smokers," NEJM, Vol. 330, no. 15, 1994, pg. 1029-1081.

Holtzaan, R.B., and F.H. Ilcevidt,"Lead-210 and polonium-210 in tissues of cigarette smokers," Science, Vol. 153, pg. 1259-1260.

Huggins, C. B., "Selective induction of hormone-dependent mammary adenocarcinoma in the rat," J. Lab Clinical Med., Vol. 109, 1987, pg. 262-266.

Kurtz, Howard, "Ex-tobacco official's charges made public," The Houston Chronicle, November 18, 1995. 8A.

Landrigan, Philip J., "The prevention of occupational cancer," CA, Vol. 46, no. 2, March/April 1996, pg 67-69.

Lewis Sr., R.J., Hazardous Chemical Desk Reference, 3rd Edition, Van Nostrand Reinhold, New York, 1963.

Little, J.B., E. P. Radford Jr., H.L. McCombs, and V.P. Hunt, "Distribution of polonium in pulmonary tissues of cigarette smokers," NEJM, Vol. 273, 1965, pg. 1343-1351.

Matthew, B.G, and D. N. Granger, "Free Radicals: reactive metabolites of oxygen as mediator of postischemic reperfusion injury," pg. 135-134, in Splanchnic Ischemia and Multiple Organ Failure, Ed. A. Marston, et al, C. V. Mosby, Washington, D.C.

McCusker, K., "Mechanism of respiratory tissue injury from cigarette smoking," American Journal of Medicine, Vol. 93, (suppl 1A), 1992.

Packer, L., "Protective role of vitamin E in biological systems," Am. J. Clin. Nutr. 1991, Vol. 53, (Suppl), pg. S1050-1055.

Perri, E.S., and E.J. Baratta, "Polonium-210 in tobacco products and human tissues," Radiat. Data Rep.,Vol. 7, pg. 485-488.

Richie, J, and S. Hecht, et al, "A Report to the American Association for Cancer Research," April 10, 1994, in The Houston Post, April 11, 1994.

Robert, Joseph C., The story of tobacco in America,The University of N. Carolina Press, Chapel Hill, 1967, pg. 241-242.

Schwartz, John, "Heart disease link to tobacco studied," The Houston Chronicle, May 4, 1996, from presentation to Molecular Medicine Society annual meeting 1996.

Shapiro, Eben, "Cigarette firms release list of ingredients," The Wall Street Journal, April 13, 1994.

"Tobacco Additives," National Public Radio, April 8, 1994.

Tso, T.C., N.A. Hallden, and L.T. Alexander, "Radium-226 and polonium-210 in leaf tobacco and tobacco soil," Science , 146, pg. 1043-1045.

U.S. Department of health and human services: The health benefits of smoking cessation. U.S. Department of health and human services, public health service, Center for Disease Control, Center for Chronic Disease Prevention and Health Promotion, Office on Smoking and Health, DHHS Publication No (CDC) 89-8416, 1990.

Wallace, L., E. Pellizzari, T.D. Hartwell, R. Perritt, and R. Ziegenfus, "Exposure to benzene and other volatile compounds from active and passive smoking," Arch. Environmental Health, Vol. 42, 1987, pg 272-9.

White, Larry C., Merchants of Death , The American Tobacco Industry, by Beech Tree Books, William Morrow and Company, 105 Madison Ave., New York, NY 10016, copyright 1988.

Chapter nine:

Aguayo, S.M., "Determinants of susceptibility to cigarette smoke," Am.J. Respir. Care Medicine, Vol. 149, 1994, pg. 1692-1698.

Boring, C.C., et al, "Cancer Statistics, 1994," CA, Vol. 44, no. 1, 1994.

Brody, Jane E., "Increasingly, a smokescreen of glamour is hiding the dangers of cigars," The New York Times, May 29,1996, B9.

"Cancer facts and figures-1995," American Cancer Society, January 1995.

CDC, "Cigarette smoking-attributable mortality and year of potential life lost-United States, 1990," MMWR, Vol. 42, no. 33, 1993.

"Cigarette is suspected in fire at fraternity," The New York Times, May 17, 1996, A8.

"Cigarette smoking among adults-United States, 1993," MMWR, Vol. 43, pg. 925-930.

"Cigarette smoking among adults-United States, 1992," MMWR, Vol. 43, no. 19, May 20, 1994, pg. 341-346.

Collins, Glen, "As a prop for the 90's, the cigar flourishes," The New York Times, April, 1996, A1.

Collins, Glen, "Cigar mania revitalizes Connecticut industry," The New York Times, August 13, 1995.

Condor, Bob, "Cigar smokers also exposed to health risks," The Houston Chronicle, February 2, 1996, 1D.

Dresibach, Robert H., Handbook of Poisoning, Lange Medical Publications, California, 1977.

"Environmental tobacco smoke in the workplace: lung cancer and other health effects," DHHA Publication no (NIOSH) 91-108, in JAMA, Vol. 266, no. 4, pg. 490.

EPA, "Respiratory health effects of passive smoking," 1992.

Feder, Barnaby J. "Ready to test new cigarette, maker worries about rules," The New York Times, April 8, 1996.

Fielding, J.E., "Smoking: Health effects and control," in Public Health and Preventive Medicine, Appleton & Lange, 1992, pg. 716-723.

Flam, F., "Scientists identify lung-cancer gene," The Houston Chronicle, April 4, 1996, 2A.

Glover, E.D., K.L. Schroeder, J.E. Henningfield, et al, "An interpretive review of smokeless tobacco research in the United States: Part I," J. Drug Education, Vol. 18, no. 4, 1988, pg. 285.

Greer, R.O., and T. C. Poulson, "Oral tissue alterations associated with the use of smokeless tobacco by teenagers," Oral Surgery, Oral Medicine, Oral Pathology, Vol. 56, no. 3, September 1983, pg. 275-284.

Hilts, Philip J., "Scientist say Philip Morris withheld nicotine findings," The New York Times, April 29, 1994.

The Houston Chronicle, June 27, 1994.

Hwang, Suein L., "Critics say 'smokeless' cigarettes are aimed at women," The Wall Street Journal, May 31, 1996, B1.

Hwang, Suein L., and Alix M. Freedman, "Smokers may mistake 'clean' cigarette for safe," The Wall Street Journal, April 30, 1996, pg. B1.

Jackson, D. Z., "Smoke-filled bribery," The Boston Globe, Sept. 20, 1992.

Katzenstein, L., American Health, Jan/Feb 1994.

Lamm, D.L., and F.M. Torti, "Bladder cancer, 1996," CA, Vol. 46, no. 2, March/April 1996, pg. 93-112.

Levy, D., "Horrible price paid for not knowing," USA Today, May 19, 1994.

MacKenziek T.D., C.E. Bartecchi, and R.W. Schrier, "The human costs of tobacco use," NEJM, Vol. 330, No. 14, pg. 975-980.

Marwick, C., "Tobacco control report card fails some federal entities, gives all tough future assignments," JAMA, Vol. 271, no. 9, pg. 645-647.

McCusker, K., "Mechanism of respiratory tissue injury from cigarette smoking," AJM, Vol. 93, (suppl 1A), 1992.

McGinnis, J.M., and W. H. Foege, "Actual causes of death in the United States," JAMA , Vol. 270, 1993, pg. 2207-12.

Miller, N.S., and J.A. Cocores, "Nicotine Dependence: diagnosis, pharmacology and treatment," J. Addictive Diseases, Vol. 11 , no.2, 1991 pg. 51-65.

Mohr, U., and G. Reznik, "Tobacco Carcinogenesis," In Harris CC(ed.): Pathogenesis and therapy of lung cancer. New York, Marcel Dekker, 1978, pg. 263.

National Cancer Institute, "Smoking, Tobacco, and Cancer Program-annual report 1983," NIH Pub. No. 84-2687, Sept. 1984.

National Center for Health Statistics, "Advance report of final mortality statistics, 1991," Monthly Vital Stat. Rep., Vol. 42, (supp2), 1993, pg. 1-61.

Nelson, D.E, et al., "Surveillance of smoking-attributable mortality and years of potential life lost, by state-United States, 1990," CDC, MMWR, Vol. 43, no. ss-1, June 10, 1994, pg. 1-8.

Newcomb, Polly A., and Paul P. Carbone, "The health consequences of smoking-Cancer," Medical Clinics of North America, Vol. 76, no 2, March 1992. (general reference)

Niewohner, D., J. Kleinerman, and D. Rice, "Pathologic changes in the peripheral airways of young cigarette smokers," NEJM, Vol. 291, 1974, pg. 755-758.

Niparko, J.K. and M.E. Johns, " Otolarynogology-Head and Neck Surgery," JAMA, Vol. 273, no. 21, June 7, 1995, pg. 1705.

Njolstad, I, E. Arnesen, and G. Lund-Larsen, "Smoking, serum lipids, blood pressure, and sex differences in myocardial infarction," Circulation, Vol. 93, no. 3, February 1, 1996, pg. 450-456.

Parish, S., R. Collins, L. Peto, J. Youngman, K. Barton, R. Jayne, P. Clarke, V. Appleby, S. Lyon, S. Cederholm-Williams, J. Marshall, and P. Sleight, "Cigarette smoking, tar yields, and non-fatal myocardial infarction: 14,000 cases and 32,000 controls in the United Kingdom," BMJ, Vol. 311, August 19, 1995, pg. 471-477.

Parker, S.L., T. Tong, S. Bolden, and P. A. Wingo, "Cancer Statistics, 1996," CA, Vol. 46, no.1, January/February 1996, pg. 5-27.

Randerath, E., D. Mittal, and K. Randerath, "Tissue distribution of covalent DNA damage in mice treated dermally with cigarette 'tar': preference for lung and heart," Carcinogenesis, 1988, Vol. 9, pg. 75-80.

"Reducing the health consequences of smoking: 25 years of progress- A report of the surgeon general," U.S. Department of health and human services. 1989, Washington, D.C.: U.S. GPO.

Reuter, August 29, 1995.

Roth MD, Jack, The Houston Chronicle, May 5, 1994.

Schwartz, John, "Battle cry is sounded on tobacco," The Houston Chronicle, July 14, 1995.

"Smoking, Tobacco and Cancer Program, 1985-1989 Status Report," U.S. Department of Health and Human Services, Public Health Service, NIH, NCI, NIH Pub. No. 90-3107,1990.

Stellman, J. M., and S. D. Stellman, "Cancer in the workplace," CA, Vol. 36, no. 2, March/April 1996, pg. 70-92.

U.S. Department of Health and Human Services: "Reducing the health consequences of smoking : 25 years of progress," Surgeon General's Report, Public Health Service, Centers for Disease Control, Center for Chronic Disease Prevention and Health Promotion, Office on Smoking and Health, DHHA Pub. No (CDC)89-8411, 1989.

U.S. Department of health and human services: "The health benefits of smoking cessation," U.S. Department of Health and Human Services, Public Health Service, Center for Disease Control, Center for Chronic Disease Prevention and Health Promotion, Office on Smoking and Health, DHHS Publication No (CDC) 89-8416, 1990.

U.S. Department of health and human services: "The health consequences of smoking: Cancer," A report of the Surgeon General. U.S. Department of Health and Human Services, Public Health Service, Office of the Assistant Secretary for Health, Office on Smoking and Health, DHHS Publication No (PHS) 82-50179,1982.

Vedantam, Shankar, "The fear factor: High anxiety over low risks," The Houston Chronicle, April 5, 1996, 8A.

Warner, K.E, "Profits of doom," AJPH, Vol. 83, no. 9, 1993.

Wynder, E.L., and Grahm, E.A., "Tobacco smoke as a possible etiological factor in bronchiogenic carcinoma," JAMA, Vol.143, 1950, pg. 329-336.

Chapter ten:

"5,600 Infants deaths tied to mothers' smoking," The New York Times, March 13, 1995.

Brody, Jane E., "And now smokers face," The New York Times, June 19, 1996.

Brody, Jane E., "Swiss study links smoking to a risk of breast cancer," The New York Times, May 5, 1996.

CDC, "Cigarette Smoking-Attributable Mortality and years of potential life lost-United Stares, 1990," MMWR, 1993; Vol. 42, pg. 645-649.

CDC, MMWR, Vol. 43, pg. 789-791,797.

CDC, MMWR, Vol. 44, no. 6, Feb. 17, 1995, pg.102-105.

"Cigarette smoking among adults-United States, 1993," MMWR, Vol. 43, 1994, pg. 925-930.

Cooke, R. "Odds of tubal pregnancy rise with smoking," The Houston Chronicle, February 21, 1994.

Cotton, Paul, "Smoking cigarettes may do developing fetus more harm than ingesting cocaine, some experts say," JAMA, Vol. 271, no. 8, 1994, pg. 576-577.

DiFranza, Joseph R., and R. A. Lew, "Effect of maternal cigarette smoking on pregnancy complication and sudden infant death syndrome," J. of Family Practice, Vol. 40, no. 4, April 1995, pg. 385-394.

Drews, C.D, C.C. Murphy, M. Yeargin-Allsopp, and P. Decoufle, "The relationship between idiopathic mental retardation and maternal smoking during pregnancy," Pediatrics, Vol. 97, no. 4, April, 1996, pg 547-553.

Ernster, Virginia L., "How tobacco companies target women," World Smoking & Health, Vol. 16, No. 2, 1991., pg.8.-11.

Ernster,V.L., "Women and Smoking," AJPH, Vol. 83, No. 9, pg. 1202.

Fox, S.H., T.D. Koepsell, and J.R. Daling, "Birth weight and smoking during pregnancy-effect modification by maternal age," Amer. J. Epidemiology, Vol. 139, no. 10, 1994, pg. 1008-1015.

Gritz, E., "Women and smoking: educating them to stop," World Smoking & Health, Vol. 16, no. 2, 1991, pg. 3-7.

Hopper, J.L, and E. Seeman, "The bone density of female twins discordant for tobacco use," NEJM, Vol. 330, No 6, 1994, pg. 387.

"Infant mortality-United States, 1993," MMWR, Vol. 45,1996, pg. 211-215.

Jones, Graeme, et al, To the Editor: "Cigarette smoking an vertebral body deformity," JAMA, Vol. 274, no. 23, Dec. 20, 1995, pg. 1834-35.

Li, De-Kun, B.A. Mueller, D.E. Hickok, J.R. Daling, A.G. Fantel, H. Checkoway, and N.S. Weiss, "Maternal smoking during pregnancy and the risk of congenital urinary tract anomalies," AJPH, Vol. 8, no. 2, 1996, pg. 249-253.

Morabia. A, M. Bernstein, S. Heritier, and N. Khatchatrian, "Relation of breast cancer with passive and active exposure to tobacco smoke," Amer. J. of Epidemiology, Vol. 143, no. 9, 1996, pg. 918-928.

Nelson, H.D, M.C. Nevitt, J.C. Scott, K.L. Stone, and S.R. Cummings, "Smoking, alcohol, and neuromuscular and physical function of older women," JAMA, Vol. 272, no. 23, December 21, 1994, pg. 1825-1831.

Novello, A., "Can we prevent the Virginia Slims woman from catching up with the Marlboro man?," World Smoking & Health, Vol. 16, no. 2, 1991, pg. 2.

Nyboe, J, G., M. Jensen, P. Appleyard, and P. Schnohr, "Smoking and the risk of first acute myocardial infarction," Am Heart J. , Vol. 122, 1991, pg. 438-447.

Parker, S. L., T. Tong, S. Bolden, and P.A. Wingo, "Cancer Statistics, 1996," CA, Vol. 46, no. 1, January/February 1996, pg. 5-27.

"Passive smoking link is found in newborns," The New York Times, February 23, 1994.

Peto, R, A.D. Lopez, J. Boreham, M, Thun, and C. Health, Jr.,"Mortality from tobacco in developed countries: indirect estimation from national vital statistics," The Lancet, Vol. 339, 1992, pg. 1268-1278.

"Smokers 59% more likely to bear retarded children," The New York Times, April 19, 1996, A11.

Smoking, Tobacco & Health, U.S. Department of Health and Human Services, Public Health service, CDC, Office on Smoking and Health, DHHS Pub. no. (CDC) 87-8397, 1989.

Wilcox, A.J., "Birth weight and perinatal mortality: the effect of maternal smoking," American Journal of Epidemiology, Vol. 93, 1971, pg. 443-456.

Willett, W. C, A. Green, M.J. Stampfer, F. E. Speizer, G. A. Colditz, B. Rosner, R.R. Monson. W. Stason, and C.H. Hennekens, "Relative and absolute excess risks of coronary heart disease among women who smoke cigarettes," NEJM, Vol. 317, 1987, pg. 1303-1309.

Chapter eleven:

"5,600 infant deaths tied to mothers' smoking," The New York Times, April 13, 1995.

ASH, Smoking and Health Review, Vol. XXIII, no 5, 1993.

Asmussen, I. and K. Kjeldsen, "Intimal ultrastructure of human umbilical arteries: observations of arteries from newborn children of smoking and non-smoking mothers," Circulation Research, Vol. 36, 1975, pg. 579-589.

"Asthma mortality and hospitalizations among children and young adults-US, 1980-1993," MMWR, Vol. 45, 1996, pg. 350-353.

"Asthma toll is up sharply, U.S. reports," New York Times, May 3, 1996, C18.

Barnes, D.E., P. Hanauer, J. Slade, L. Bero, and S.A. Glantz, "Environmental tobacco Smoke: The Brown and Williamson Documents," JAMA, Vol. 274, no. 3, July 19, 1995. pg. 248-253.

Bartecchi, C.E., T.D. MacKenzie, and R.W. Schrier, "The Human costs of tobacco use," NEJM, Vol. 330, no. 13, pg. 907-912.

Bo-qing, Z., and W. W. Parmley, "Hemodynamic and vascular effects of active and passive smoking," American Heart Journal, Vol. 130, no.6, December, 1995, pg. 1270-1275.

Brody, Jane E., "Swiss study links smoking to a risk of breast cancer," The New York Times, May 5, 1996.

Brownson, R.C, M.C. Alavanja, E. T. Hock, and T. S. Loy, "Passive smoking and lung cancer in nonsmoking women," AJPH, Vol. 82, 1992, Pg. 1525-30.

Brunnemann, K.D., J.E. Hoffmann, "Analysis of tobacco-specific N'-nitrosamines in indoor air," Carcinogenesis, 1992, Vol. 13, pg. 2315-2418.

Byrd, J.C., "Environmental Tobacco Smoke: Medical and legal Issues," Medical Clinics of N. America, Vol. 76, no. 2, March 1992, pg. 377-398.

Calian, Sara, "Philip Morris tries to snuff our curbs on overseas smokers," The Wall Street Journal, June 5, 1996, B7.

Celermajer, D S., M.R. Adams, P. Clarkson, J. Robinson, R. McCredie, A. Donald, and J. E. Deanfield, "Passive smoking and impaired endothelium-dependent arterial dilatation in healthy young adults," NEJM, Vol. 334, no. 3, Jan. 18, 1996, pg. 150-154.

Chilomonczyk, B.A., "Association between exposure to environmental tobacco smoke and exacerbation's of asthma in children," NEJM, Vol. 328, no. 23, pg. 1664.

Consumer Reports, May 1994, pg. 318.

DiFranza, Joseph R., and R. A. Lew, "Effect of maternal cigarette smoking on pregnancy complication and sudden infant death syndrome," The J. of Family Practice, Vol. 40, no. 4, April 1995, pg. 385-394.

DiFranza, Joseph R., and R. A. Lew, "Morbidity and Mortality in children associated with the use of tobacco products by other people," Pediatrics, Vol. 97, no. 4, April 1996, pg. 560-568.

Elders, J.M., "Reducing the risk of sudden infant death syndrome," JAMA, Vol. 272, no. 21, December 7, 1994, pg. 1646.

Elipoulos, C., J. Klein, M.K. Phan, B. Knie, M. Greenwald, D. Chitayat, and G. Koren, "Hair concentrations of nicotine and cotinine in women and their newborn infants," JAMA, Vol. 271, no. 8, pg. 621-623.

Environmental Protection Agency, "Respiratory health effects of passive smoking: lung cancer and other disorders," Washington, D.C. : Office of Health and Environmental Assessment, December 1992, EPA/600/6-90/006/F.

"Environmental tobacco smoke in Workplace; Lung Cancer and other health effects", JAMA, Vol. 266, no 4, July 24/31, 1991, pg. 471. [DHHA publication no. (NIOSH)91-108].

Eriksen, M.P., Charles A. LeMaistre, and G.R. Newell, "Health hazards of passive smoking," American Review of Public Health, Vol. 9, 1988, pg. 47-70.

Fielding, J.E., and K. J. Phenow, "Health effects of involuntary smoking," NEJM, Vol. 319, no. 22, 1988, pg. 1452-1460.

Filippine, G., M. Farinotti, G. Lovicu, P. Maisonneuve, and P. Boyle, "Mothers' active and passive smoking," International Journal of Cancer, Vol. 57, 1994, pg. 769-774.

Fontham, E.T.H., P. Correa, P. Reynolds, et al, "Environmental tobacco smoke and lung cancer in nonsmoking women: a multicenter study," JAMA, Vol. 271, 1994, Pg. 1752-1759.

Freedman, Alix M., "Grand jury probes secondhand-smoke studies," The Wall Street Journal, February 15, 1996, B1.

Friedman, G.D, D.B Pettiti, and R. D. Bawol, "Prevalence and correlates of passive smoking," AJPH, Vol. 73, 1983, pg. 401-405.

Glantz, Stanton A. and W.W. Parmley, "Passive smoking and heart disease: Mechanisms and risk," JAMA, Vol. 273, no. 13, April 5, 1995, pg. 1047-1053.

Guyton, A.C., Structure and function of the nervous system, W.B. Saunders Co., Philadelphia, 1976.

Hammond, S., K, G. Sorensen, R. Youngstrom, and J. K. Ockene, "Occupational exposure to environmental tobacco smoke," JAMA, Vol. 274, no. 12, September 27, 1995. pg. 956-960.

Hilts, Philip J., "Tobacco foes see fake data in smoke peril," The New York Times, December 21, 1994.

Hirayama, T., "Non-smoking wives of heavy smokers have a higher risk of lung cancer: a study from Japan," BMJ, Vol. 282, 1981, pg. 183-185.

Klonoff-Cohen, Hillary S., et al, "The effect of passive smoking and tobacco exposure through breast milk on sudden infant death syndrome," JAMA, Vol. 273, No. 10., March 8, 1995.

Lesmes, G. R, and K. H. Donofrio, "Passive smoking: The medical and economic issues," AJM, Vol. 93 (suppl 1A), July 15, 1992, pg. 1A, 38S-42S.

Levy, Doug, "Smoking data tampered with, researchers say," USA Today, November 2, 1994.

Mannino, D.M., M. Siegel, C. Husten, D. Rose, and R. Etzel, "Environmental tobacco smoke exposure and respiratory diseases in children," American College of Chest Physicians, abstract P1783, 1994.

National Research Council, Committee on Passive Smoking, "Environmental tobacco smoke: measuring exposures and assessing health effects," Washington, D. C.: National Academy Press, 1986.

Newcomb, Polly A. and Paul P. Carbone, "The health consequences of smoking-Cancer," Medical Clinics of North America, Vol. 76, no 2, March 1992.

Penn, A, and C.A. Snyder, "1,3, butadiene, a vapor phase component of environmental tobacco smoke, accelerates arterioscleroitc plaque development," Circulation, Vol. 93, no. 3, February 1, 1996, pg. 552-557.

Peto, J., and R. Doll, "Passive smoking," British Journal of Cancer, Vol. 54, 1986, pg. 381-383.

Pirkle, J. L, K.M. Flegal, J.T. Bernert, and D. J. Brody, "Exposure of the US Population to environmental tobacco smoke, The Third national health and nutrition examination, survey, 1988 to 1991," JAMA, Vol. 275, no. 16, April 24, 1996, pg. 1233-1240.

Reynolds, P, and E.T.H. Fontham, "Passive smoking and lung cancer," Annals of Medicine, Vol. 27, 1995, pg. 633-640.

Schwartz, John, "Research documents smoking's heavy toll on fetuses and infants," The Houston Chronicle, April 12, 1995, From the *J. of Family Practice*.

Shapiro, E., "R.J. Reynolds fights back in campaign," The Wall Street Journal, May 23, 1994.

Siegel, Michael, "Involuntary smoking in the restaurant workplace," JAMA, Vol. 270, no. 4, July 28, 1993, pg. 490-493.

Skolnick, A.A., "First AHA statement on tobacco and children," JAMA, Vol. 272, no 11, September 21, 1994.

Spitzer. W.O., V. Lawrence, R. Dales, et al, "Links between passive smoking and disease: a best-evidence synthesis. A Report of the working group on passive smoking," Clinical Invest. Medicine, Vol. 13, 1990, pg. 17-42.

Stockwell, H. G., A. H. Goldman, G.H. Lyman, et al. "Environmental tobacco smoke and lung cancer risk in nonsmoking women," J. National Cancer Institute, Vol. 84, 1992, pg. 1417-1422.

"Study: Smoking by spouse caries heart-disese risk," from *The American Heart Journal*, in The Houston Chronicle, August 8, 1996, 32A.

Stone, Richard, Science, Vol. 257, July 31, 1992.

Svendsen, K, L.H. Kuller, J. M. Maritn, and J. K. Ockene, "Effects of passive smoking in the multiple risk factor intervention trial," American Journal of Epidemiology, Vol. 126, 1987, pg. 783-795.

Swartz, John, "Research documents smoking heavy toll on fetuses and infants," The Houston Chronicle, April 12, 1995.

Taylor, A.E, D. C. Johnson, and H. Kazemi, "Environmental tobacco smoke and cardiovascular diseased; a position paper from the Council on Cardiopulmonary and Critical Care," American Heart Association, Circulation, Vol. 86, 1992, pg. 699.

U.S. Dept. of Health and Human Services. "The Health Consequences of smoking: Cancer, A Report of the Surgeon General," U.S. Dept. of Health and Human Services. U.S. Public Health Service, Office on Smoking and Health, 1982. DHHS, pub. PHS 82-5-179.

Vineis, P., H. Bartsch, N.Caporaso, A.M. Harrington, F.F. Kadlubar, et al, "Genetically based N-acetyltransferase metabolic polymorphism and low-level environmental exposure to carcinogens," Nature, Vol. 369, May 12, 1994, pg. 15.

The Wall Street Journal, May 18, 1994, C22.

Warner, K.E, G.A. Fulton, P. Nicolas, and D. R. Grimes, "Employment implications of declining tobacco product sales for the regional economies of the United States," JAMA, Vol. 275, no. 16, April 24, 1996, pg 1241-1246.

Wells, A. Judson, "Passive smoking as a cause of heart disease," J. American College of Cardiology, Vol. 24, no 2, 1994, pg. 546-554.

Chapter twelve:

Bero, L.A., A. Galbraith, and D. Rennie, "Sponsored symposia on environmental tobacco smoke," JAMA, Vol. 271, no. 8, 1994, pg. 612-617.

Bero, L.A., D.E. Barnes, P. Hanauer, John Slade, and Stanton A. Glantz, "Lawyer control of the tobacco industry's external research program: The Brown and Williamson Documents," JAMA, Vol. 274, no. 3, July 19, 1995. pg.. 241-247.

Cohen, L.P., and M. Geyelin, "Probe reopens into nonprofit tobacco group," The Wall Street Journal, February 8, 1996, A3.

Freedman, Alix and Cohen, L.P., "How cigarette makers keep health question open year after year," The Wall Street Journal, February 11, 1993.

Geyelin, Milo, "A Missouri law firm finds tobacco to be a lucrative cash crop," The Wall Street Journal, March 28, 1996, A1.

Levy, D., "Horrible price paid for not knowing," USA Today, May 19, 1994.

McGinley, L., "Tobacco research council, financed by industry, is criticized in Congress," The Wall Street Journal, May 27, 1994.

St. Petersburg Times, May 27, 1994.

Taylor, P., The Smoke Ring, Pantheon Books, New York, 1984.

White, Larry C., Merchants of Death, Beech Tree Books, New York 1988.

Chapter thirteen:

"Antismoking TV ads dropped after threat of suit by Reynolds," The Wall Street Journal, October 14, 1994.

ASH Smoking and Health Review, Volume XXVI, no. 2, March-April 1996.

Ayres Jr., B. D., The New York Times, May 15, 1994.

Ayres Jr., B.D., "Stations pull ad critical of tobacco industry," The New York Times, October 16, 1994.

Califano Jr., Joseph A., Governing America, Simon and Schuster, New York, 1981.

Califano, Jr., Joseph A., "Revealing the link between campaign financing and deaths caused by tobacco," JAMA, Vol. 272, no. 15, Oct. 19, 1994, pg. 1217-1218.

"Environmental tobacco smoke in Workplace; Lung Cancer and other health effects," JAMA, July24/31, 1991, Vol. 266, no 4, pg. 471. [DHHS publication no. (NIOSH)91-108.

Fisher, Ian, "Tobacco funds go to black officials," The New York Times, November 19, 1995, A21.

Gostin, L.O, A.M. Brandt, and P.C. Cleary, "Tobacco liability and public health policy," JAMA, Vol. 266, no. 22, December 11, 1991.

Gray, Jerry, "House committee votes to continue tobacco subsidies," The New York Times, June 28, 1995.

Jensen, E. and E. Shapiro. "Philip Morris suit against ABC News seeks $10 billion, alleges defamation," The Wall Street Journal, March 25, 1994.

Levy, D., "Government also a victim of concealed smoke study," USA Today, May 18, 1994.

Marwick, C., "Tobacco control report card fails some federal entities, gives all tough future assignments," JAMA, Vol. 271, no. 9, pg. 645-647.

National Public Radio, "Tobacco Additives," April 8, 1994

Salwen, Kevin G., "Smoking ban may bring gain in productivity," The Wall Street Journal, March 28, 1994.

Schmitt, Eric, "Senate approves bill to phase our farming subsidies," The New York Times, February 8, 1996, A1.

Shapiro, Eric, "Philip Morris sues city over no smoking rules," The Wall Street Journal, February 2, 1994.

"Smoking Tobacco & Health," U.S. Department of Health and Human Services, Public Health Service, CDC, Office on Smoking & Health, DHHS Pub. No. (CDC) 87-8397, 1989.

Taylor, P., The Smoke Ring, Pantheon Books, New York, 1984.

Chapter fourteen:

Brownlee, S., S.V. Roberts, M. Cooper, E. Goode, K. Hetter, and A. Wright, "Should cigarettes be outlawed?," U.S. News & World Report, April 18, 1994.

Califano, Jr., Joseph A., "Revealing the link between campaign financing and deaths caused by tobacco," JAMA, Vol. 272, no. 15, Oct. 19, 1994, pg. 1217-1218.

Fisher, Ian, "Tobacco funds go to black officials," The New York Times, November 19, 1995, A-21.

Fritsch, Jane, "Tobacco companies pump cash into republican party's coffers," The New York Times, September 13, 1995. A1.

Greenberg, Paul. "PAC'S should become a campaign issue," The Houston Chronicle, April 5, 1996, 38A.

Kaplan, Sheila, "Tobacco Dole," Mother Jones, May/June 1996.

Moore, S., Wolfe, S.M., Lindes, D., Douglas, C.E., "Epidemiology of failed tobacco control legislation," JAMA, Vol. 272, no. 15, October 19, 1994, pg. 1171-1175.

Mother Jones, May/June 1996.

Samules, B., C. Douglas, C. Wolfe, and P. Wilbur, "Tobacco money, tobacco people, tobacco policies," Advocacy Institute Report, August 1992.

Seelye, Katharine Q., "Tobacco Politics Falter Even in Congress," The New York Times, April 2, 1994.

Specht J, "Foes have tobacco industry huffing, puffing," The Houston Post, May 7, 1994.

Taylor, P., The Smoke Ring, Pantheon Books, New York, 1984.

U.S. Public Interest Research Group, March 14, 1996.

Wartzman, R., "Campaign-finance reform may prove the test of republican resolve to change Washington," The Wall Street Journal, November 18, 1994.

"Well-Healed: Inside lobbing for health care reform," Washington, DC: Center for Public Integrity; 1994, pg. 62-63.

Chapter fifteen:

The American Lung Association, "Statistical update on lung diseases, 1991," U.S. Department of Health and Human Services, 1983.

ASH, Smoking and Health Review, Vol. XXIII, No. 5, 1993.

Califano, J. A., "Congress overlooking obvious Medicare savings," The Houston Chronicle, November 1, 1995.

Carter, Jimmy, "A healthy tobacco tax could help farmers too," The Houston Chronicle, February 11, 1994.

Centers for disease control and prevention, "Cigarette smoking-attributable mortality and years of potential lost U.S, 1990," MMWR, Vol. 42, 1993, Pg. 645-649.

Cooper, Helene, "Tobacco's troubles jeopardize the jobs of surprising few," The Wall Street Journal, April 14, 1994.

Cotton, Paul, "Smokers may pay, but not their own way," JAMA, Vol. 271, no. 9, March 2, 1994, pg. 644-645.

DeLay, Representative Tom, Personal Communication, February 16, 1994.

Escobedo, L.G, and J. P. Peddicord, "Smoking prevalence in US birth cohorts: The influence of gender and education," AJPH, Vol. 86, no 2, February 1996, pg. 231-236.

Hilts, Philip J., "Sharp rise seen in smokers' health care costs," The New York Times, July 8, 1994.

Hodgson, T. A., "Cigarette smoking and lifetime medical expenditures," Milbank Q, Vol. 70, 1992, pg. 81-125.

Janofsky, M., "Mississippi insists that tobacco giants 'pay for their sins," Houston Chronicle, May 24, 1994.

Lesmes, G. R., and K. H. Donofrio, "Passive smoking: The medical and economic issues," AJM, Vol. 93 (Suppl 1A), July 15, 1992, pg. 1A, 38S-41S.

Levin, Myron, "Budget office blocks smoke case statistics: Lobbying efforts prevent reporting," The Houston Chronicle, August 19, 1995, 8A.

MacKenzie, Thomas D., C.E. Bartecchi, and R.W. Schrier, "The Human Costs of Tobacco Use," NEJM, Vol. 330, no. 14, April 7, 1994, pg. 975-980.

Mansnerus, Laura, "Making a case for death," The New York Times, May 5, 1996, pg. 4-1.

"Maryland seeks attorneys for possible tobacco suit," The Wall Street Journal, November 17, 1995.

"Medical-Care expenditures attributable to cigarette smoking, United States, 1993," MMWR, Vol. 43, no. 26, July 8, 1994, pg. 469-472.

"Medicare's big cigarette burn," The New York Times, May 18, 1994.

Merrill, J.M., K. Fox, and H. Chang, "The cost of substance abuse to America's health care system, Report 1: Medicaid Hospital costs," New York, NY: Center on Addiction and Substance Abuse at Columbia University, 1994.

MMWR, Vol. 43, No. 19, pg.341-346.

Mother Jones Interactive, 1995, and U.S. PIRG.

Nelson, D.E., S.L. Emont, R.M. Brackbill, et al., "Cigarette smoking prevalence by occupation in the United States," J. Occupational Medicine, Vol. 36, no 5, pg. 516-525.

Nickens, Tim, "Chiles signs law intended to burn tobacco companies," The Houston Chronicle, May 27, 1994.

Pettigrew Kraft, B., "Pre-trial hearings start in landmark anti-tobacco lawsuit," The Houston Chronicle, December 19, 1994.

Rice, Dorothy P., SCSF, 1986, in White, Larry C., Merchants of Death , The American Tobacco Industry, Beech Tree Books, William Morrow and Company, New York, 1988

Rich, S., "Smoking hits a new low, and urge to quit is rising," The Houston Chronicle, December 23, 1994.

Roth, Bennett, "Putting out cigarettes called costly," The Houston Chronicle, April 29, 1994.

Schelling, T.C. "Economics and Cigarettes," Preventative Medicine, Vol. 15, 1986, pg. 549-60.

Shapiro, E., "More young adults smoke cigarettes U.S. data shows," The Wall Street Journal, May 20, 1994.

Shopland, D.R, S.J. Niemcryk, and K.M. Marconi, "Geographic and gender variations in total tobacco use," AJPH, Vol. 82, no.1, pg. 103-106.

Simmons, John, To the editor: JAMA, Vol. 275, no 4, January 24/31, 1996, pg 276.

"Smoking-related deaths and financial costs: estimates for 1990," Rev.ed. Washington, D.C. Office of Technology Assessment, 1993.

"Smoking and health in the Americans: a 1992 report of the Surgeon General, in collaboration with the Pan American Health Organization: executive summary," Atlanta: Department of Health and Human Services, 1992. (DHHS publication no. (CDC) 92-8421).

The Wall Street Journal, October 31, 1995, pg.A-1.

Wells, A. Judson, "Passive smoking as a cause of heart disease," J. American College of Cardiology, Vol 24, no. 2, August 1994, pg 546-554.

White, J. R, and H.F. Froeb, "Small airways dysfunction in nonsmokers chronically exposed to tobacco smoke," NEJM, 1980, pg. 270-273.

Woo, Junda, "Mississippi want tobacco firms to pay its cost of treating welfare recipients," The Wall Street Journal, May 24, 1994.

Woo, Junda, "Tobacco firms face greater health liability," The Wall Street Journal, May 5, 1994.

Wynder E. L., and S. D. Stellman, "Comparative epidemiology of tobacco-related cancers," Cancer Research, Vol. 37, 1977, pg. 4608-4622.

Chapter sixteen:

Collins, Glenn, "Selection of judge stirs debate over tobacco companies's suit," The New York Times, August 15, 1995.

FDA, "Regulations restricting the sale and distribution of cigarettes and smokeless tobacco products to protect children and adolescents; Proposed Rule," Federal Register, August 11, 1995, 21 CFR Part 801. pg. 41314-41375.

Fisher, Ian, "Tobacco funds go to black officials," The New York Times, November 19, 1995, A21.

Hilts, Philip J., "Tobacco held to be drug that must be regulated," The New York Times, July 13, 1995.

Hilts, Philip J., "FDA panel takes step toward setting control on nicotine," The New York Times, August 2, 1994.

Kessler, David A., "Nicotine addiction in young people," NEJM, Vol. 333, no. 3, July 20, 1995, pg. 186-189.

Kilborn, Peter T., "Clinton approves a series of curbs on cigarette ads," The New York Times, August 24, 1996, A1.

Knutson, Lawrence L., "Dole chided for tobacco remark," The Houston Chronicle, June 16, 1996, 10A.

Mahar, Maggie, "Tobacco's smoking gun," Barron's, May 16, 1994.

McGinley, Laurie, "GOP takes aim at FDA, seeking to ease way for approval of new drugs, medical products," The Wall Street Journal, December 12, 1994.

McGinley, Laurie, "What David Kessler wants any how he'll try to get it," The Wall Street Journal, June 23, 1994.

McGinley. Laurie, "Cigarettes now on market are addictive, FDA drug abuse advisory panel finds," The Wall Street Journal, August 3, 1994.

Mother Jones, May/June 1996.

"Nicotine Attack: Cigarette regulation is formally proposed; Industry sues to halt it," The Wall Street Journal, August 11, 1995, A1.

The New York Times, June 17, 1996, A9.

U.S. Public Interest Research Group, March 96, 1996

Chapter seventeen:

Altman, David G., "Tobacco control advocacy," Stanford Center for Research and Disease Prevention, California Department of Health Services, 1993.

American. Journal of Hospital Pharmacy, Vol. 51, May 15, 1994.

"Assessment of the impact of a 100% smoke-free ordinance on restaurant sales - West Lake Hills, TX, 1992-1994," MMWR, Vol. 44, 1995, pg. 369-372.

Glantz, S. A, and L.R.A. Smith, "The effect of ordinances requiring smoke-free restaurants on restaurant sales," AJ PH, Vol. 84, no. 7, July 1994, pg. 1081-1085.

Hilts, Philip J., "Smoking ban wins Clinton' support," The New York Times, Feb. 8, 1994.

Hilts, P. J., "U.S. sees a smoking ban saving $39 billion," New York Times, April 21, 1994.

Hwang, Suein L., "Letter from a tobacco company to an art professor, August 1970," The Wall Street Journal, July 21, 1995.

King Jr., Ralph T., "Willie Brown, favorite of the tobacco industry, lets San Francisco proceed with cigarette suit," The Wall Street Journal, July 2, 1996, A14.

Marwick, Charles, "Tobacco control report card fails some Federal entities, gives all tough future assignments," JAMA, Vol. 271, no. 9, March 2, 1994, pg. 645-647.

New York Times, April 4, 1994.

Referendums, a comparative study of practice and theory, Editors: David Butler and Austin Ranney, American Enterprise Institute for public policy Research, Washington, D.C. 1978

Skolnick, A.A., "Anti-tobacco advocates fight 'illegal' diversion of tobacco control money," JAMA, Vol. 2271, no. 18, 1994, pg. 1287-1390.

Todd, J.S. et al. [Editorial]. "The Brown and Williamson Documents -Where do we go from here?," JAMA, Vol. 274, no. 3, July 19, 1995. pg. 256-258.

Waxman, Henry, "Stop the drugging of our children," Los Angeles Times, April 11, 1994.

White, Larry C., Merchants of Death, Beech Tree Books, New York, 1988.

Appendix

"AMA wants tobacco-free mutual funds," The Wall Street Journal, April 24, 1996.

Benoqitz, N.L., R. Kuyt, P. Jacob III, R.T. Jones, and A.L. Osman, "Cotinine disposition and effects," Clinical Pharmacology and Therapeutics, Vol. 34, 1983, pg. 604-611.

Benowitz, N.L., P. Jacob III, R.T. Jones, and J. Rosenberg, "Interindividual variability in the metabolism and cardiovascular effects of nicotine in man," J. Pharmacol Exp.Ther, Vol 221, 1982, pg 368-372.

Benowitz, N.L., "Pharmacologic aspects of cigarette smoking and nicotine addiction," NEJM, Vol. 319, no. 20, 1988, pg 1318-1330.

Benowitz, N.L., and P. Jacob III, "Daily intake of nicotine during cigarette smoking," Clinical Pharmacol Ther., Vol. 35, 1984, pg. 499-504.

Clarke, P.B., C. B. Pert, and A. Pert, "Autoradiographic distribution of nicotine receptors in rat brain," Brain Res., Vol. 323, 1984, pg. 390-395.

Collaborative Group for the Study of Stroke in Young Women, "Oral contraceptives and stroke in young women: associated risk factors," JAMA, Vol. 231, 1975, pg 718-722.

EPA, "Respiratory health effects of passive smoking: Lung Cancer and other disorders," Office of Health and Environmental Assessment, Washington, D.C. 1992. EPA/600/6-90/006F.

Gehlbach, S.H., W.A. Williams, L.D. Perry, and J.S. Woodall, "Green-tobacco sickness: an illness of tobacco harvesters," JAMA, Vol 229, 1974, pg. 1880-1883.

Glantz, S.A., and W.W. Parmley, "Passive smoking and heart disease: epidemiology, physiology, and biochemistry," Circulation, Vol. 83, no. 1, 1991, pg. 1-12.

Goodman and Gilman's, The Pharmacological Basis of Therapeutics, Sixth edition, Editors: A. G. Gilman, L.S. Goodman. and A. Gilman, Macmillan Publishing Co., Inc., New York, 1980

Handbook of Poisoning, R. H. Dreisbach, Lange Medical Publications, 1977.

Hilts, Philip J., "Cigarette Makers Dispute reports on addictiveness," New York Times, April 15, 1994.

Jones, D., and J. Cox, "What would our lives be like?," USA TODAY, June 9, 1994.

Luck, W., and H. Nau, "Exposure of the fetus, neonate, and nursed infant to nicotine and cotinine from maternal smoking," NEJM., Vol. 311, 1984, pg. 672.

McGinley, L., "Tobacco-research council, financed by industry, is criticized in Congress," The Wall Street Journal, May 27, 1994.

McKinlay, S.M., N.L. Bifano, and J.B. McKinlay, "Smoking and age at menopause in women," Annals Internal Medicine, Vol. 103, 1985, pg. 350-356.

"Mutual fund investors advised to sniff out tobacco," JAMA, Vol. 275 no.16. April 24, 1996, pg 1222.

Nicod, P., R. Rehr, M.D. Winniford, W.B. Campbell, B.G. Firth, and L.D. Hillis, "Acute systemic and coronary hemodynamic and serologic responses to cigarette smoking in long-term smokers with artherosclerotic coronary artery disease," J. American College of Cardiology, Vol. 4, 1984, pg. 964-971.

NIOSH, Current Intelligence Bulletin 54, June 1991, Environmental Tobacco Smoke in the workplace.

Pool, W.F., C.S. Godin, and P.A. Crooks, "Nicotine racemization during cigarette smoking," Toxicologist, Vol. 5, 1985, pg 232.

Rebecca Pearl, , " Tobacco Additives," National Public Radio, April 8, 1994.

Recer, P., "Best-selling snuffs lead in carcinogens," from the *J. of the National Cancer Institute,* in The Houston Chronicle, December 20, 1995.

Shapireo, S., D. Stone, L. Rosenberg, D.W. Kaufman, P.D. Stolley, and O.S. Miettinen, "Oral-contraceptive use in relation to myocardial infarction," Lancet, Vol. 1, 1979, pg. 743-747.

Stellman, J.M. and S.D. Stellman, "Cancer and the Workplace," CA, Vol 46, no. 2, pg. 70-92, 1996.

Tilashalski, K., B. Rodu, and C. Mayfield, "Assessing the nicotine content of smokeless tobacco products," JADA, Vol. 125, May 1994, pg 590-594.

"Tobacco Holdings," The New York Times, March 17, 1996, 7F.

Abbreviations used in bibliography

AJM	American Journal of Medicine
AJPH	American Journal of Public Health
Arc.Int.Med.	Archives of Internal Medicine
BMJ	British Medical Journal
CA	Ca-A Cancer Journal for Clinicians
JADA	Journal of the American Dental Association
JAMA	Journal of the American Medical Association
MMWR	Mortality and Morbidity Weekly Review
NEJM	New England Journal of Medicine

Environmental Tobacco Smoke is Responsible

for the Death of One Nonsmoking Person

Every 6 1/2 Minutes.

Appendixes

Page

APPENDIX A: The Tobacco Industry: Major Companys and Products

COMPANY (Parents & Divisions)	1993 Net Tobacco Revenue (Billions)	BRANDS
Philip Morris, USA; Dave's Tobacco Co.	$26.2	Marlboro, Benson & Hedges, Merit, Virginia Slims, Bristol, Bucks, Alpine, Players Navy Cut, Cambridge, Parliament, Saratoga, Philip Morris, Basic, Dave's, Park 500
R.J. Reynolds Tobacco USA; (RJR Nabisco Inc.) Moonlight Tobacco Co.	$8.0	Winston, Salem, Camels, Doral, Magna, Vantage, More, NOW, Monarch, Best Value, Century, Sterling, Jumbos, Sedona, Bees, Metro, Politix, Red Kamel, Moonlight.
U.S. Tobacco Co. (UST)	$0.924	Copenhagen, Skoal, Borkum Riff, Don Tomas
Lorillard Tobacco Co. (Lowes Corp)	$0.959	True, Kent, Newport, Old Gold, Spring, Triumph, Max 120's, Satin, Style
Liggett Group Inc. (Brooke Group Ltd.)	NA	Eve, Lark, L&M, Chesterfield
American Tobacco Co, (American Brands, Inc.) [a]	$1.51	Carlton, Lucky Strike, Pall Mall, Tareyton, American, Malibu, Misty, Montclair, Riviera, Prime, Private Stock, Silva Thins, Summit
Brown & Williamson Tobacco Corp. (B&W) British American Tobacco Co. (B.A.T. Industries)	$19.9	Barclay, Belair, Kool, Raleigh, Richland, Viceroy, Capri, GPC

[a] B.A.T. acquired American Tobacco Co. April 1994.

Other Manufactures and Sellers of Tobacco Products

Brook Group
Culbro (General Cigar)
DiMon
Hanson
Mafco Consolidated Group
Sara Lee
Schweitzer-Mauduit International
Standard Commercial
Universal
Helme Tobacco Co.
Alfred Dunhill
Davidoff
Temple Hall
Swisher International
Havatampa Inc.
Conwood Co., L.P.
National Tobacco Co.
Pinkenton Tobacco Co.
Mac Andrews & Forbes

Non-Tobacco Brands Sold by Tobacco Companies:

Loews	CBS, CNA Financial Insurance Co., Loews Hotels, Bulova, CBS, Champion International.
Philip Morris, Plank Road Brewery	Kraft Foods, Jell-O, Kool-Aid, Cool-Whip, Entenmann's Cakes, Oscar Mayer, Churny Co., General Foods Bakery Co., Lewis Rich Co., Maxwell House, Seven Seas Salad Dressings, Miller beer, Red Dog beer, Icehouse beer, Post cereals, Nabisco cereals b.
RJR Nabisco	Oreo, Ritz, Chips Ahoy!, Wheat Thins, SnackWell, Fleischmann's, Planters, Life Savers, Breath Savers, Del Monte Foods.
UST	Wine: Chateau St. Michelle, Conn Creek, Columbia Crest, Villa Mount Eden.
B.A.T.	Farmer New World Life, Ohio State Life Insurance Co.

[b] Philip Morris purchased Nabisco Cereals from RJR Nabisco in 1993.

APPENDIX B:

Composition of Mainstream Tobacco Smoke

and IARC or EPA Category of Carcinogenicity.

Table I
Major Components of the Vapor Phase

Carbon monoxide		Hydrogen cyanide	
Carbon dioxide		Hydrazine	*Probable carcinogen*
Carbonyl sulfide		Ammonia	
Benzene	*Group 1 carcinogen*	Methylamine	
Toluene		Dimethylamine	
Formaldehyde	*Group 2A carcinogen*	Nitrogen oxides	
Acrolein		N-Nitrosodime-thylamine	*Group 2A carcinogen*
Acetone		N-Nitrosodieth-ylamine	*Group 2A carcinogen*
Pyridine		N-Nitrosopyrr-olidine	*Probable carcinogen*
3-Methylpyridine		Formic acid	
3-Vinylpyridine		Acetic acid	
Methyl chloride		1,3-Butadiene	*Group 2A carcinogen*
Acetaldehyde			

Composition of Mainstream Tobacco Smoke

and IARC or EPA Category of Carcinogenicity.

Table II

Major Components of the Particulate Phase

Particulate matter		Cholesterol	
Nicotine		γ-Butyrolactone	*Probable carcinogen*
Anatabine		Quinoline	
Phenol	*Cancer Promoter*	Harman (1-methyl-9H-pyrido-[3,4-β]-indole)	
Catechol	*Co-carcinogen*	N-Nitroso-nornicotine	*Nitrosoamine*
Hydroquinone		NNK	*Nitrosoamine*
Aniline	*Probable carcinogen*	N-Nitroso-diethanolamine	*Probable carcinogen*
2-Toluidine		Cadminum	*Group 1 carcinogen*
2-Naphthylamine	*Group 1 carcinogen*	Nickel	*Group 1 carcinogen*
4-Aminobiphenyl	*Group 1 carcinogen*	Zinc	
Benzo[a]pyrene	*Probable carcinogen*	Polonium-210	*Known carcinogen*
Benz[a]anthracene	*Group2A carcinogen*	Benzoic acid	
Lactic acid		Succinic acid	
Glycolic acid		Polychlorinated dibenzo-p-dioxins (PCDD)	
		Polychlorinated dibenzofurans (PCDF)	

International Agency for Research on Cancer (IRAC) assessments of chemical carcinogenicity.

Category	**Carcinogenicity**
Group 1	Carcinogenic to humans
Group 2A	Probably carcinogenic to humans
Group 2B	Possibly carcinogenic to humans
Group 4	Probably not carcinogenic to humans

APPENDIX C:
Composition of Environmental Tobacco Smoke
and IARC or EPA Category of Carcinogenicity.

Carbon monoxide		Hydrogen cyanide	
Carbon dioxide		o-Cresol	*Group 2A carcinogen*
Benzene	*Group 1 carcinogen*	m + p-Cresol	*Group 2A carcinogen*
Toluene		Nitrogen oxides	
Formaldehyde	*Group 2A carcinogen*	Phenol	*Promoter*
Acrolein		Hydroquinone	
Acetone		N-Nitrosopyrrolidine	*Probable carcinogen*
Ammonia		NNK	*Nitrosoamine*
Pyridine		N-nitrosonornicotine	*Nitrosoamine*
3-hydroxypyridine		N-nitrosoanatabine	*Nitrosoamine*
3-Vinylpyridine		N-nitrosoanabasine	*Nitrosoamine*
Limonene		Dimethylnitrosamine	*Nitrosoamine*
Neophytadiene		Ethylmethylnitrosamine	*Nitrosoamine*
Isoprene		Diethylnitrosamine	*Nitrosoamine*
Benz[a]anthracene	*Group2A carcinogen*	Acetaldehyde	
Benzo[a]pyrene	*Probable carcinogen*	Propionaldehyde	
Nicotine		nC27-nC33	
Styrene		Catechol	*Co-carcinog-en*
Pyrrole		Phenanthrene	
Acetonitrile		Fluoranthene	
Acrylonitrile	*Group 2A carcinogen*	2-Naphthylamine	*Group 1 carcinogen*
Naphthalene		Nickel	*Group 1 carcinogen*
Anthracene		Lead	
Pyrene		Chromium	*Group 1 carcinogen*
4-Aminobiphenyl		Cadmium	*Group 1 carcinogen*

APPENDIX D:

Nicotine Concentrations of Smokeless Tobacco Brands

BRAND	TYPE	NICOTINE mg	NICOTINE Percent*	pH	MANUFACTURE
Hawken	Snuff	3.2	0.59%	5.4 - 5.7	Conwood Co., L.P
Beech-nut	Loose Leaf	na	0.77%	na	National Tobacco Co.
Red-Man	Loose Leaf	na	0.87%	na	Pinkenton Tobacco Co.
Lancaster	Loose Leaf	na	1.10%	na	Helme Tobacco Co.
Day's Work	Plug	na	1.63%	na	Pinkenton Tobacco Co.
Cannon-Ball	Plug	na	1.67%	na	Conwood Co., L.P
Skoal Bandits, straight	Snuff	10.1	2.16%	5.4 - 5.7	US Tobacco
Kodiak	Snuff	10.9 – 12.0	2.99%	7.5 - 8.2	Conwood Co., L.P.
Copenhagen	Snuff	10.9 – 12.0	3.20%	7.5 - 8.2	US Tobacco
Skoal, long-cut	Snuff	10.9 – 12.0	3.33%	7.5 - 8.2	US Tobacco
Skoal, long-cut, Wintergreen	Snuff	na	3.35%	7.5 - 8.2	US Tobacco

APPENDIX E

Tobacco Industry Sponsored Organizations and Publications:

Pro-Tobacco Organizations:

The Australian Tobacco Council

The Center for Indoor Air Research **(CIAR)**

Council for Tobacco Research **(CTR)**

National Smokers Alliance

Restaurants for a Sensible Voluntary Policy

The Smokeless Tobacco Council

The Tobacco Institute

Pro-Tobacco Publications:

American Smokers Alliance

American Smokers Journal

Choice

Healthy Buildings

National Smokers Alliance

Smokers' Advocate

Organizations Sympathetic to the Tobacco Industry:

Citizens for a Sound Economy

Competitive Enterprise Institute

Progress & Freedom Foundation

Washington Legal Foundation

APPENDIX F

Product Insert:

TOBACCO: CIGARETTES, CIGARS, PIPE TOBACCO.

A cigarette is a nicotine delivery device that provides systemic delivery of nicotine (about 1mg. each) following inhalation of its combustible products. Nicotine is the pharmacologically active ingredient. WARNING: MAY BE HABIT FORMING. All other components are biologically hazardous. Nicotine is a tertiary amine composed of a pyridine and a pyrrolidine ring. It is a colorless to pale yellow, freely water soluble, strongly alkaline, oily, volatile, hygroscopic liquid, present in the tobacco plant. Nicotine has a characteristic pungent odor and turns brown on exposure to air or light. Of its two stereoisomers R and S, S(-)-nicotine is the more active and is the more prevalent form in tobacco. During the combustion of tobacco, racemization increases the R-isomer to 10%.[1] The free alkaloid is absorbed rapidly through the respiratory tract.

Chemical name: S-3-(1-methyl-2-pyrrolidinyl) pyridine

Molecular Formula: $C_{10}H_{14}N_2$

MolecularWeight: 162.23

Ionization Constants: pKa1=7.84, pKa2=3.04

Octanol-Water Partition Coefficient: 15:1 at pH7.

Chemical composition of tobacco smoke:[3]

Contains 4000 compounds in the gas and particle phases. Rapid inhalation creates different chemicals than slow gently inhalation.
Gas phase contains: Carbon dioxide, nitrogen oxides, ammonia, volatile nitrosamines, hydrogen cyanide, sulfur-compounds, nitriles, hydrocarbons, aldehydes and ketones, e.g. formaldehyde.
Particulate phase contains: Nicotine, water, and tar.
Tar is a polycyclic aromatic hydrocarbons. Tar is what is left after water and nicotine are removed. Tar contains 60 documented carcinogens, such as: nitrosamines and aromatic amines, (role in bladder cancer), polycyclic hydrocarbons (exceedingly potent carcinogens), benzo[a]pyrene (Initiate and accelerate development of coronary lesions), metallic ions and several radioactive compounds, such as polonium 210, and DDT (banned insecticide).

Warning: Polonium-210, is a radioactive isotope found in tobacco. Radioactive compounds are known to cause cancer.

Partial chemical composition of tobacco smoke:

VAPOR PHASE	VAPOR PHASE	PARTICULATE PHASE	PARTICULATE PHASE
Carbon monoxide	Hydrogen cyanide	Particulate matter	Cholesterol
Carbon dioxide	Hydrazine	Nicotine	γ-Butyrolactone
Carbonyl sulfide	Ammonia	Anatabine	Quinoline
Benzene	Methylamine	Phenol	Harman
Toluene	Dimethylamine	Catechol	N-Nitroso-nornicotine
Formaldehyde	Nitrogen oxides	Hydroquinone	NNK
Acrolein	N-Nitroso-dimethylamine	Aniline	N-Nitroso-ethanolamine
Acetone	N-Nitroso-dethylamine	2-Toluidine	Cadmium
Pyridine	N-Nitroso-pyrrolidine	2-Naphthylamine	Nickel
3-Methylpyridine	Formic acid	4-Aminobiphenyl	Zinc
3-Vinylpyridine	Acetic acid	Benzo[a]pyrene	Polonium-210
MethCyl chloride	1,3-Butadiene	Benz[a]anthracene	Benzoic acid
Acetaldehyde		Lactic acid	Succinic acid
		Glycolic acid	PCDDs, PCDF's

Partial list of chemical additives that may be contained in the tobacco: [2]

Additives	Properties	EPA Classification
1. Nicotine sulfate	Addictive drug; Toxin	
2. Di-n-hexyl ether	Enhances combustion; gasoline additive	
3. Dehydroxy-metho-puro lactone	Flavor	
4. Mega stigma trianone	Untested food additive	
5. Maltatol	Artificial sweetener; Not FDA approved	
6. Tobacco extract	Contains nicotine, and carcinogens	
7. Ammonia	Toxic irritant; "Impact booster"- Releases 'free'- nicotine.	
8. Angelica root extract	Carcinogen; Toxin	**Toxin**
9. Sclareol	Toxin; Pro-convulsant; Causes convulsions in animals	**Toxin**
10. Guranic acid	Liver toxin	**Toxin**
11. Ethyl Furoid, (2-furoate)	Liver toxin; Biological warfare agent.	**Toxin**
12. Methaprine	Insecticide; Toxin	**Toxin**
13. Freon-11, (no longer used)	Chloroflurohydrocarbon; When burned, forms phosgene, a suffocating and highly poisonous war gas.	

Experts say carbon monoxide, nicotine, and tar are the most likely contributors to health hazards. Probable contributors are: acrolein, hydrocyanic acid, nitric oxide, nitrogen dioxide, cresols, and amohenols. Suspected hazards include acetaldehyde, acetone, acetonitrile, acrylonitrile, ammonia, benzene, and other gases. In the particulate phase, butylamine, dimethylamine, DDT, endrin, furfural, and others are also suspected as hazardous. [5]

CLINICAL PHARMACOLOGY

Pharmacodynamics

Nicotine, the chief alkaloid in tobacco products, binds stereoselectively to acetylcholine receptors at the autonomic ganglia, in the adrenal medulla, at neuromuscular junctions, and in the brain. Nicotine readily crosses the blood-brain barrier and is rapidly taken up by the brain. [6] Widely distributed in brain, nicotine binds specifically to the hypothalamus, hippocampus, thalamus, midbrain, brain stem and the cerebral cortex. [7]

Pharmacologic Action

Two types of central nervous system effects are believed to be the basis of nicotine's positively reinforcing properties. A stimulating effect, exerted mainly in the cortex via the locus ceruleus, produces increased alertness and cognitive performance. A "reward" effect via the "pleasure system" in the brain is exerted in the limbic system. At low doses the stimulant effects predominate, while at high doses the reward effects will predominate. Intermittent intravenous administration of nicotine activates neurohormonal pathways, releasing acetylcholine, norepinephrine, dopamine, serotonin, vasopressin, beta-endorphin, growth hormone, and ACTH.

The cardiovascular effects of nicotine include peripheral vasoconstriction, tachycardia, and elevated blood pressure.

Acute and chronic tolerance to nicotine develops from smoking tobacco or ingesting nicotine preparations. Acute tolerance (a reduction in response for a given does) develops usually in less than one hour. Full sensitivity is reached about 1 1/2 hours after a cigarette. The heart rate effects of nicotine will persist during the day, and overnight, despite the development of short-term tolerance.

The cardiovascular effect of smoking every 30 minutes during waking hours for 5 days was determined. The heart rate was elevated (about 10 beats/min) and blood pressure increased (about 5 mm Hg). In the healthy individual, nicotine increases the heart rate and blood pressure, cardiac stroke volume and output, and coronary blood flow. [8]

Withdrawal from nicotine, in addicted individuals, is characterized by craving, nervousness, restlessness, irritability, mood lability, anxiety, drowsiness, sleep disturbances, impaired concentration, increased appetite, minor somatic complaints (headache, myalgia, constipation, fatigue), and weight gain. Nicotine toxicity is characterized by nausea, abdominal pain, vomiting, diarrhea, diaphoresis, flushing, dizziness, disturbed hearing and vision, confusion, weakness, palpitations, altered respiration, and hypotension.

Pharmacokinetics

Absorption: Tar is quickly absorbed by the lung. The small airways and alveoli of the lung rapidly absorb nicotine. Nicotine reaches the brain in eight seconds, faster than by intravenous administration. Pipe and cigar smoke is absorbed through the mucous membranes.[9] The bioavailability of nicotine, depending upon the intensity and the method used to smoke, ranges from 3 to 40 percent. The dose of nicotine delivered ranges from 0.3 to 3.2 mg. per cigarette.[10]

Nicotine rapidly enters the systemic circulation. The volume of distribution following IV administration of nicotine is approximately 2 to 3 L/kg. The half-life of nicotine averages 2 hours, range from one to four hours.[11] The major elimination is by the liver, and average plasma clearance is about 1.2 min. To a small degree, the kidney and lung metabolize nicotine. More than 20 metabolites of nicotine have been identified, all of which are believed to be less active than the parent compound. The primary metabolites of nicotine are nicotine-*N*-oxide, and cotinine. Cotinine, has a plasma half-life of 15 to 20 hours, and concentrations that exceed nicotine by ten fold. [12]

Plasma protein binding of nicotine is <5%. Therefore, changes in nicotine blinding from use of concomitant drugs or alterations of plasma proteins by disease states would not be expected to have significant consequences.

The primary urinary metabolites are cotinine (15% of the dose) and trans-3-hydroxycotinine (45% of the dose). About 10% of nicotine is excreted in the urine with high urine flow rates and urine acidification below pH 5.0.

INDICATIONS AND USAGE

None. All smokers should be instructed to stop smoking immediately.

CONTRAINDICATIONS

The use of tobacco products, cigarettes, cigars, pipe tobacco, chewing tobacco, snuff, is contraindicated in humans.

WARNINGS

Nicotine from any source (active or passive) can be toxic. Smoking causes lung cancer, heart disease, and emphysema and may adversely effect the fetus and the pregnant woman. Therefore patients that smoke should be encouraged to attempt cessation of smoking immediately, using educational, behavioral intervention or pharmacologic approaches.

Drug Dependence.

Nicotine can produce drug dependence and therefore has the potential for abuse. Psychic dependence, physical dependence, and tolerance may develop upon repeated use.

Pregnancy Warning

Tobacco smoke, which has been shown to be harmful to the fetus, contains nicotine, hydrogen cyanide, and carbon monoxide. Nicotine freely crosses the placental barrier, and has been detected in amniotic fluid and neonatal blood.[13] Nicotine has been shown in animal studies to cause fetal harm.

Safety Note Concerning Children

The amounts of nicotine that are tolerated by adult smokers can produce symptoms of poisoning and could prove fatal if ingested by children. Ingestion of tobacco by children causes seizures, hypotension, and respiratory failure.[14] One cigarette taken orally can be lethal.

Keep out of the reach of children and pets.

PRECAUTIONS

Patients should be urged to stop smoking immediately.

Cancer

Neoplastic diseases are probably due to one or more of the following know carcinogens in tobacco smoke: BENZENE, FORMALDEHYDE, HYDRAZINE, N-NITROSODIMETHYLAMINE, N-NITROSOPYRROLIDINE, TAR, o-TOLUIDINE, 2-NAPHTHYLAMINE, 4-AMINOBIPHENYL. BENZ(a)ANTHRACENE, BENZO(a)PYRENE, QUINOLINE, N'NITROSONORNICOTINE, NNK, N-NITROSODIETHANOLAMINE,

CADMIUM, NICKEL, POLONIUM-210.[15] Smoking causes cancer of the lung, larynx, oral cavity, esophagus, bladder, breast, and pancreas. Synergism of the ciliotoxic actions with environmental carcinogens has been described.[16]

Cardiovascular or Peripheral Vascular Diseases

Cardiovascular diseases related to smoking include: coronary artery disease, atherosclerosis, cerebrovascular disease, peripheral vascular disease, Burger's disease, and atherosclerotic vascular disease.[17] Patients with existing coronary heart disease are more susceptible to smoking-induced myocardial ischemia, and coronary spasm. The risks of nicotine are higher in patients with cardiovascular and peripheral vascular diseases. Nicotine and carbon monoxide increase platelet aggregation, leading to an increased risk of thrombus formation and myocardial infarction.[18]

Accelerated Hypertension

Smoking constitutes a risk factor for development of malignant hypertension in patients with accelerated hypertension.

Renal or Hepatic Insufficiency

Nicotine is extensively metabolized primarily by the liver, and its total system clearance is dependent on liver blood flow. Some influence of hepatic impairment of drug kinetics (renal clearance) should be anticipated.

Endocrine Diseases

Nicotine causes the release of catecholamines by the adrenal medulla. Patients with hyperthyroidism, pheochromocytoma or insulin-dependent diabetes are at higher risk. Smoking is associated with early menopause in women. [19]

Peptic Ulcer Disease

Nicotine delays healing in peptic ulcer disease. Smoking is a major risk factor for the recurrence of peptic ulcer disease.

Drug Interactions

Polycyclic aromatic hydrocarbons found in tobacco smoke will accelerate the metabolism of drugs by cytochrome P-448 enzymes. Smoking may alter the pharmacokinetics of certain concomitant medications. Smokers may required an increased dose of the following drugs: Antipyrine,

acetaminophen, caffeine, imipramine, desmethyldiazepam, lidocaine, oxazepam, pentazocine, phenacetin, propranolol, theophylline, insulin, and adrenergic antagonists (e.g. prozosin, labetalol). [20]
Smokers may require a lower dose of adrenergic agonists (isoproterenol, phenylephrine).
Cigarette smoking and the use of oral contraceptives may increase the risk of stroke and myocardial infarction in women. [21, 22]

Carcinogenesis, Mutagenesis, Impairment of Fertility

Nicotine itself does not appear to be a carcinogen in laboratory animals. Nicotine is nitrosalated in burning tobacco and in the curing process of smokeless tobacco. The N-nitrosamines formed by nitrosalation are highly carcinogenic.
Nicotine and its metabolites increased the incidence of tumors in the cheek pouches of hamsters and for stomach of F344 rats, respectively, when given in combination with tumor-initiators. One study, which could not be replicated, suggested that cotinine, the primary metabolite of nicotine, may cause lymphoreticular sarcoma in the large intestine in rats. Neither nicotine nor cotinine were mutagenic in the Ames *Salmonella* test. Nicotine induced repairable DNA damage in an *E. coli* test system. Nicotine was shown to be genotoxic in a test system using Chinese hamster ovary cells. In rats and rabbits, implantation can be delayed or inhibited by a reduction in DNA synthesis that appears to be caused by nicotine. Studies have shown a decrease in litter size in rats treated with nicotine during gestation.

PREGNANCY

The harmful effects of cigarette smoking on maternal and fetal health are clearly established. These include low birth weight, an increased risk of spontaneous abortion, and increased perinatal mortality.

Teratogenicity

Cigarette smoking during pregnancy is associated with an increased risk of spontaneous abortion, low birth weight infants, kidney malformations, and perinatal mortality. Nicotine and carbon monoxide are considered the most likely mediators of these outcomes. The effects of cigarette smoking on fetal cardiovascular parameters have been studied near term. Cigarettes increased fetal aortic blood flow and heart rate and decreased uterine blood flow and fetal breathing movements. Nicotine passes freely into breast milk. An infant has the ability to clear nicotine by hepatic first pass clearance' however, the efficiency of removal is probably lowest at birth.

DRUG ABUSE AND DEPENDENCE

Psychic dependence, physical dependence, and tolerance may develop upon starting smoking. In 80% of smokers, cessation of the use of tobacco is followed by a withdrawal syndrome, which may vary from person to person. Withdrawal from nicotine in addicted individuals is characterized by craving, nervousness, restlessness, irritability, mood lability, anxiety, drowsiness, sleep disturbances, impaired concentration, increased appetite, minor somatic complaints (headache, myalgia, constipation, fatigue), and weight gain.

OVERDOSAGE

Overdosage from Ingestion

Persons ingesting tobacco products should be referred to a health care facility for management. As little as one pure drop of nicotine, or the amount contained in 2 cigarettes can be lethal. Due to the possibility of nicotine-induced seizures, activated charcoal should be administered. In unconscious patients with a secure airway, instill activated charcoal via a nasogastric tube. Atropine can be given as an antidote. Phentolamine 1-5mg IV or IM can be given to control signs of sympathetic hyperactivity, such as hypertension.[23]

SAFETY AND HANDLING

Burning cigarettes are a fire hazard. Handle carefully, cigarette burns can be serious. Do not smoke while intoxicated. Do not smoke in bed. Do not smoke during dry conditions in forested areas.

Avoid direct contact of tobacco with skin. Do not touch the eyes after handling. If tobacco is handled, wash skin with water.

Tobacco harvesters are at risk of green-tobacco sickness. Cutaneous absorption of nicotine results in nausea, vomiting, pallor, weakness, dizziness, light-headedness, headache, and sweating.[24]

Proper Disposal

Be certain cigarette is extinguished before disposal. Dispose in a way to prevent its access by children or pets. Do not smoke during dry conditions in forested areas. Cigarette butts are considered a hazardous toxic waste product. Do not litter. Runoff from areas containing large accumulation of cigarette butts, such as door ways to buildings, could cause contamination of ground water.

WARNING:

Federal law prohibits selling to children under 18 years of age.

References:
[1] Pool, W.F., C.S. Godin, and P.A. Crooks, "Nicotine racemization during cigarette smoking", Toxicologist, Vol. 5, 1985, pg. 232.
[2] Pearl, Rebecca, National Public Radio, Report on Tobacco Additives, April 8, 1994.
[3] Goodman and Gilman's "The Pharmacological Basis of Therapeutics," Sixth edition, Editors: A. G. Gilman, L.S. Goodman. and A. Gilman, Macmillan Publishing CO., Inc., New York, 1980
[4] EPA, "Respiratory health effects of passive smoking: Lung Cancer and other disorders", Office of Health and Environmental Assessment, Washington, D.C. 1992. EPA/600/6-90/006F.
[5] Goodman and Gilman's "The Pharmacological Basis of Therapeutics," Sixth edition, Editors: A. G. Gilman, L.S. Goodman. and A. Gilman, Macmillan Publishing CO., Inc., New York, 1980.
[6] Benowitz, N.L., "Pharmacologic aspects of cigarette smoking and nicotine addiction", NEJM, Vol. 319, No. 20, 1988, pg 1318-1330.
[7] Clarke, P.B., C.B. Pert, and A. Pert, "Autoradiographic distribution of nicotine receptors in rat brain', Brain Res. Vol 323, (1984), pg.. 390-395.
[8] Nicod, P., R. Rehr, M.D. Winniford, W.B. Campbell, B.G. Firth, and L.D. Hillis, "Acute systemic and coronary hemodynamic and serologic responses to cigarette smoking in long-term smokers with artherosclerotic coronary artery disease", J. American Coll. Cardiol, Vol. 4, 1984, pg 964-971.
[9]Goodman and Gilman's "The Pharmacological Basis of Therapeutics," Sixth edition, Editors: A. G. Gilman, L.S. Goodman. and A. Gilman, Macmillan Publishing CO., Inc., New York, 1980.
[10] Benowitz, N.L., and P. Jacob III, "Daily intake of nicotine during cigarette smoking." Clinical Pharmacol Ther. Vol. 35, 1984, pg. 499-504.
[11] Benowitz, N.L., P. Jacob III, R.T. Jones, and J. Rosenberg, " Interindividual variability in the metabolism and cardiovascular effects of nicotine in man", J. Pharmacol Exp.Ther, Vol. 221, 1982, pg 368-372.
[12] Benoqitz, N.L., F. Kuyt, P. Jacob III, R.T. Jones, and A.L. Osman, "Cotinine disposition and effects", Clin. Pharmacol. Ther. Vol. 34, 1983, pg. 604-611.
[13] Luck, W., and H. Nau, "Exposure of the fetus, neonate, and nursed infant to nicotine and cotinine from maternal smoking", N EJM, Vol. 311, 1984, pg. 672.
[14] Benowitz, N.L., "Pharmacologic aspects of cigarette smoking and nicotine addiction", NEJM, Vol. 319, No. 20, 1988, pg 1318-1330.
[15] NIOSH, Current Intelligence Bulletin 54, June 1991, Environmental Tobacco Smoke in the workplace.

[16,17] Goodman and Gilman's "The Pharmacological Basis of Therapeutics," Sixth edition, Editors: A. G. Gilman, L.S. Goodman. and A. Gilman, Macmillan Publishing CO., Inc., New York, 1980, pg. 559
[18] Glantz, S.A., and W.W. Parmley, " Passive smoking and heart disease: epidemiology, physiology, and biochemistry," Circulation, Vol. 83, No. 1, 1991, pg. 1-12.
[19] McKinlay, S.M., N.L. Bifano, and J.B. McKinlay, "Smoking and age at menopause in women", Ann. Inter. Med. , Vol 103, 1985, Pg 350-356.
[20] Benowitz, N.L., "Pharmacologic aspects of cigarette smoking and nicotine addiction", NEJM, Vol. 319, No. 20, 1988, pg 1318-1330.
[21] Collaborative Group for the Study of Stroke in Young Women. "Oral contraceptives and stroke in young women: associated risk factors", JAMA, Vol. 231, 1975, pg 718-722.
[22] Shapireo, S., D. Stone, L. Rosenberg, D.W. Kaufman., P.D. Stolley, and O.S. Miettinen, "Oral-contraceptive use in relation to myocardial infarction", Lancet, Vol .1, 1979, pg 743-747. .
[23] Handbook of Poisoning, R. H. Dreisbach, Lange Medical Publications, 1977.
[24] Gehlbach, S.H., W.A. Williams, L.D. Perry, and J.S. Woodall, "Green-tobacco sickness: an illness of tobacco harvesters", JAMA, Vol 229, 1974, pg 1880-1883.

APPENDIX G:

Mutual Funds that Own Significantly Large Amounts of Tobacco Stocks, (7-31-95 to 1-31-96)

Mutual Fund Name	Value in Millions
Investment Co. of America	$464.8
Vanguard Index 500	$174.7
Fidelity Puritan	$314.2
Fidelity Contrafund	$175.1
Fidelity Growth & Income	$702.9
Income Fund of America	$297.7
Fidelity Equity Income II	$308.9
Fidelity Asset Manager	$260.6
Vanguard Windsor II	$334.2
Fidelity Equity Income (RJR & Philip Morris)	NA
Fidelity Adv. Growth Opportunity "A" (Philip Morris)	NA

Mutual Funds that Own NO Tobacco Stocks:

Calvert Social Investment Managed A	1-800-769-1204
Ariel Capital Management	1-800-292-7435
Paxworld Fund	1-800-767-1729
Green Century Fund	1-800-321-1928
Neuberger & Berman Socially Responsive Fund	1-800-877-9700

APPENDIX H:

Pro-Health, Tobacco Control Advocacy Groups

Action on Smoking and Health, (ASH)
2013 H. Street N.W.
Washington, D.C. 20006
202-659-4310

Advocacy Institute
1707 L. Street, N.W.
Suite 400
Washington, D.C. 20036
202-659-8484

Americans for Nonsmokers Rights, (ANR)
2530 San Pablo Ave.
Suite J
Berkeley, CA 94702
510-841-3032

Campaign for Tobacco-Free Kids
515 North State St.
Chicago, Ill 60610
202-452-1184

Doctors Ought to Care (DOC)
5510 Greenbriar, Suite 235
Houston, TX 77005
713-798-7729

INFACT
256 Hanover Street
Boston, MA 02113
617-742-4583

Stop Teenage Addiction to Tobacco (STAT)
121 Lyman street, Suite 210
Springfield, MA 01103
413-732-7828

For More Information Contact:

The National Cancer Institute
Building 31, Room 10A24
Bethesda, MD 20892
1-800-4-CANCER

The American Cancer Society
1599 Clifton Road, NE
Atlanta, GA 30329
1-800-ACS-2345

The American Heart Association
1-800-AHA-USA1

The American Lung Association
1740 Broadway
New York, NY 10019-4374
212-315-8700

The Coalition on Smoking OR Health
1150 Connecticut Ave. N.W.
Suite 820
Washington, D.C. 20036

Centers for Disease Control and Prevention
Mail Stop K-50
4770 Buford Highway
Atlanta, GA 30341
404-488-5705

APPENDIX I:

BYLAWS for Pro-health Tobacco Control Coalition

Bylaws of ____________________

ARTICLE I
NAME, NEED, MISSION STATEMENT, FUNCTIONS, OFFICE

__________________(name)__________ - a Pro-health Tobacco Control Coalition

Statement of need:

Tobacco use is the number one preventable cause of death, and kills 434, 000 Americans annually.

83,000 Americans die from the cumulative effects of breathing secondhand smoke annually.

Advertising is the main reason over 3 million teens smoke today.

Most tobacco use starts before the age 14.

Mission Statement

We are dedicated to eliminating tobacco use as a major cause of premature death, by preventing tobacco use and encouraging cessation, reducing minors access to tobacco, curtailing tobacco advertising and promotion, and promoting smoke-free environments through advocacy, education and service.

Functions:

To serve as the coordinating body for the exchange and dissemination of information and resources for tobacco education.

To identify and disseminate information of public policy issues regarding tobacco use as a health hazard.

To coordinate the use of member resources to achieve the coalition's mission.

To pursue appropriate tobacco use prevention projects.

Office and Meeting Place

The principal office and meeting place of the coalition shall be in the City of __________, County of __________, State of.______________.

The coalition also may have offices at other places as the board of directors may from time to time designate or as the business of the coalition may require.

ARTICLE II
BOARD OF DIRECTORS

Authority:

The powers of the coalition shall be exercised by or under the authority of, and the business and affairs of the coalition shall be managed under the direction of, the board of directors of the coalition.

Executive Officers:

The officers of the Board of Directors shall comprise a president, vice president, secretary, and 5 standing committee chairpersons: public policy, education, communication, membership, and finance (optional).

No member shall hold more than one executive position.

Duties of the Executives

The duties of the executives will be determined by consensus of the board of directors, and from time to time reviewed and changed if deemed necessary, unless otherwise provided by these Bylaws.

President:

The president shall be the chief executive officer of the coalition and shall, subject to the direction and control of the board of directors, have general supervision, direction, and control of the business and affairs of the coalition. He shall preside at all meetings of the coalition and directors and be an ex-officio member of all the standing committees, including the executive committee, and shall have the general powers and duties of management usually vested in the office of president of a corporation and shall have such other powers and duties as may from time to time be prescribed by the board of directors or these Bylaws.

Vice-President:

In the absence or disability of the president, the vice-president shall perform all the duties of the president and, when so acting, shall have all the powers of, and be subject to all the restrictions upon, the president. The vice-president shall have such other powers and perform such other duties as may from time to time be prescribed by the board of directors or these Bylaws.

Secretary:

The secretary shall keep a book of minutes of all meetings of directors and coalition general meetings, with the time and place of holding, whether regular or special, the names of those present at directors' meetings, the number of members present or represented at coalition meetings, and the proceedings thereof. The secretary shall certify and keep the original and a copy of the Bylaws as amended or otherwise altered to date. The secretary shall give notice of all meetings of directors, and general coalition and special meetings required to be given by the provisions of these Bylaws.

Term of Office:

The directors shall be elected at the annual meeting of the coalition and hold office until the next annual meeting and until their successors have been elected and qualified.
The term of each officer shall be one year, and limited to 2 consecutive terms.

Vacancies:

A vacancy on the board of directors shall exist in the case of death, resignation, or removal of any director or in case the authorized number of directors is increased or in case the members fail to elect the full authorized number of directors at any annual or special meeting of the coalition at which any director is elected.
Vacancies on the board of directors may be filled by the affirmative vote of a majority of the remaining directors or by election at an annual, or special meeting of members called for that purpose.

Removal:

Any or all of the directors may be removed, with or without cause, at a special meeting of coalition members called expressly for that purpose by the vote of 2/3 of the coalition members of record.

ARTICLE III
MEMBERSHIP

Membership:

Membership is open to health care professionals and institutions, medical and paramedical organizations, public health officials and departments, community organizations, and individuals that subscribe to the mission of the coalition.

Parties Interested in membership may apply by means of an application form.

The board of directors must approve all applications before an applicant is considered a member of record.

The board of directors may, with or without cause, terminate the membership rights of any member, by written notice delivered to the member by the secretary or president.

Rights of Members:

The coalition shall not affect the independence of members to carry out tobacco control programs individually or within another organization.

Each member of record shall be entitled to one vote on at the annual coalition meeting to elect a board of directors, except by other provisions of these Bylaws.

Each member of record is authorized to attend annual and general coalition meetings, and is entitled to bring a prospective member as a guest.

Resignation from Membership:

A member may resign with a written notice to the president or secretary, and thereby forfeits all membership rights.

Responsibility of Members:

All members will support the mission of NAME

Each organization and agency must designate an official representative, and one alternate, to attend meeting and participate on a committee.

Each member is responsible for his or her own expenses incurred while doing coalition business.

Members may not accept interviews by the media, or act as an unauthorized spokesman for the coalition in any way, by any medium.

ARTICLE IV
MEETINGS

Place of Meetings:

All meetings of the coalition shall be held at the principal executive office of the coalition or at such other place as may be determined by the board of directors.

Annual Coalition Meetings:

The annual meeting of the coalition shall be held on the __________ day of the month of ________, if not a holiday, at __ o'clock __.M., at which time the coalition shall elect a board of directors and transact other business. If this date falls on a holiday, then the meeting shall be held on the following business day at the same hour.

General Coalition Meetings:

The general meetings of the coalition shall be held on the __________ day of each month, if not a holiday, at ___ o'clock __ .M.

Board of Directors Meetings:

The Board of Directors meetings shall be held on the __________ day of each month, if not a holiday, at ___ o'clock __.M., at which time the board of directors will transact business. There shall be no fewer than 4 board of director meetings a year.

Special Meetings:

Special meetings of the coalition may be called by the president, or the board of directors, from time to time as needed, or by 2/3 vote of the members of record.

Notices of Meetings:

Notices of coalition meetings, general, executive, or special, shall be given to members of record by or at the direction of the president or secretary of the coalition, or the person calling the meeting.

Such notices shall be given either personally, by fax or by mail. Notices shall be given not less than 10, or more than 60 days before the date of the meeting.

Such notice shall state the place, date, and hour of the meeting and, in the case of a special meeting, the purpose or purposes for which the meeting is called.

VOTING:

Board of Directors Voting:

Only the directors of record shall be entitled to vote at a board of directors meeting. Each director shall be entitled to one vote on each matter submitted to a vote at a meeting of board of directors, except by other provisions of these By-laws.

Annual Meeting Voting:

If a quorum is present at the annual coalition meeting, directors shall be elected by a plurality of the votes cast by the members present. The board of directors shall determine what percentage of the members of record constitutes a quorum.

Proxies:

Any member may vote either in person or by proxy executed in writing by the director and filed with the secretary of the coalition. Every member entitled to vote may authorize another person to act by proxy by filing a written proxy, executed by such person, with the secretary of the coalition.

ARTICLE V
COMMITTEES

Executive Standing Committees:

The executive committees serve at the pleasure of the board, each of which shall be comprised of one elected director. The Executive committees shall be public policy, education, membership, communications, and finance (optional).

ARTICLE VI
AMENDMENT OF BYLAWS

By Directors:

The board of directors may amend or repeal the Bylaws, or adopt new Bylaws, unless:

The coalition members, by vote at a special meeting, amend, repeal, or adopt a particular bylaw that expressly provides that the board of directors may not amend that bylaw.

By Coalition Members:

The coalition may amend, repeal, or adopt the Bylaws even though the Bylaws may also be amended, repealed, or adopted by the board of directors.

This action may only be taken at a special meeting of the coalition, may be called by the president, the board of directors, by the holders of at least 2/3 of all the members of record.

Coalitions that are considering incorporating as a nonprofit corporation, 501 (C) (3), are advised to consult an attorney.

APPENDIX J:

Chronology of the Tobacco War and Death Toll

Year	Event	Death Toll from Tobacco
1964	· First Surgeon Generals Report on Smoking and Health	0
1965	· Federal Cigarette Labeling and Advertising Act	394,000
1971	· Cigarette Ads Banned on TV and radio.	1,794,000
1976	· FTC Investigates unfair tobacco advertising.	3,240,000
1979	· HEW investigates tobacco promotion to children.	4,220,000
1980	· Congress weakens FTC to stop tobacco investigation.	4,565,000
1981	· White House eliminates HEW's budget for tobacco investigation. · Congress votes no to end tobacco subsidies	4,935,000
1982	· No-net-cost provision added to tobacco subsidies.	5,315,000
1984	· Comprehensive Smoking Education Act, strengthens warnings.	6,105,000
1988	· Smoking banned on short airline flights. ·Surgeon General declares nicotine addictive.	7,788,000
1993	· EPA classifies ETS as Class A Carcinogen	9,933,000
1994	· Congressional Hearing on Nicotine and Tobacco. · FDA investigates tobacco for possible regulation. · Congress votes down SFEA	Over 10 Million

Index

Symbols

A

B

C

D

F

G

H

I

J

K

L

M

N

P

S

T

U

V

Y